Wide Awake
Thinking, Reading, and Writing Critically

Sara Hosey
Nassau Community College

Fran O'Connor
Nassau Community College

PEARSON

Boston Columbus Indianapolis New York San Francisco Upper Saddle River
Amsterdam Cape Town Dubai London Madrid Milan Munich Paris Montreal Toronto
Delhi Mexico City São Paulo Sydney Hong Kong Seoul Singapore Taipei Tokyo

Senior Acquisitions Editor: Lauren Finn
Head of Marketing: Roxanne McCarley
Project Coordination, Text Design, and
   Electronic Page Makeup: Cenveo
Cover Designer: John Callahan

Cover Image: © tale/Shutterstock
Senior Manufacturing Buyer: Roy
   Pickering
Printer/Binder: Edwards Brothers
Cover Printer: Demand Production Center

Credits and acknowledgments borrowed from other sources and reproduced, with permission, in this textbook appear on the appropriate page within text or on page 309.

Library of Congress Cataloging-in-Publication Data

Hosey, Sara.
  Wide Awake: Thinking, Reading, and Writing Critically / Sara Hosey, Fran O'Connor.
    pages cm
  Includes index.
  ISBN 978-0-205-72440-6
  1. College readers. 2. Critical thinking—Study and teaching (Higher) I. O'Connor, Fran,
    author. II. Title.
  PE1417.H677 2013
  808'.0427--dc23

                       2012041191

10 9 8 7 6 5 4 3 2—EDW—16 15 14 13

www.pearsonhighered.com

ISBN 10:   0-205-72440-X
ISBN 13: 978-0-205-72440-6

Brief Contents

Part 2
Wide Awake to Reading

Detailed Contents

Part 1 Wide Awake to Writing

1 Chapter One
Critical Reading and Writing
Identifying Audience and Purpose　　　　**1**

6 Chapter 6

From Paragraphs to Essays   53

Part 2   Wide Awake to Reading

9 Chapter Nine
Disability Studies
Questioning "Normal"   **96**

10 Chapter Ten
What to Eat
Difficult Decisions About Food in America   **131**

13 ## Chapter Thirteen

Social Networking

14 ## Chapter Fourteen

How to Be Happy

Preface
to Instructors

How to Use Wide Awake:
Thinking, Reading, and Writing Critically

*W*ide Awake: Thinking, Reading, and Writing Critically offers
students concrete writing instruction in an accessible and
engaging style as well as a collection of fresh and compelling
essays. Emphasizing the importance of consciousness and choice in
the reading and writing processes, *Wide Awake Thinking, Reading,
and Writing Critically* asks readers to attend to the world around
them and to recognize and determine how they will participate in
that world. The philosophy of *Wide Awake* is simple: One should make
conscious decisions, knowing that decisions lead to consequences.

Deliberateness is a theme for the writing instruction provided here.
To be "wide awake" is to be alert, and hopefully, to be deliberate. This
text emphasizes writing as a process of selection and rejection: Every
time a person sets pen to paper (or finger to keyboard), she begins to
make hundreds of complex and related choices concerning how she
wishes to express herself. Highlighting the concept of choice in writing,
this text offers strategies and suggestions for various writing situations.

Overall, *Wide Awake* is designed to facilitate the development of
analytical close-reading skills, including the ability to recognize the
importance of textual references in reading responses, as well as attention to thematic connections within and outside of a discipline. Equally
as important, however, is the emphasis *Wide Awake* places on developing students' abilities to think critically and write deliberately, ultimately heightening their consciousness about the immediate (school,
job, neighborhood) and the remote (state, country, world, cyberspace).

The reading selections are anchored in contemporary issues relevant to students' lives; these issues are not only of urgent importance, but are those which students are confronted with daily. These readings invite students to challenge accepted notions about life in America, to pose complex questions about the world around them, to reflect on their own experiences, and to apply the ideas they are learning about to their everyday lives.

This text specializes in readings within underexplored topics, such as what it means to have a disability in American culture and what it means to be happy, in addition to readings that probe current notions of what education ought to be, how communication technologies affect our lives, what constitutes "the environment" (and why we should care about it), and how to eat healthily. These readings are all connected by the theme of being "wide awake," and there are a number of overlaps between the considerations of topics in each chapter.

Writing Instruction

Eight rhetoric chapters comprise Part 1 and discuss considering audience and purpose; prewriting, drafting, and critical reading; writing introductions, conclusions, and thesis statements; and composing paragraphs while providing effective support. Also explored are more advanced skills such as argumentation; synthesis; summary, paraphrase, and quotation; and the researched essay. Each of these chapters provides an overview, describes possible choices, includes examples, and offers exercises and writing assignments so that students can immediately apply concepts they have learned. Academic expectations—particularly those that may differ from those of students' precollege years—are addressed throughout the writing instruction section.

Each rhetoric chapter in Part 1 also includes a "Prereading Check-In" question designed to stimulate thinking about the writing issue addressed in the chapter, "Write Back" opportunities that invite students to immediately apply the skill described, "Follow-up Activity" asks students to continue to practice the skills they have learned, and "Tip Box" that provides advice and information regarding common sources of student-teacher misunderstandings, including the basics of email etiquette and the use of Internet sources such as Wikipedia in college essays.

Anthology Topics

The six anthology chapters that comprise Part 2 explore pressing contemporary issues, including education in America, disability studies, and the popularity of social networking. *Wide Awake* presents student and instructor with a breadth of readings, including one "classic" text per chapter, as well as an array of genres from periodicals, anthologies, and the Internet, in order to facilitate thinking, critiquing, evaluating, and making decisions about the important issues that affect our lives every single day.

The rich selection of readings in the anthology section is designed to appeal to a variety of students. Because of significant thematic overlap between the chapters, students can begin to see the interrelatedness of issues in addition to recognizing how ideas build on and inform each other. Students may consider, for example, the relationship between industrial food production and environmental corruption.

The following anthology topics, while all concerned with how personal responses, experiences, and choices are affected and in turn can affect larger institutional, political, or global forces, appear in an order that suggests a move from the highly personal to the public, such as the institution of American education. Placing the chapter "How to Be Happy: The Question of Choice" last is meant to suggest that, in the end, most human activities have as their goal the acquisition of some kind of happiness: Why concern ourselves with what we should or shouldn't eat, with politics and government, or with examining and reforming education, if not for the betterment of our society and, by extension, ourselves?

Disability Studies: Questioning "Normal"

Despite the contemporary rage for "diversity," it is only recently that a general understanding of the significance and the value of human variation has truly entered into scholarly discussions. An emerging discipline, disability studies calls for the recognition of disability as itself a valuable analytical category, comparable to categories such as race, class, and gender. This unit offers a selection of some of the best writing by and about people with disabilities; these pieces encourage critical discussion and thinking by challenging accepted ideas about "the normal" and the "natural" and highlighting the extent to which "disability" itself is socially constructed.

What to Eat: Difficult Decisions About Food in America

Like ecology, food science has become increasingly politicized in recent years. The rising price of food, coupled with increasing consumer skepticism about the integrity of industrial foods, has resulted in widespread reconsiderations of the basic question of sustenance. The authors presented in this unit critique contemporary food production, outline the connections between "big food" and government policies, problematize naturalized notions about the purpose of food as well as the "ideal" body type, and propose responses and solutions to contemporary food issues.

Ecological Consciousness: A Challenge for the 21ˢᵗ Century

Many colleges and universities, including the State University of New York system, have announced their decisions to "go green." The SUNY system, for example, is not only asking its colleges to "green" their buildings and infrastructure, but their curriculum as well. Further, cities and suburbs are providing incentives to encourage businesses and citizens to embrace green technology, and individuals everywhere are making day-to-day choices in order to decrease their "carbon footprints." These initiatives are harbingers of things to come: More colleges and universities will recognize the necessity of interdisciplinarity, and more instructors will look to incorporate units on the environment in their composition courses. The readings in this chapter discuss current ecological issues, both theoretical and practical, as well as various aspects of humans' complex relationship with nature.

Choosing School: American Education in the 21ˢᵗ Century

For good reason, a chapter focused on education is a fairly standard feature of many composition readers. While all of the topics included in *Wide Awake: Thinking, Reading, and Writing Critically* are in some ways relevant to many students' lives, education is an issue that is clearly related to their immediate concerns and endeavors. In addition, most students have an abundance of first-hand experience at being in school. Bringing together familiar investigations of the notion of enlightenment (such as Plato's "The Allegory of the Cave") and more contemporary commentaries on schooling (such as the work of Mike Rose), this section asks students to think critically about the very purpose of education. The selections in this unit consider the goals of the American system of universal education, the ostensible crisis in education, and proposals for the improvement of our educational system.

Social Networking: The Promise and Pitfalls of a Web 3.0 World

Twitter, Facebook, and YouTube, among other technologies that have been touted as potentially democratizing, bring us closer to one another but also, paradoxically, expose us to the "slings and arrows" of modern life as, for example, virtual strangers feel free to criticize our online personalities, philosophies, and beliefs. The readings in this chapter, including Malcolm Gladwell's article, "Why the Revolution Will Not Be Tweeted," ask students to consider how these technologies affect the ways we learn, the ways we interact, and the ways we conceive of our own persons.

How to Be Happy: The Question of Choice

Happiness is perhaps the ultimate human goal, the reason that many of us give as the hoped-for result of our conscious choices. What, however, is happiness? Wherever did 21st-century Americans get the idea that we have some sort of right to be happy? Drawing on recent investigations, both popular and scientific, this unit invites students to look at this elusive goal from a variety of perspectives and worldviews. This chapter contains discussions of what it means to be happy and how we can potentially increase our happiness.

The Anthology Apparatus

Provided with the "connective tissue" in the form of end-of-chapter suggestions and cross-references as well as questions designed to point instructors and students to related or oppositional readings in other chapters within the text, instructors can design their own curriculum with *Wide Awake: Thinking, Reading, and Writing Critically*.

"Prereading Check-In" questions low-stakes opportunities for students to record initial ideas, are of two kinds: The first question asks students for their personal reaction to a topic, perhaps inviting them to reflect on their experiences; the second question asks them to respond to controversies or to discover what they already know about a topic. These questions are designed to focus students' reading, to demonstrate to them how much they already know, and to invite them to recognize their personal connections to the topics.

"Choosing to Read Critically Questions" are also of two kinds: The first pair of questions asks students to demonstrate reading comprehension; the second pair asks them to examine the text's rhetorical strategies. Additionally, some of the questions may allow students to exercise and further develop their summarizing, quoting, and paraphrasing skills.

Each pair of "Choosing to Respond Questions" includes a question that asks students to comment on the article drawing on their own experiences or observations as well as a question that asks the student to respond to the larger controversy or topic that the selection engages. Each pair of "Wide Awake to Connections Questions" includes a question that asks the student to conduct further research into some aspect of the reading and an intertextual question that asks the student to connect the selection he or she has just read with another selection from elsewhere in the book.

Lastly, each anthology chapter concludes with "Questions and Suggestions for Further Research and Writing," ideal opportunities for formal essays. Students are encouraged to synthesize information from multiple articles within the chapter; to make connections to ideas presented in other anthology chapters; to conduct further research on some aspect of the topic; to consider mass media depictions/handlings of issues within the topic; and to do independent research in their campus or community.

Instructor's Manual

The Instructor's Manual to accompany *Wide Awake* will provide three week-by-week syllabi, peer review worksheets for three different essays, guidelines for assigning essays, and cross-references for using articles with similar concerns from different anthology chapters.

Acknowledgments

The authors would like to extend gratitude to Lauren Finn, our editor, and Sandra Manzanares, our editorial assistant. Thanks to Dr. Timothy

Strode for his guidance early in the project. Thanks also to Jess Rao, Esq. for his support and feedback. Finally, thank you to the reviewers:

K.A. Wisniewski, Stevenson University
Guy Shebat, Youngstown State University
Andrew Rusnak, Jr., The Community College of Baltimore County Essex
Rebecca Rudd, Citrus College
Marty Price, Mississippi State University
Heal McKnight, Kirkwood Community College
Glenn D. Klopfenstein, Passaic County Community College
Dale Ireland, California State University, East Bay
Thomas Girshin, Ithaca College
Larry C. Bush, Pensacola State College
Elizabeth Whitmore Funk, Marymount University
Lauren Ingraham, University of Tennessee at Chattanooga
Jamie McDaniel, Pittsburg State University
Lisa Neilson, Marist College
Julia Ruengert, Pensacola State College
Lori Vail, Green River Community College
Monica Walker, The Community College of Baltimore County
Craig Frischkorn, Cecil College
Susan Carlson, Pittsburg State University
Barbara Solak, Tunxis Community College
Jason Roberts, Sierra College
Ruth Rassool, College of the Canyons
Keith Mitchell, The University of Massachusetts Lowell
Michael Martin, Marygrove College

Preface
to Students

What to Expect from Wide Awake:
Thinking, Reading, and Writing Critically

To be "wide awake" is to be alert, and hopefully, to be deliberate about our beliefs, our commitments, and our choices in life. Bringing together influential, respected, and innovative writers and thinkers considering topics such as the **environment, food politics, social networking, disability studies, education, and happiness,** *Wide Awake: Thinking, Reading, and Writing Critically* is designed to provide you with concrete writing instruction as well as fresh and exciting readings on a variety of cutting-edge topics. These readings invite you to reflect on your own experiences, to pose questions about complex issues, and to challenge accepted notions about life in the United States of America.

Consciousness and Choice

>> **Prereading Check-In**
Please take a few moments to consider and respond to the following questions.
Why did you choose to attend this college? What do you hope to achieve by attending college?

Choice: Anticipating and Evaluating Consequences

The prewriting questions above have asked you to consider the significance of your academic choices. While it's important to remember that

TIP BOX: Time Management

Recent research has demonstrated that one of the biggest obstacles to first-year students' success is not intelligence or motivation but time management: the ability to anticipate the workload and to meet deadlines. Taking the time to plan out your semester may be the first step to effectively managing your schoolwork. You might choose to get a calendar in which to record blocks of time for weekly assignments as well as major due dates and exams.

there are always circumstances beyond one's control (one might have family obligations that demand time and attention or one might feel over- or under-prepared for some classes), it's equally as important to remember that there are circumstances one can control. For example, you can make a choice to work hard on your writing this semester. Attending to your writing will almost guarantee that your writing will improve. Of course, this does not mean you'll get an "A" for the class; everyone knows that you can work hard and still not get the grade that you'd like. However, if you focus on improving your writing this semester, you will become a better writer, able to compose responses and arguments more clearly and effectively than you have before.

Making Choices in Your Writing

Every time you set a pen to paper, or finger to keyboard, you make multiple—and often unconscious—choices about how you want to express yourself. This textbook will ask you to *pay attention*, to be deliberate in your composition, and to look critically at your own and others' writing.

Think about traveling to a destination you visit often, such as a friend's house or a place of work. When going somewhere familiar, we often travel intuitively; the only time we really pay attention to how we're getting there is when there's a roadblock or a detour and we are forced to change our approach. Sometimes we may discover that we've been missing out on a better—quicker, easier, or more scenic—way of going.

Writing can be like traveling in this way. When many of us compose, we often just sit down and write, without really noticing what we're doing. The only time we change our approach is when we get writer's block or run into some other kind of problem that prevents us from proceeding as we normally would.

However, just as you might want to explore different traveling routes, you might want to consider trying out different and new ways of composing. That is, you don't always have to approach writing in the same way. Perhaps another way of proceeding might be more direct, effective, and/or enjoyable. This textbook will ask you to be more aware of yourself as a writer, what you do and why you do it, so that you can choose to be more effective, both in your sentences and in your essays overall.

Many beginning writers think that good writing is all a matter of being talented or even being lucky. Certainly, talent and luck sometimes play a role; however, truly good writing is a combination of skills, interest, care, and deliberate decisions. The more alert you are to your ideas, your practices, and your choices as a writer, the more your writing will become interesting, confident, and compelling.

1 Chapter One

Critical Reading and Writing:
Identifying Audience and Purpose

Chapter Objectives

- Determine appropriate situations for "just reading" versus critical reading.
- Implement techniques for critical reading.
- Identify audience and purpose in others' writing and formulate a response.
- Distinguish between formal and informal voices in speaking and writing.
- Identify your audience and purpose and choose an appropriate voice for your documents.

>> Prereading Check-In

When you are asked to read something for class, how, where, and when do you read it? Explain whether or not you feel that your habits are effective.

Crucial to your development as a reader and a writer is the ability to identify other authors' reasons for writing. In addition, being aware of your own primary goals and audiences will enable you to more deliberately select the strategies you use in your writing.

"Just Reading" Versus Critical Reading

Sometimes students are unsure of how closely they are expected to read assignments for various classes; some students assume they can "just read" or skim their assignments, while others spend hours highlighting entire pages.

The boxes below describe two different approaches to written material. While "Just Reading" can be very effective for tackling many different types of materials, "Critical Reading" will often prove more appropriate when dealing with the readings assigned in composition classes.

"Just Reading"	Vs.	Critical Reading
Just reading is getting the main idea or skimming a piece to get the overall gist.		Assigned readings may be complex, and they may be models for the type of writing and thinking that students are expected to do. Sometimes an assigned text needs to be read carefully and more than once.
Some people—students and instructors—have difficulty reading anything that isn't about one of their personal interests. In order to make the task less painful, they read while watching television or doing something else on the computer.		Different things work for different people, but if you find yourself easily distracted, you can and should choose to read and study in a place that allows you to concentrate. As mentioned above, some of the assigned readings are challenging and, often, your instructor will expect you to struggle with and through a reading.
Underlining and taking notes may not be necessary. All of the material is equally important.		Having a pen in your hand may actually compel you to focus on the words and sentences as well as on the rhythm of the selection. Underline sentences and ideas that you think are important, confusing, right, wrong, or interesting. The next step is to identify and respond to what you have underlined. To **annotate** is to take notes in the margins, picking out ideas that you agree and disagree with and briefly responding to them. Remember to only underline concepts that you feel are crucial; too much underlining will make it difficult for you to figure out why you underlined a section in the first place.

"Just Reading"	Vs.	Critical Reading
Questions and information before and after the assigned reading aren't necessary for understanding the piece.		In *Wide Awake*, questions before and after each selection are designed to support you as you develop your original ideas about topics, develop your specific responses to articles, and, finally, develop ideas for further inquiry. In addition, the biographical note about each author may provide clues as to his or her purpose and audience.

TIP BOX Exercise Your Reading Muscles

The best way to become a stronger and more comfortable reader is to practice: read something every day. Many strong readers compare reading to any other kind of exercise or physical training: it's unpleasant and difficult if you rarely do it, but once you get into the habit, it becomes easier and more enjoyable. After a while, you may start to feel uncomfortable if you go a day or two *without* doing it. If you're not sure what to read, start picking up a daily newspaper, check out the fiction section of your local library, or look at some online magazines or blogs that deal with one of your interests.

Critical Reading: Choosing to Be Wide Awake

In many of your college classes, and particularly in humanities classes, you will be expected to read actively and alertly. This means reading carefully, working to understand any material that you might find difficult, keeping track of the author's ideas, and being aware of your responses to those ideas.

To read critically means that you don't simply accept everything that an author puts forward or argues. In order to develop your response to a piece, you might begin by identifying **key words** and **phrases** (that is, words and phrases that seem important and that might give you some ideas about the author's reason for writing), **rhetorical strategies** (how and what the author does with his or her writing in order to convey his or her point), as well as the author's **voice** and **tone** (the author's individual way of writing and his or her feelings about the subject). Further, ask yourself whether or not you found the piece compelling—and the reasons why you did or didn't find it compelling. Were you entertained? Do you feel persuaded? Was the information you needed communicated effectively? Did you find the author's tone and/or style effective? Does what he or she argues make sense? Are there holes in the logic?

Identifying Audience and Purpose in Others' Writing

Recognizing other authors' *audiences* and *purposes* can help you to become a strong critical reader. An author's audience is the individual or group that the author imagines will read her or his work. The purpose is the writer's goal: does he or she hope to entertain, to persuade, to educate, to commemorate, to advertise, to motivate?

You may already be very skilled at identifying other writers' agendas: read each quotation below and write down the authors' primary audience and purpose. Then, in the column marked "Key Words and Phrases," make a note of what specific words helped you to identify the audience and purpose.

	Presumed Audience	Presumed Purpose	Key Words and Phrases
"Comfort. Safety. Reliability. With two rows of seats and extra storage in the trunk, we're here for you and your expanding family."			
"Once upon a time, there was a child named Cinderella. Cinderella's mother died and her father remarried another woman, Cinderella's stepmother. Cinderella's stepmother was very cruel to Cinderella."			
"Our government needs to stop paying lip service to the importance of education and start actually paying for a first-class educational system. If you choose to vote for me, I promise to demand that we invest more money in our local schools."			

You may have found the above exercise pretty easy to do. That's because you're probably already quite good at recognizing certain kinds of rhetoric: you're aware when someone is trying to advertise to you, to entertain you, or to convince you. Thus, the phrase "Once upon a time," for example, might be familiar to you, not only perhaps from your own childhood, but also from mass media uses of the phrase. The name "Cinderella" might also have jumped out at you as a key indicator telling you where the quotation was from, who it was for, and what it was designed to do. Breaking things down into parts like this is a step of the **analytical work** that goes into critical reading. (Analysis is discussed further in Chapter 2.)

Of course, it will be more difficult to detect audience and purpose in less familiar and more difficult texts. When confronted with more challenging pieces, use the same skills as those you used in the exercise above—pick out words and phrases that seem important, spell out the associations that certain words and phrases have for you—in addition to looking up unfamiliar words and, when you need to supplement your understanding or the assignment calls for it, conducting research.

Preparing Your Response: Checking in with Yourself

A strategy you might use to anticipate the direction and thrust of an author's discussion is to think and/or write about the topic before you read the assigned text. For example, if you've been assigned Laura Perez's "A Forgotten Child Remembers: Reflections on Education," an article about the author's experiences in school included in Chapter 12, you might spend some time reflecting on your own pre-college experiences as well as your philosophies about the goals of education. While your thinking and writing might not address exactly the same topics as Perez's piece, you'll be better prepared to read the article critically because you have entered Perez's "conversation" by thinking and writing about her topic. In addition, you will remember more clearly which ideas were your own and which were Perez's.

Further, after thinking about your own experiences and observations, you may feel more engaged as you read Perez's work. At one point in the reading, Perez argues that "teachers are not emotionally connected to their students." What do you think of this claim? Should teachers have emotional connections to their students? How do Perez's experiences compare to your own educational experiences?

When engaging in critical thinking and reading, it's helpful to be aware of your own assumptions and attitudes so that you can more accurately gauge your responses to different perspectives: are you reacting emotionally, logically, or both? Our backgrounds can certainly color our responses to an issue. Perhaps you plan to work in the field of education, or perhaps one of your parents was a school principal, or perhaps, socially, high school was extremely difficult for you. Any of these situations might have an effect on how you view American education today. Once you have recognized your own stake in the issue, you can then begin to critically read the text without allowing strong reactions to block your comprehension of it.

Sometimes we might agree with a viewpoint simply because it supports an opinion we already hold. While there's nothing wrong with appreciating the ideas of those with whom you agree—and informing yourself further will help as you develop your own ideas—you want to make sure that you're "wide awake" when you're reading for school. In this case, that means being aware of and interrogating your assumptions and attitudes, especially if those are attitudes that you haven't really considered before. At the same time, it is important to try to understand positions we don't agree with and to ask ourselves why we don't agree with them. Being able to understand—and to mount a counterargument to—positions we oppose is a crucial skill in college writing.

Identifying Audience and Purpose in Your Writing

WRITE BACK   Choosing Your Audience and Purpose

Please write a paragraph in response to each of the prompts below.

Imagine that you have an interview for a job you'd really like. Before the interview, your prospective employer has asked you to write up a brief description of yourself. Draft the one-paragraph profile of yourself that you'd include in the email.

Imagine that a favorite relative is putting together a "family newsletter" and has asked you to contribute a paragraph about yourself that tells everyone what you've been up to. Or, if you'd prefer, imagine that you're writing the description for a friend or a group that you were once a part of.

Now imagine that you are creating a profile for an online social network such as Facebook. Write that profile below.

The three paragraphs you've composed in response to the above prompts are probably quite different from each other. That is a good thing; what those differences demonstrate is that you already know how to tailor your writing according to audience and purpose. We choose to use different styles and tones when addressing people such as employers and instructors than we do when addressing friends or even, sometimes, family members. For example, while you may have great respect for your Facebook friends, they probably wouldn't be offended if you use a less-than-formal style when you write to them; in fact, some people might find formal language inappropriate or alienating on a website such as Facebook. On the other hand, your email to the prospective boss should probably contain phrases such as "Dear" and "Sincerely" and shouldn't contain any grammatical errors. A lack of formal language or the presence of grammatical errors might indicate to the potential employer that you haven't taken the task seriously and that you don't really care about getting the job.

Identifying Your Audience

College writing is writing for an audience. However, who that audience is isn't always completely clear. Of course, you are writing for your instructor, the person who will probably be evaluating your work and assigning it a grade. You may also be writing for your peers; peer review and participation in workshops are important elements of many composition classes. Finally, you may be writing for an audience beyond the classroom: an admissions committee, a newspaper or blog, a family member, or members of another community who might find your work interesting or enlightening.

In order to make things less complicated, this text concentrates on conventional academic standards, or those expectations that many instructors for different classes often have for academic essays. Although you will have many opportunities to use an informal tone in your writing (many professors will ask you to compose informal "responses" or "journals" both during class time and for homework), your major essays should probably adopt a formal tone—at least in your weighted assignments (rather than informal journals or response papers). As you write for academic audiences, then, you will probably be expected to maintain a formal tone, avoiding slang and swear words, using complete and correct sentences, and keeping away from a style that is too conversational.

Formal and Informal Voices: Speaking Versus Writing

Although most of us recognize that we don't—or shouldn't—write the way that we speak, it is also important to understand how these modes of communication may work differently. Face-to-face conversations certainly rely on words, but, for their success, they also rely heavily on gestures, facial expressions, tone of voice, and intonation. However, in written communication, we can no longer depend on these conversational aids. Notice how some people use abbreviations such as "LOL" when they write emails and texts because they don't want the recipient to misinterpret their message or tone. Thus, when composing written responses, it's helpful to remember the absence of gestures, facial expressions, and voice inflection.

Furthermore, when speaking, we often rely on tone of voice to communicate meaning. For example, you might say, "Yes, he's the nicest guy," and genuinely mean it; on the other hand, it would be easy to imagine saying that exact phrase and meaning it sarcastically. While we can't rely on tone of voice when writing (and it's rarely a good idea to employ sarcasm in your formal essays), there are ways of communicating tone in your written work. Your tone suggests your attitude toward both your subject and your reader. For example, ask yourself: are you dealing with a serious topic? Will you use an informal or a formal voice? The tone you choose is fundamentally related to your perceived audience.

Punctuation, sentence length, sentence organization, and word choice go a long way toward alerting audiences to intent or meaning. Consider, for example, informal and formal responses to the question "Are you available for an appointment on the 15th?" Informally, one might respond: "Yeah." In speech and/or among friends, "yeah" might mean: "Yes, that time works well for me" or, possibly, "Although I'm not truly happy with that time, I won't argue and I'll be ready then." As you can see, sometimes short sentences, contractions, and slang can convey a lot of information in speech or informal writing.

A formal response to "Are you available for an appointment on the 15th?" might be: "Thank you for the offer. Yes, I am available to meet on the 15th, and I look forward to our appointment." Clearly, the second example seems more appropriate for written communication. In addition, the formal response attempts to express more precise ideas and leaves less room for misunderstanding.

TIP BOX Email Etiquette

When you're writing an email related to work or school, you should follow professional and/or academic protocol. Treat these types of correspondences as letters: stay formal (no "u" for "you"), mind your spelling and grammar, and, at least for a first in a series of emails, include a salutation (Dear Professor or Dear Mr./Ms. Blank). It's bad form to send an attachment without any information in the body of the email; one way of addressing this is to state, "Attached please find" and describe the documents you've attached. In addition, if you're handing in an assignment as an email attachment, you should ask the professor to let you know that the document was received.

Also, whenever you email someone in a position of authority, particularly if you are asking that individual for something (the assignment, a recommendation, information about a job), you should make sure to send a follow-up email expressing your thanks.

Finally, it's probably a good idea to have separate email accounts: one for family and friends and one for school and work. Colorful email addresses such as "sexymetfan22" and "spoiledrotten18" are best used informally; your school and work email addresses should be less personal.

Identifying Your Purpose

Just as you do when critically reading another's work, you should be aware of your own audience and purpose when you write. Is the piece you're creating meant to inform, describe, persuade, or entertain? Are you possibly attempting to do several of those things at once? Articulating your goals can help you to become a more deliberate writer.

For example, if you write a cover letter to a prospective employer, your purpose is to convince that employer that you would be an excellent candidate for a position. If you're writing an opinion piece for your school newspaper, you may be attempting to influence, as well as inform, and even entertain your peers. In writing academic papers, you often have multiple purposes: at times, you want to convince the professor of an idea or argument that you are forwarding, as well as demonstrate to your professor that you understand the subject matter and that you deserve some sort of positive evaluation of the assignment. This is another situation in which it is important to know your audience. Understanding what kind of writing your professor is expecting from you is the first step toward fulfilling the assignment and showing that you have mastered the material.

Understanding your purpose will allow you to more effectively organize your work, select a tone, and, as discussed in later chapters, choose appropriate evidence to support your ideas.

Conclusion

Reading critically means to read while paying attention to how a text is put together, what assumptions it takes for granted, and whether or not you find the text engaging and compelling. Adjusting your tone and style according to perceived audience and purpose is the best way to appeal to your readers. Remember that formal academic essays are often designed not only as intellectual exercises, but also as tools for your professors to see whether or not you have comprehended and applied the ideas you are learning in class.

Follow-up Activity #1: Imagining Audience and Purpose

Choose two items from the following list and write a short paragraph for each, keeping in mind your intended audience and purpose. Switch with a partner and don't tell him or her which items you chose; your partner should read your work and see if he or she can identify your audience and purpose through the key words and phrases you've provided. (Alternately, this assignment can be handed in to your instructor.)

1. A Wikipedia entry for the subject "Cinderella"
2. A "position wanted" ad; that is, an advertisement describing an individual's skills and the desired position
3. The first few sentences of an obituary for a famous person
4. An email from a student to a professor asking about a homework assignment
5. The first few sentences of a newspaper article about a crime
6. The first few sentences of a newspaper article about a recent sporting event
7. The first few sentences of a college-application essay
8. The first few sentences of a comedian's stand-up routine
9. The first few sentences of an infomercial script
10. Directions telling someone how to take care of your pet while you are away on vacation

Follow-up Activity #2:
Identifying Audience and Purpose

Pick an article at random from the second half of this book. Don't read the information that precedes the article (which includes information about the author and the article's overall point). Instead, read the first two or three paragraphs and then write a paragraph describing whom you think the article's audience is and what the author's purpose is. Pick out specific words and phrases to back up your ideas about whom this article is for and why the author wrote it.

Chapter Two

Using Evidence and Analysis

Chapter Objectives

- Locate specific textual evidence to support your claims.
- Analyze various types of textual evidence.
- Identify others' use of textual evidence.

Evidence can take the form of facts, statistics, examples, and analysis (the explanation or discussion of how the evidence works), are the key components in much academic writing. You already draw on evidence and analysis whenever you defend an idea or observation that someone else might disagree with. This chapter reviews how to use evidence and analysis strategically to back up and explain the positions you take in your essays.

Providing Specific Evidence

Have you ever gone to a movie with a friend and, as you walked out to the lobby or sat together on the couch afterward, discovered that the two of you disagreed in your evaluations of the film? One of you might have said, "That was so dumb," while the other one said, "That was so great!"

In making simple statements like those above, you're often trying to convince others to see things your way. You might say to your companion, "That movie was so unrealistic" in order to back up your claim that the film is "dumb" and your friend might say, "But the special effects were amazing!" in order to back up her idea that the film was "great."

When you provide reasons or even facts to back up your ideas, you're actually providing **evidence**. For example, if you were to say that specific elements of the **text**, such as the computer graphics or the acting, were particularly unconvincing, you would be breaking down the text into smaller parts (the special effects, the acting) and thus providing evidence to support your point of view.

Below are excerpts from two movie reviews: the first is Kenneth Turan's review of *Harry Potter and the Deathly Hallows—Part 2* from the *Los Angeles Times*. The second is Peter Travers' review of *The Social Network* from *Rolling Stone*. Even if you are not familiar with the films, note how the authors make claims about each film's merits and then backs up those claims with specific examples from the text.

From Turan's "Harry Potter and the Deathly Hallows—Part 2":

> The Harry Potter films, like the boy wizard himself, have had their creative ups and downs, so it's especially satisfying that this final film, ungainly title and all, has been worth the wait. Though no expense has been spared in its production, it succeeds because it brings us back to the combination of magic, adventure and emotion that created the books' popularity in the first place.
>
> [A] consistent factor in the Potter universe is the production's refusal to skimp or pinch pennies. That willingness to do whatever it took to bring Stuart Craig's exceptional production designs to life no matter how painstaking the task is central to the new film's success as well.
>
> To give just two examples, more than 200,000 golden coins and thousands of other pieces were created to convincingly fill a vault at Gringotts bank, and so much furniture and objects were bought to make Hogwarts' enormous Room of Requirement look more crowded than Charles Foster Kane's storehouse that the set dressing department was busy for months buying up bric-a-brac. Nothing's too good for our Harry.

From Travers' "The Social Network":

> [*The Social Network* is] bracingly smart, brutally funny and acted to perfection without exception. . . . [Actor Jesse] Eisenberg delivers a tour de force, nimbly negotiating Sorkin's rat-a-tat dialogue and revealing how alienation and loneliness actually fuel Mark's ambition. More crucially, Eisenberg lets us see the chinks in Mark's armor, unearthing long-buried feelings when Napster co-founder Sean Parker (Justin Timberlake) enters the scene, ready to take Facebook to the next level. . . . Timberlake is phenomenal, a revelation, even. You expect him to nail Sean's charming hustle, and he does, working a restaurant meeting with Mark and Eduardo like a twentysomething Dr. Evil. "A million dollars isn't cool," he says. "You know what's cool? A billion dollars." Sean, with a rep for drugs and very young women, sinks his hooks in. . . . It's a role to die for, and Timberlake the mesmerizer just crushes it.

WRITE BACK   Review a Film

Write a two-paragraph review of a movie you've seen recently.

In the first paragraph, announce whether or not the film is worth seeing and provide your overall reason for this position (i.e., the film is unrealistic, humorous, socially significant). In the second paragraph, provide concrete evidence to back up your position. Use one or two details from the film, such as an important moment, a quote, or a production element (lighting, sound, direction), and show how that piece of evidence relates back to your overall position (that the film is or is not worth seeing).

Analyzing Your Evidence

Analysis is the act of breaking something down into parts and seeing how those parts work together. There are many different kinds of analysis: in the sciences, for example, analysis might mean looking at the parts of a cell (the cell wall, the mitochondria, the nucleus) in order to better understand how the cell as a whole functions. In literature, analysis often means breaking a literary text down into words and phrases and seeing how those words and phrases work together to create the text's overall effect. This chapter discusses the analysis you are performing both when you read and discuss the merits of another author's work and the analysis you perform when you look at textual evidence, such as the details of a film. (See Chapter 6 for further discussion of how to effectively incorporate evidence and analysis in your writing.)

Thus, when analyzing a visual text (such as an image, a film, or a work of art), we often look critically at how it uses signs and symbols to create meaning. For example, although the message it communicates might seem obvious at first, many writers have used the red, octagonal "stop" sign as a visual text that lends itself to further analysis and discussion. In analyzing a stop sign, one might ask: What is the color red associated with? Does the octagonal shape have significance? What does "stop" mean? How do we know that it means to stop our vehicle and not to stop doing something else? Do you stop at a stop sign even when there's no one around? Further, how do you feel or behave when you "run" a stop sign? Do you immediately look in your rearview mirror to see if you've been spotted by a police officer? How does failing to stop at a stop sign alter our relationship to law enforcement and, by extension, to our society? Finally, what can the stop sign tell us about our society?

Although the answers to some of these questions may seem obvious, you are thinking analytically when you focus on how the parts work together (the red, the shape, the letters) to communicate meaning and when you take time to interpret the implications of that meaning.

Developing Your Analysis: Why, How, and So What?

The above "Write Back" asks you to support your opinion about a film by using evidence or details from the film. Your discussion of that evidence, or the way in which you demonstrate that your evidence relates to your larger claim, is a form of analysis.

In writing an analysis, you basically interpret your evidence or data. One way of understanding how to effectively interpret evidence is to see your discussion as proceeding in response to a series of questions. Consider the following dialogue that is meant to demonstrate how one's analysis might develop in response to the questions "why," "how," and "so what"?

John: My claim is that this movie is bad and not worth seeing.

Elyse: Why? Can you back up that claim?

John: My reason is that the movie is unrealistic.

Elyse: How so?

John: For example, in one scene, the main character is shot twice and run over by a car. Then he gets up, chases down the bad guys, and beats them up.

Elyse: So what?

John: That example demonstrates that the movie shows things that could never happen in "real life."

While the above exchange is a little artificial, Elyse's questions are models for the kinds of questions that you can ask when you are developing your own—or reading another's—analysis.

Identifying Others' Analytical Work

Below is an excerpt from Tom Vanderbilt's *Traffic: Why We Drive the Way We Do and What It Says About Us*. In it, Vanderbilt close-reads, or analyzes, country-singer Chely Wright's song "The Bumper of My SUV." Note how Vanderbilt discusses the assumptions we all make about each other, as well as the ways that seemingly neutral objects, such as types of automobiles and bumper stickers, can function to convey meaning. Also notice how Vanderbilt makes a claim, uses evidence, and then analyzes his evidence (demonstrating how his evidence works).

From *Traffic: Why We Drive the Way We Do and What It Says About Us*
by Tom Vanderbilt

[In] Chely Wright's "The Bumper of My SUV," the song's protagonist complains that a "lady in a minivan" has given her the finger because of a United States Marine Corps bumper sticker on her SUV. "Does she think she knows what I stand for / Or the things that I believe," sings Wright, just because the narrator has a bumper sticker for the U.S. Marines on the aforementioned bumper of her SUV? The first issue here is the struggle over identity; the narrator is upset that her identity has been defined by someone else. But the narrator may be protesting too much: How *else* would we know the things that you stand for or believe if you did not have a bumper sticker on your SUV? And if you are resentful at having your identity pigeonholed, why put a pigeonholing sticker on your bumper in the first place?

In being offended, the SUV driver has made several huge assumptions of her own. First, she has presumed that the finger had something to do with the bumper sticker, when in fact it could have been directed at a perceived act of aggressive driving on her part. Or could it have been the fact that this single driver was tooling around in a large SUV, inordinately harming the environment, putting pedestrians and drivers of cars at greater risk, and increasing the country's dependence on foreign oil? Second, by invoking a "lady in a minivan," later echoed by references to "private schools," she is perpetuating a preemptive negative stereotype against minivans: that their drivers are somehow more elitist than the drivers of SUVs—which makes no sense as SUVs, on average, cost more than minivans. The narrator is guilty of the same things she accuses the minivan driver of.

WRITE BACK:

1. Identify the key phrases and ideas that Vanderbilt uses to back up his analysis. How compelling do you find his evidence? Are there other ways of interpreting the evidence he provides?
2. To what extent do you think you judge other people based on the type of car they drive (or don't drive)? How and why do you arrive at these judgments? (For further discussion of behind-the-wheel snap judgments, locate and read Rob Walker's articles "Hummer Love" and "Stuck on You," written for the "Consumed" column in the *New York Times Magazine*.)

TIP BOX Using an Analytic Principle for Clarity

One way to proceed when writing an analysis is to immediately announce and describe the analytical principle or principles you will be employing in your essay. For example, a *feminist analysis* of a work of fiction might focus on depictions of gender roles. In another example, you may summarize a text, such as Graham Pullin's "An Introduction to Universal Design" (included in Chapter 9, "Disability Studies: Questioning 'Normal'"), in order to write an analysis of your school or workplace to see whether or not they are designed "for the whole population." In order to perform this type of analysis, you should first clearly state the argument of the piece you will be using as well as what you plan to reveal about the second text (the one you will be analyzing).

Conclusion

When you identify how parts work together to create a whole, you are engaging in critical reading and analysis. Analysis is a crucial element of much college writing; the ability to present and analyze evidence is a skill you'll be asked to use in both humanities and science classes.

Follow-up Activity #1: Analyzing the Dollar Bill

The following multipart activity will ask you to continue thinking about and practicing selecting and analyzing evidence. You may be assigned to complete one or all of the following steps.

PART I: MAKE A LIST

Before you read any further, take out a dollar bill from your pocket, wallet, or bag, look at it, and record what you see. Make a list of all the images and symbols that appear. When you are satisfied that you have gotten down all possible details, please continue reading.

PART II: READ ANOTHER STUDENT'S ANALYSIS

The following is a first draft of a short, student-authored essay. The writer was asked to look at a dollar bill, create a list of the symbols that appear on it, and to "close-read," or analyze, and interpret one or two of those symbols. Her task was to pick out elements to focus on and to explore the implications of those elements, asking what, if anything, the dollar bill can tell us about American culture and values. The writer didn't perform any research for this piece; instead, she drew on her observations as well as her own knowledge and ideas about what she perceived.

Here is the list of elements that Callaghan created:

George Washington, pyramid, eye, eagle, "In God We Trust"

Mary Callaghan

Analysis of the One-Dollar Bill

The Ambiguous Symbols of the Dollar Bill

From eagles to flags to famous presidential portraits, Americans use a variety of popular symbols to represent values such as freedom, democracy, victory, and independence. The American one-dollar bill is saturated with images. One of the less-familiar features is the image of an eye on the top of a pyramid. The meaning behind this symbol may be less obvious than others, leaving it open for interpretation. I argue that the eye and the pyramid are complex symbols that reflect both negative and positive aspects of American society and history.

Given the amount of time and effort required to construct them, pyramids are symbols of hard work. The art of building a pyramid must be very precise in order to create a masterpiece. This hard work and creativity can be compared to the careful and tedious efforts put into building this country and its government. Further, like the pyramid, American laws and the framework of our government are supported by the strong bottom layer of democratic values. The Constitution, the laws, and the outline of America can be considered something of a masterpiece, much like a fully constructed pyramid.

In addition, the pyramids are ancient. This suggests that the ideas of our government are based on those of an earlier time; our government uses both ideas and symbolism associated with ancient Egypt. In constructing the government, the forefathers of the United States drew on the ideas from several different philosophers, leaders, and governing styles, each contributing to the final product much like blocks on a pyramid.

However, the pyramids, I believe, were constructed by slaves working in the harshest of conditions. They toiled their entire lives working on great pyramids they probably never got to see finished. While the dollar bill is perhaps not directly referencing slavery, it does seem important that at the time of our country's founding, we still had people in slavery. This may spark thoughts of those people who this country failed, people who were denied freedom, equal rights, and proper recognition as Americans. African Americans, women, and other minorities have spent decades working and fighting for the rights that the Constitution should have granted everyone without question. Like the slaves, most of these people lived lives deprived of justice and died while it seemed their efforts were still in vain.

On top of the pyramid is an eye. Like the pyramid, the eye could have both good and bad implications. First, because of the phrase "In God We Trust," the eye might be read as God's eye watching over America. In addition, this eye could symbolize how our government uses its authority to watch over American citizens. Governmental figures might feel compelled to compare themselves with an all-seeing eye. While this is important for our safety, the eye could also represent surveillance.

Finally, in a democratic society, we have the opportunity and obligation to elect our leaders, and the votes of the citizens are essential building blocks to the structure of the pyramid. Governmental figures may, therefore, only assume their position on top with the support of the entire pyramid. Thus, the eye is both a symbol of authority but also represents the way the American people "keep an eye" on their leaders.

PART III: WRITE BACK

Respond to Callaghan's analysis by answering the following questions.

1. If you have noticed signs and symbols on the dollar bill that Callaghan hasn't, then you have the makings of your own argument. What other signs and symbols did you notice? Pick another detail and write a one-paragraph analysis of that element.

2. Write two paragraphs responding directly to Callaghan. In one paragraph, describe for her the part or parts of the essay that you liked or found convincing. In the second paragraph, tell her what she could continue to work on developing or explaining in her essay.

3. Go further: spend some time researching and reading about the various symbols you noticed. A simple Google search of "symbols dollar bill" will result in some fascinating information (as well as many sites promoting conspiracy theories about the U.S. government). Write a three- to four-paragraph analysis of the dollar bill incorporating the research you have done. (See Chapter 8, "Research and Writing" for a discussion of how to incorporate and cite sources.)

Chapter Three

Getting Started:
Prewriting, Developing a Topic, and Drafting

Chapter Objectives

- Identify prewriting techniques.
- Select a challenging and engaging topic.
- Articulate the importance of your chosen topic and select supporting evidence.
- Implement various drafting approaches to create a document.

>> Prereading Check-In

How do you feel when you are writing? If you like to write, explain what you like about it. If you don't like to write, explain what it is that you find unpleasant. If you like writing some types of things and not others, explain what and why.

Writing assignments for college classes are generally quite varied. Some instructors will give you detailed instructions that explain what you are expected to explore in your essay, while others will ask you to demonstrate certain skills, such as the ability to present and defend a thesis (discussed in Chapter 4) or the ability to incorporate multiple sources (discussed in Chapter 8), while allowing you to select your own topic. Still other assignments fall somewhere in between: the instructor provides you with a list of possible topics and questions to explore, but the ultimate direction of the essay is up to you. When approaching any assignment in which you have a degree of choice, you may want to begin by establishing what your interests are, what you think and want to say about your topic, and how, specifically, you will proceed.

In addition to describing prewriting strategies that can help you figure out what you think about both general or specific issues and topics, this chapter discusses how you might go about selecting and developing a topic and offers some suggestions as to how to get started writing.

Prewriting Techniques

Prewriting is anything you do in order to get yourself to start thinking and writing. Just as an athlete might want to warm up her muscles by moving around and stretching, writers often "warm up" with prewriting techniques. This section reviews two techniques that many writers use in order to warm up: **brainstorming** and **freewriting**.

Note: Although "prewriting" suggests that you use these tools before you start writing (and they are very effective at this stage of the process), they can also be effective at later stages as well. If you're afflicted by "writer's block" or get stumped in the middle of your essay, it may be helpful to do some freewriting or brainstorming in order to get yourself back on track. In addition, many writers freewrite about their process in order to reflect on and better understand what they have accomplished, where they are going with their writing, and what they still need to do.

Brainstorming: Allowing Ideas and Connections to Emerge

Brainstorming, done individually or in groups, is simply letting your mind come up with ideas without judgment. So, for example, if a student is asked to brainstorm on attitudes toward food in America, he might generate a list of commercials for fast-food restaurants that he'd seen, television programs that present losing weight as a competition, people he knew who were on diets, articles he'd read that focused on food and eating, times in his life when he ate poorly, holidays associated with eating, and more. He would use brainstorming to come up with and record ideas and then later to start to figure out which ideas he found exciting and interesting and wanted to possibly follow up on by further developing, researching, or writing.

In addition to academic settings, brainstorming is often used in the corporate world; the idea of "thinking outside the box" is an invitation to allow your mind to roam and to follow up on ideas, even if they initially seem impossible or ridiculous.

Some writers prefer to visually represent the relationship between their ideas rather than simply jotting them down. Called **diagramming** or **clustering**, this is the practice of mapping out for yourself what you're thinking about and, ideally, demonstrating the relationships.

Brainstorming Exercise

Part I:
Alone or with a group of other students, brainstorm on the topic of "happiness." Write down whatever ideas come to mind.

Part II (optional):
After developing a list or group of ideas, select one topic to develop into a longer discussion or essay.

The following diagram was created in response to a prompt asking a student to explore the relationship between material possessions and happiness.

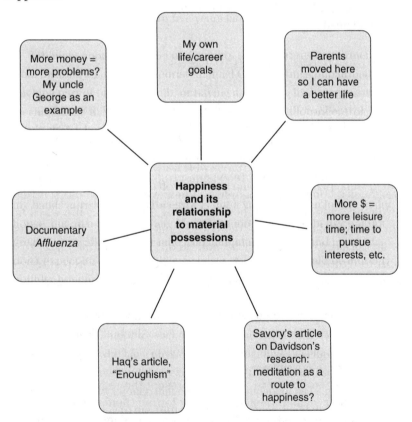

The above diagram gives the author a sense of how the secondary ideas are related to her main idea; you might notice that the ideas on

the left side of the page seem to problematize the idea that money can buy happiness, while the ideas on the right side begin to suggest that material wealth can bring some level of comfort. Each of the circles could be its own paragraph supporting the author's main contention.

Rather than visual mapping, other students might choose to make lists of their ideas and to later organize those lists according to what ideas they think are the strongest or most important.

Freewriting: Turn Off the Editor

Freewriting is a lot like brainstorming in that you really have to turn off your internal editor, or stop judging your ideas and allow yourself to free-associate. When you freewrite, you put down whatever you feel like writing. If you wanted to, you could simply write, "I'm the best" over and over again. One goal is to never stop moving your pen or stop typing, even if what you are writing doesn't make any sense.

In a "directed freewrite," you still turn off your editor but you make an effort to stay on topic. For example, your instructor might tell you to do a freewrite on your paper's progress, in which case you might write about what you have done so far and what you still need to do. Or, as in the exercise below, the instructor might ask you to freewrite on an issue so that you can start getting some of your ideas down. (Many of the "Prereading Check-In" questions in this textbook are designed to help you establish your initial reactions to and thoughts about a topic.) A directed freewrite can be particularly helpful when you're trying to come up with a topic for an essay or if you get stuck in the middle of an essay and you need to figure out what to do next.

The following is a student freewrite answering the above "Write Back" prompt. Underline any phrases or ideas that the student might want to pursue if he was writing an essay on this topic.

WRITE BACK   **Freewrite**

Write about whatever comes to mind—places, memories, concepts— when you think of the word "nature."

Nature. It makes me think of how we used to go camping when me and Joe were little. Maybe we didn't go that often, but I feel like we were always going then. That was also before the divorce, so maybe

*I'm idealizing a little bit. We would go "Up North." I remember fish-
ing, too. My dad still fishes a lot but he goes to different places now.
Actually, the lake we used to go to is really popular, which stinks,
because the whole idea is to get away from other people. I guess.
Sometimes it feels like there isn't any place left that's really wild or
away from other people. At least not in this country. Is that a good
thing? I don't think so. Last year I visited my friend in Tucson and
she took me into the desert and that felt pretty desolate. We couldn't
get a phone signal or anything. It felt very far away and that was
kind of scary and also what made it kind of cool.*

TIP BOX **Allowing for Great Ideas**

There are other ways to free up your creativity and get yourself thinking in
addition to brainstorming and freewriting. These activities might be talking into
a voice recorder or sharing your ideas with a friend, tutor, or instructor who
takes notes for you and gives you feedback. You may want to try out a few
different techniques and see what works for you.

In addition, many people report that they have their best ideas when they're
most relaxed (for example, in the shower). Thus, some writers overcome
"writer's block" by taking a nap, doing yoga or meditating, going for a run or
walk, or talking out their ideas with friends.

Choosing a Challenging and Engaging Topic

As discussed at the beginning of this chapter, you will often be in
the position of choosing a topic from within a larger theme, such as
"Choosing School: American Education in the 21st Century" or "Social
Networking," two of the chapters in the anthology of this book. In this
case, you will often have to decide which aspect of the larger topic you
want to focus on. Many successful writers freewrite and/or brainstorm
as soon as they receive an assignment in order to capture their ideas
and determine what they will be most interested in pursuing. Some

---

TIP BOX **Keep an Idea File**

Hold onto everything you write this semester—even if it's an informal freewrite or brainstorm—because it might come in handy later if and when you're
preparing an essay.

writers feel that freewriting and brainstorming reveal ideas and opinions that they didn't even know they had.

As you select your topic, it might help to keep some commonsense advice in mind: choose a topic that actually interests you, that will challenge you, and that you feel will allow you to fulfill the assignment.

Choosing to Challenge Yourself

When it comes to selecting from a list of possible topics, you might be tempted to choose a topic because it looks "easy." However, there are two potential pitfalls here. First, it might actually be quite difficult to write a strong and sophisticated essay about a topic that doesn't seem to demand any hard work or thinking. A student, for example, might think that writing a four-page paper analyzing the representation of race in one of her favorite movies, *American History X* (1998), won't be a challenge. When she turns in the paper, however, she's done little more than describe the action of the film. The paper comes back with the comments: "too much plot summary. What's your point?" The task of analyzing a film is actually much more complicated than simply telling what happens; in fact, writing critically about mass media may be one of the *hardest* kinds of essays you can do in a composition class. While the topic of "race in *American History X*" is not itself too easy, the student's approach—watching and summarizing the movie—is.

Another pitfall of an "easy" topic is that it might not give the writer a lot of ideas for development. For example, a very "hot button" topic these days is texting while driving. A student might be tempted to write a paper on this topic condemning texting while driving because it seems like a cut-and-dried issue. However, would anyone argue that texting while driving is a good idea? In order to develop an essay that is interesting for both writer and readers, the writer must get past the obvious ("texting while driving is a bad idea").

Now, while the topic of "texting and driving" is a little worn, it could actually yield a complex and interesting essay if the writer finds a fresh way to approach the issue. The point is, of course, that you're in a writing class in order to improve as a writer, not to fall back on old, and perhaps unhelpful, habits or, as in the above examples, to discover the "easiest" way to do things. In fact, you might find that choosing topics that seem difficult or challenging often result in your increased engagement with the assignment and, ultimately, in your development as a writer.

> ## TIP BOX How to Read an Assignment
>
> The first step to successfully completing an assignment is, of course, making sure you understand what it is you're being asked to do. After establishing the assignment's straightforward requirements, such as due dates, page length, and minimum source requirements, you should look for some key words and phrases that indicate what kinds of writing skills you will be expected to demonstrate. Look at the verbs, or words such as summarize, respond, describe, explain, argue, analyze, compare, and contrast. Some assignments will ask you to perform more than one of the above tasks; for example, you might be asked to "summarize and respond" to another author's work. In another example, you might be asked to "analyze" a situation in a "thesis-driven" essay. Analysis is discussed in Chapter 2 of this book; thesis statements are discussed in Chapter 4, arguments in Chapter 5, and summaries in Chapter 8. Ultimately, if you are at all confused by the terminology of the assignment or about what you are supposed to do, you should ask your instructor for elaboration and assistance.

Developing Your Topic

Beginning writers sometimes have a hard time selecting a topic that is appropriate for the page and research requirements of the assignment. Sometimes topics are way too broad: it's unrealistic to try to cover "World War II" in a five- or seven-page paper. On the other hand, you don't want to choose a topic that's so limited that you find yourself repeating ideas and phrases or pulling in irrelevant details just to meet the page requirement. This section discusses strategies for developing your topic while keeping in mind the parameters of the assignment, as well as determining and presenting why what you have to say is important.

Broadening Your View

Once you've established what it is you'd like to write about, spend some time thinking about and recording the major points that you want to make in the essay. Try to imagine how many paragraphs you'll need in order to fully address each point.

Expert writers develop fascinating—and lengthy—papers discussing a single stanza of a poem or what might seem to be a small historical event. However, there are times when a topic might be too narrow to fully explore in a well-developed essay. If you find that you can only come up with one or two points to make about your topic, you might reconsider the scope. For example, the topic of texting and driving described above is too limited: the student's only major point was that texting and driving is bad because it can cause car accidents. However, if he reconsidered his approach, he might be able to add some nuance or complexity to his topic. He could expand his topic to discuss how texting is negative in teens' lives in general—beyond just their driving habits. Or he could broaden his topic to allow for a discussion of new laws against texting and driving; he could even shift his topic in order to address whether or not these laws are appropriate or effective.

Sometimes students feel that their topics are too limited and their essays are too short (not meeting the page minimum) because they don't have anything else they want to say or add in the essay. After putting hours of work into the paper, the student could choose to change topics and work on something new at the last minute. This, of course, is probably not the best practice.

If you find yourself in the position of having nothing else to say, perhaps you need to ask more probing questions about your topic. Check in with yourself: are you hiding from the work? If so, you might do some brainstorming or freewriting in order to further pursue the "how and why" questions that might add complexity to the discussion.

Narrowing Your Topic

While some students might start off with topics that are too limited, more often topics start off as general ideas (i.e., "controversies around education" or "The American Civil War") that need narrowing and development. This section discusses the kinds of questions you can ask in order to focus your topic. These include: What do I want to say about my subject, and to whom do I want to say it? To be more specific, what populations am I writing about? Which aspects of my topic are important? Why does what I'm writing about matter?

Here's an example of how asking and answering questions can help you to move from the general to the specific as well as to establish why what you will write is important and interesting.

General Topic: The American Civil War
Who am I writing about?
African Americans who fought as soldiers in the Northern army
Which aspects of my topic are important?

> I will discuss how these individuals became enlisted, where and
> when they fought, and what their contributions were.
> **Why does what I'm writing about matter?**
> The discussion of these soldiers can help us to better understand
> the war in general and the participation of people of color in our
> armed forces more specifically.

Here's another example, although this student jots down a number
of areas that interest him before he arrives at his focus.

Topic?	The Internet
Who?	Teenagers or children.
Which aspects?	Cyberbullying or something with kids looking at porn or maybe predators on the Internet.
Why does it matter?	**While there are a lot of problems that come with letting kids use the Internet, I think that cyberbullying is an issue we have to address. It has been a problem in my town and has increased so much that victimized teens have committed suicide.**

Notice how both of the above topics start out very general ("the Civil
War" and "the Internet") and that figuring out who is being addressed
and which aspects are important helps students arrive at a much more
specific focus.

Topic Checklist

Do a quick check-in with yourself once you've settled on a topic. Is
your topic

- appropriate in terms of the length of the essay?
- going to allow you to demonstrate the types of skills the instructor would like to see you using (such as incorporating sources or forwarding a thesis)?
- appropriate in terms of the subjects/questions the instructor has asked you to write about?
- interesting and important?
- something that you will be able to find sources on if you are asked to conduct research?

A wonderful resource, of course, is your instructor. He or she will be
able to help you decide if your topic should be narrowed or broadened.

Determining Why It Matters

In the previous section, each example ends by asking the student to explain why what he or she is writing about matters. Whenever we write, we want to be making a contribution to the larger conversation that is going on about our topic.

Sometimes a topic matters because you plan to introduce a new way of looking at or understanding an issue, as demonstrated by the example above that explores the topic of the American Civil War. For the "texting while driving" topic, the author might decide that, although most people say that they agree that texting while driving is dangerous, the statistics show that many people are still doing it so the point is worth making again. Finally, the topic of cyberbullying in the above example is important to the author because it is something he has seen increasing not only nationally but also in his own community. The author's personal connection to the topic provides urgency for him; hopefully that urgency will carry over into the essay.

Different Approaches to Drafting

Once you've established your interests, ideas, and topic, it will be time to start writing the essay. Some writers say that they already know what they want to say and how they want to say it before they start composing their essay. They sit down and write it from the introductory paragraph right through to the concluding paragraph. While this strategy might work well for some individuals, it is clearly not for everyone. In fact, many writers find it more effective to write their introductions last. (For more discussion of introductory paragraphs, see Chapter 6.) This section provides an overview of different approaches to drafting your essay. Try one or two that you have not used before.

TIP BOX   **Create the Conditions for Success**

When it's time to write your essay, make sure that you provide yourself with the time and space you need in order to give your topic the sustained attention that any assignment calls for. That is, don't sabotage yourself by trying to write your paper a half an hour before class, in your car, or while you are on your phone. Instead, choose to turn off the phone completely, stay off the Internet, and find a quiet place to think and write.

Getting It Down

Some writers find that once they've selected a topic and brainstormed some ideas, the best way for them to proceed to is simply start writing, not worrying about grammar or polish, but getting the ideas down on paper in some sort of organized form. They often skip the introduction and start on the first "body" paragraph, or the first point they want to make.

One warning: this strategy is only effective when the writer makes time to revise the essay and polish it later. Sometimes students intend to write a second draft, but when they've finished the first, they feel exhausted and decide that the first draft is "good enough." If this sounds like something that happens to you, it is time to break the habit, especially when preparing essays for your composition class.

Creating an Outline

Many students find it helpful to generate an outline or a list of their ideas in the order they will present them. Outlines can be very valuable in that they provide you with a sense of the overall structure and direction of the essay. In addition, when you write each paragraph to correspond with each point on the outline or on the list, you can easily see where you are going and how you might choose to transition or move into your next point. (Because many students are already familiar with formal outlines, they are not discussed here; however, a quick Google search of "formal outline" will yield many helpful websites.)

Building Around the Evidence

Evidence, which is discussed in both Chapters 2 and 6, is the data you include in your essay. Evidence can include personal experience and observation, facts and statistics, and quotations, summaries, and paraphrases from other authors. Some writers establish what they will use for evidence, figure out the order in which they will present their evidence, and then build their paragraphs around the evidence. One way to do this is to construct an outline or a list of your evidence. An old-fashioned technique is to write the evidence on index cards and then stack the cards according to the order in which you would like to present each piece of information (you can flip through and reorganize easily). The index-card method is also helpful for visual learners and thinkers who might want to lay out all of the major points and evidence in front of them in order to see how they relate to and build on each other. A more contemporary practice would be to create a computer document into which you cut and paste your evidence, moving it around to see what works the best.

Conclusion

Essay writing is an opportunity to deepen your learning and develop your writing skills. As you choose a topic, figure out what interests you and what will challenge you. Use prewriting techniques like brainstorming and freewriting to get you "warmed up" and attuned to your ideas and interests, as well as to further explore and develop whatever topic you've chosen to focus on. Once you settle on a topic, keep asking yourself why it matters or why it is important and make sure that these stakes are clear to your reader as well. Find what works for you as you begin drafting, and always make sure to leave time for one—if not multiple—revisions.

Follow-up Activity #1: Narrowing Your Topic

Practice narrowing the following topics by supplying possible answers to the questions that follow. There are no "right answers" here; just pursue any idea within the topic that interests you.

Topic: Disability
Who?
Which aspects?
Why does it matter?

Topic: Food
Who?
Which aspects?
Why does it matter?

Follow-up Activity #2: Developing Main Ideas

In the following exercise, designed to help you practice developing and organizing ideas, you will either work alone or in a group to formulate three or four main points for each topic. Each point would be discussed in its own paragraph in the essay. If you can't come up with three or four major points, revise the topic in order to make it more interesting and workable.

Note: It's okay if some of your points make opposite arguments; interesting essays often allow for complex or multiple points of view.

Example:

TOPIC: UNIFORMS IN PUBLIC HIGH SCHOOLS

Point 1: Uniforms might eliminate some of the competition over wealth and status.

Point 2: This might also result in less bullying.

Point 3: Having everyone dressed in the same neat and formal clothing sends a message that school is not a fashion show but a place for seriousness and hard work.

Point 4: Unfortunately, forcing all students to dress the same limits their freedom of expression regarding fashion.

TOPICS:

1. Incivility on the Internet.
2. Schools providing/not providing education about the outdoors and nature.
3. Depictions of individuals with disabilities in movies and on television.

4 Chapter Four
The Thesis Statement

- Take a position on a topic to move from an observation to an argument.
- Distinguish between observation and argument.
- Construct effective thesis statements.
- Construct preliminary thesis statements.
- Identify strategies for developing thesis statements.

>> **Prereading Check-In**

Write a paragraph arguing one of the following positions:

Smoking should be banned/not banned in all public places.

We should/should not put a "fat tax" on junk foods.

Everyone/not everyone should go to college.

Choosing to Take a Position

The "Prereading Check-In" above asks you to take a position and write a paragraph supporting that position. For example, you may write a paragraph that starts with the sentence "Smoking should be banned in all public places," followed with sentences providing the reasons that it should be banned. In doing so, you are presenting and defending a **thesis statement** or an overarching point. Although the above exercise is short, thesis statements work as the organizing principle of your essays. Not only do they announce what you will prove in your essay, but every paragraph in your essay should refer back to and support your thesis statement.

Here are some examples of thesis statements taken from articles that appear in the later anthology of readings:

In his article "Health Care Should Be a Personal Responsibility" (Chapter 10: What to Eat), Radley Balko writes, **"Instead of manipulating or intervening in the array of food options available to American consumers, our government ought to be working to foster a sense of responsibility in and ownership of our own health and well-being."**

In "An Inconvenient Truth About Youth" (Chapter 11: Ecological Consciousness), Laura Wray and Constance Flanagan write that **"the inconvenient truth today is that youths' willingness to conserve gas, heat and energy has taken a precipitous plunge since the 1980s."**

Each of the above quotations serves as the thesis statement for the entire article. While you might find other sentences or statements in each article that seem to capture the author's main ideas, the above statements are good examples of refined thesis statements because they provide the overall argument or point of the article. That is, Radley Balko hopes to show that the government's involvement in fighting obesity is misguided and that individuals should be held responsible for their health, and Wray and Flanagan argue that young people are less likely than older folks to act to protect the environment. (Wray and Flanagan go on to suggest that the older generation should try to model better environmental behavior.)

A thesis statement, then, is the contention, or proposition, that the author states clearly and then backs up throughout the entire piece. A strong thesis statement is an essential part of many successful compositions.

From Observation to Argument

Notice that each of the above examples does not simply state the topic or present an observation. For example, Balko doesn't write "I will discuss the government" and Wray and Flanagan don't write, "environmentalism is a movement." Instead, in both of the examples, the authors go further to make clear what he or she will say *about* their topic or issue. Balko suggests that the government's approach to the issue of obesity is a problem that needs to be addressed; in

WRITE BACK   Identifying Others' Theses

Read the relevant article and then finish the following sentence by including Gunlock's thesis statement in a quotation.

In Julie Gunlock's "Federalizing Fat" (Chapter 10, What To Eat), Gunlock argues_____ .

TIP BOX Highlighting the Argument

While not all college essay assignments demand that you develop an argument, many professors across disciplines expect students to be able to argue—and back up (support)—a point. Argument is discussed further in the next chapter.

One strategy that you might find effective is to phrase your thesis statement in the following way: "In this paper, I will argue that_____." If you or your instructor is uncomfortable with this phrasing, in particular the use of the word "I," you can always delete it after your first draft. The usefulness of this phrase, however, is that it should remind you that *you* are putting forward a point, not just restating a fact or making a casual observation.

a similar manner, Wray and Flanagan, rather than simply observing that young people are not interested in environmentalism, suggest that this disinterest is a negative trend. This part of the thesis statement, the author's perspective on the topic, provides the thesis statement with an edge and a direction. Having a point about the topic gives you something to prove.

You can test your thesis statement by asking whether you are putting forward an observation or an argument. It would be silly, for example, to write a paper that begins "In this paper, I will argue that there is a lot of interest in celebrities in our culture." A reasonable person probably wouldn't disagree with this statement because it's just basically true. If you were to say, however, "In this paper, I will argue that our culture's interest in celebrities is sick" or "I will argue that celebrities have a responsibility to behave as role models," suddenly you are saying something *about* the topic. Certainly, reasonable people could disagree about whether or not celebrity gossip has a good, bad, or neutral effect on our society or whether or not celebrities should serve as role models.

A topic or issue matters when it is a problem (for example, Gunlock critiques government attempts to curtail childhood obesity), when you offer a solution (Wray and Flanagan suggest that government should encourage and model better conservation practices), or when you are saying something that people haven't said before or you are reframing the terms of the conversation (Balko suggests that obesity may be a problem, but that government intervention is an even bigger problem).

WRITE BACK   Adding the Argumentative Edge

Each of the following sentences is a basic observation or fact. Write a second sentence in which you say something about the topic.

EXAMPLE

Observation	Many industrial farmers inject pigs and cows with antibiotics.
Thesis Statement	The fact that some farmers inject pigs and cows with antibiotics *is a problem because,* as a result of this exposure to antibiotics in the meat we eat, humans are developing antibiotic-resistant infections.

1. Obesity is increasing in America.
2. Some colleges have ramps to accommodate students in wheelchairs.
3. *Grand Theft Auto* is a video game.

Understanding and Developing Effective Thesis Statements

The Preliminary or Working Thesis Statement

Because constructing an effective thesis statement can be a difficult task, it's often effective to *write your whole essay before you develop your final thesis statement.* One reason to do so is that writing an essay can often be (or rather, should often be) a process of discovery for the writer. Peter Taylor, a Pulitzer Prize-winning author, wrote that "writing is how you discover what you think." That's why we often need to revise our thesis statements near the end of the writing process; it is only after we've spent some time on and given sustained attention to our topic that we really know what we think about it.

Chapter 3, "Getting Started: Prewriting, Developing a Topic, and Drafting," emphasizes that a thesis statement may emerge gradually as you think about and narrow down your topic by asking questions and developing the points you will make. Even if you decide to delay writing your thesis statement until the end of the writing process, it's still a

> **TIP BOX** Flipping Your Intro and Conclusion
>
> Have you ever gotten a comment from an instructor that you should use your conclusion as your essay's introduction? Often, it is at the end of the essay that some of us really figure out what we are arguing in the essay. If you're familiar with this comment, you might consider moving some of the ideas you present in your conclusion into your introduction after you've completed a first draft.

good idea to start with a **working** or **preliminary thesis statement** or a general idea of what you will be proving in the paper.

If a Thesis Statement Were a Person

Here's an analogy that might clarify the characteristics of an effective thesis statement. Imagine thesis statements as types of personalities. We'll call them Kitty, Blando, Charming, and Sophia.

Kitty is part of a radical political group that thinks cats are incredibly intelligent and should have rights as citizens. Kitty makes extreme claims and bristles and gets angry at those who don't agree with her or don't understand why she is so fervent about her causes. Predictably, only those who agree with her views find her passionate and eloquent.

Unlike Kitty, *Blando* is often hesitant to take a position on any issue. It seems like he doesn't really have any opinions, and he offers observations such as "Old people are a valuable resource" and "Diversity is the spice of life." People get along with Blando, but he's pretty boring and, after speaking to him for a few minutes, most folks tend to drift away from him in search of more lively and meaningful conversation.

Charming is an interesting guy—full of anecdotes and information. He'll tell story after story, but as you listen to him, you'll often notice that the stories are disconnected. When Charming finally gets to the end of his story, someone else has to "interpret" it for you by saying, "What Charming means is . . ."

Sophia is pretty even-tempered, although she cares deeply about certain issues. An extremely reasonable person, Sophia is able to get along with people even if she disagrees with them. In fact, Sophia can often be overheard beginning her sentences with remarks such as "I understand your point, but . . ." or "While some people may feel that way, I feel that . . ." and "Let me see if I understand you correctly . . ."

Now, if we analyze the four—Kitty, Blando, Charming, and Sophia— as potential thesis statements, we can begin to see which statements begin, sustain, and maintain stimulating conversation and which don't.

Kitty is the type of thesis statement that is downright unreasonable. She takes positions that are really difficult for anyone else to get behind, and she resorts to repetition and irrational outbursts in order to try to force other people to see things her way.

Blando is a much more common thesis statement than Kitty: he just doesn't say anything at all. He's either so afraid of offending someone, or so unsure of his own ideas, or so lazy, that he refuses to take any positions. He has a hard time following up on his openers (i.e., "Old people are a valuable resource") because not only does he not have anything else to say about the issue, but whoever he's talking to has usually already walked away.

Charming, unlike Kitty or Blando, appeals to other people and is often very entertaining. The trouble is that his listeners don't understand the point of his stories.

So, of course, *Sophia* is the model conversationalist and thesis statement. She has something to say, and it's neither outrageous nor straight out of a greeting card. Sophia's positions are well considered and are often responses to others' ideas. (Notice that Sophia often begins by acknowledging others' positions. It's a good idea to use your thesis statement to demonstrate that you have researched your topic and you know what other people are saying about your topic, but that you have something important to contribute.) Not everyone agrees with Sophia, but she does a nice job of reasoning with others and explaining her positions on issues while providing support (in the form of examples) as she argues.

Developing the Thesis Statement

As the above analogy is meant to demonstrate, an effective thesis statement has certain qualities.

Your thesis statement should **not**:

- be a cliché. ("Friends are an important part of life.")
- be an idea you can exhaust in a one- or two-paragraph discussion. ("Texting and driving should be illegal because it is dangerous.")
- be impossible to agree with. ("Cats should have the right to vote.")
- be an observation. ("Daycare is an option for many working parents.")

Your thesis statement **should:**

- be something that others could reasonably disagree with. ("Social networking promotes only superficial relationships.")
- be complex and sophisticated. ("Recent research has troubled our former understanding of nonhuman animals as obviously inferior to humans. We need to reevaluate how we understand and appreciate animal intelligence.")
- provide a sense of the overarching point of your essay. ("Using cross-cultural comparisons, I will demonstrate that the United States can and should establish reliable, accessible, and high-quality state-funded child care.")
- provide you with a point that you will be able to expand on and defend. ("Although some teenagers abuse it, texting is a habit that can have social and academic benefits.")
- appear early in your essay, preferably in the first paragraph. (Some instructors also specify that the thesis statement should appear as the last sentence of your first paragraph.)

Your thesis statement **may:**

- be prescriptive or advise the reader to take a certain kind of action. ("We should allow the privatization of the public school system.")
- be an original idea or intervention. ("Although most people see social networking as facilitating relationships, I will argue that Facebook, in particular, actually trivializes and degrades friendships.")
- be more than one sentence. ("As a nation that is founded on principles of equality and justice, it is a contradiction that the United States of America has a huge class of people who are discriminated against economically, socially, and politically. Our treatment of 'ex-cons' who have served their time is unfair, and we must take legal steps to right this wrong.")

Talking Through Your Ideas

Ultimately, the thesis statement is a tool for you and for your reader. The thesis statement will give you a clear idea of what your focus is and what you will have to do in the paper in order to make your point. In addition, the thesis statement functions to let your reader know what it is you'll be convincing him or her of.

Talking over your thesis statement with peers can be an effective way of developing and sharpening your thesis statement. The following (which is drawn from a real conversation, although the students' names have been changed) is the development of one of Blando's boring remarks: *Old people are a valuable resource.* As you can see, by challenging Blando and talking through his ideas with him, Sophia is able to help Blando arrive at a more specific and compelling approach for his paper.

Blando: Old people are a valuable resource.

Sophia: Sure, but does anyone think they aren't? I mean, who's going to say that old people are useless?

Blando: Well, maybe people wouldn't *say* that, but have you visited a nursing home lately? People are just stuck there, forgotten about. We don't care about old people at all. You know, in China, old people are treated with reverence. Here, it's like, we just want to put them in storage until they die.

Sophia: So what you're saying is that people all pretend that we have respect for the elderly, but when it comes down to it, we don't really.

Blando: That's it.

Sophia: Not everybody is like that, though. My grandmother lives with my family.

Blando: But our culture in general doesn't really value old people. That's what I saw when I was volunteering at that nursing home last year. A lot of people's families never came to visit them. It was really sad.

Sophia: Well, just because it was sad doesn't mean that the old people themselves were valuable. I'm not trying to be cruel, but do you see what I'm saying? Being old does not equal being valuable. I don't really want to hang out with someone who's totally out of it.

Blando: But there are so many problems with what you're saying. First of all, not all of them are "out of it." Some of them were smart and engaged. One old guy was very interested in politics and current events, and he had some great perspectives. He had served in World War II. But, you know, even the ones who were kind of out of it, I mean, they're people too. They're still human beings. They deserve to be treated with dignity.

So Blando is upset by the treatment of **senior citizens** in **nursing homes in the United States;** he feels that our culture does not treat old people with **dignity.** This is much stronger and more specific than his original statement. Now, Blando has a couple of different directions that his thesis statement could take. One might be a cross-cultural

TALK BACK   Engaging in a Dialogue

Using Blando and Sophia's conversation as a model, engage in a dialogue with a partner in an attempt to further develop one of the following into strong preliminary thesis statements.

A lot of people still smoke in public places.

Teenagers spend a lot of time on their computers doing social networking stuff.

College tuitions keep increasing.

(You may choose to ask questions such as: Could I write a paper on this topic? What kinds of evidence—articles, data, observations—would I use to back up my position? Would I want to write a paper on this topic? Why or why not?)

comparison, looking at how old people are treated in other nations and cultures and discussing what the United States could learn from or teach to other nations about the treatment of seniors. Another option is that Blando could discuss *how* old folks are a "valuable resource": what is it that he feels they have to offer younger people? Finally, perhaps Blando could start to address what old and young people have to offer *each other*. For this last option, Blando might wind up writing a paper that is really about encouraging volunteerism among young Americans (which is not anywhere near "old people are a valuable resource," the thesis statement Blando began with, but that uses Blando's visits to the nursing home as an example of the type of service work that might benefit young people). His discussion with Sophia has resulted in a reevaluation of his first idea and in the development of a number of *preliminary thesis statements*.

Conclusion

A thesis statement is a tool that can help you organize your ideas as well as let your reader know what it is you'll be proving in your essay. A strong thesis statement should be appropriately narrow and, rather than simply stating an observation about your topic, should forward an arguable point about your topic.

Follow-up Activity #1:
Playing Thesis Statement Telephone

Did you ever play the game "telephone" when you were a kid? In the game, you sat in a circle, and you whispered a statement into the ear of your neighbor to the right. Your neighbor then repeated that statement into the next person's ear, and so on, until it went all the way around the circle and was whispered into the ear of your neighbor on the left. The last person then repeated the statement to the group, usually to peals of laughter because somehow your original statement ("Ellen likes Mike") had transformed during its trip around the circle ("Hell is on bikes"). Although the childhood game is silly and fun, it nevertheless reveals how a statement can be changed over time and with handling.

The follow-up below asks you to perform a more academic form of "telephone" wherein you, as a group, transform a simple topic into a working thesis statement by passing the treated topic around to each person in the group, asking him or her to further refine it or to interrogate it.

There are three topics listed below. Each person takes a topic to start with. When you have your topic, write a preliminary thesis statement. Then, pass that thesis statement to your right. The person to your right will revise/add to the statement and pass it to the student on his or her right. Passing the developing thesis statement continues until the statement returns to you. At that point, the group should decide as a whole whether or not the thesis statement is strong enough to build a discussion around or if it should be passed around the group again.

If this activity goes smoothly, you will first write your thesis statement and, while your statement is going around the group, you will have the opportunity to add to or revise two other thesis statements initially developed by the other members of your group.

Here are the topics:

1. The American high school
2. The rights of people with disabilities
3. Children and the Internet

As you revise each thesis statement, think about the questions used for narrowing topics in Chapter 3, "Getting Started: Prewriting, Developing a Topic, and Drafting" (Who? Which aspects? Why does it matter?).

In addition, you might ask yourself why this topic is important overall. Can action pertaining to this topic be taken? How can this action be taken? Time permitting, if each group has an opportunity to share its strongest statement with the class, all of you will understand more clearly that quite a bit of brainstorming and thought have to go into creating a preliminary thesis statement, and it isn't as hard as you think it is—if you get other people involved in your ideas.

Chapter Five

Argument

Chapter Objectives

- Develop your position using strategies of *pathos*, *ethos*, and *logos*.
- Consider and prepare for counter-arguments.

>> Prereading Check-In

Describe a recent argument you had with another person. What points were you trying to make? What points was the other person trying to make?

Argument: Choosing to Take a Position

The task of developing original arguments is something you may or may not have been asked to do in your precollege work, but it is a key component of many college assignments. While it may appear daunting to have to articulate your ideas on issues that you may not have given too much thought to before, this chapter will provide you with an understanding of how to state a position, employ a variety of appeals, and construct effective arguments.

As discussed in Chapter 2, "Using Evidence and Analysis," you may already be proficient at constructing arguments. Every time you say something like "I hate/love that movie/book/person," you are taking a position on a topic. If the person you're talking to has a different opinion, you may be asked to back up your opinion with evidence, as well as to explain how the evidence works. Stating your position and offering and explaining your evidence are the essence of argument.

An Example of Argument:
The Courtroom Procedural

Courtroom dramas (for example, television crime shows such as *Law and Order* or novels such as Harper Lee's *To Kill a Mockingbird* or John Grisham's *Runaway Jury*), although perhaps not completely accurate in their reflection of the workings of the legal system, can demonstrate some of the tools used to make arguments. In a typical courtroom drama, lawyers construct arguments for opposing sides. These stories are interesting because they depend on two different perspectives about the truth of a situation, such as whether an individual is guilty or not guilty, sane or insane, liable or not liable, and because the outcome of a trial has significant consequences for the characters involved.

The following excerpt from Douglas Starr's 2010 book *The Killer of Little Shepherds: A True Crime Story and the Birth of Forensic Science* describes the arguments made by the prosecuting and defense attorneys (Ducher and Charbonnier) at the trial of Joseph Vacher, a serial killer in nineteenth-century France. Importantly, the question was not whether or not Vacher committed the crime (he was clearly the perpetrator), but whether Vacher was sane or insane. Although he had been in an asylum before he began murdering, the doctors had declared him "cured." If found insane (or "not responsible" for his actions), Vacher would have been recommitted to a state-run asylum. This was troubling because there was a very good chance that he would have been released after a relatively brief time. In short, Ducher wanted to prove that Vacher was sane and thus responsible for his actions; Charbonnier wanted to prove that Vacher was insane and thus not responsible.

As you read the following selection, note Starr's masterful descriptions as well as how each attorney interprets the same evidence in order to convince the jury to see things his way.

From *The Killer of Little Shepherds:*

At four o'clock Ducher began his closing statement for the prosecution. With a solemn air and "grand gestures that seemed the result of studied preparation," he described Vacher as "probably the greatest criminal in history." He reminded the jury of the defendant's life story, from his early days as a malicious, violent child to his troubled adolescence and then his violent behavior in the regiment.

Ducher continued with his summation. He reminded the jury of Vacher's time in the asylums, where, regardless of whether he was insane or merely faking, he was released with a document attesting to his cure. Ducher . . . recounted the rest of the killing spree and the experts' evaluations of the crimes. "All have the same characteristics, the mark of the monster," he said. "Each one required a sangfroid, and remarkable presence of mind in preparation and execution."

Vacher was no lunatic, Ducher concluded, but a conscious, calculating predator.

Now it was Charbonnier's turn. His sonorous voice, with its great ability to communicate emotion, "impressed everyone," according to reporters. Motioning to Vacher, he intoned, "This is not a great criminal, but a poor, sick man whom I have come to defend . . . we still do not have proof of his complete responsibility."

Like Ducher before him, Charbonnier reviewed Vacher's life history for the jury, but through a radically different lens. He said that many of the stories about the defendant's childhood had been exaggerated. Speaking of Vacher's time in the regiment, he noted that the defendant had been a "good soldier" who had risen in the ranks and received an honorable discharge. "How could this man so proud of his sergeant stripes . . . find himself in the status of a vagabond living off of charity? Does that not certainly indicate some aberrations of his sanity?"

Charbonnier spoke about Vacher's rough treatment at the asylums, and cast doubt over whether the defendant had been cured. . . . "What is cured?" Charbonnier said of the defendant. "How much do you know about that? What's the proof?" Or could it be that once he was out of the asylum he experienced a relapse?

The attorney took the jury through each of the murders, pointing out places where one could find fault with the experts. True, "all of the crimes he committed were done in an automatic fashion," but that indicated the behavior of an insane man rather than a rational one.

Charbonnier . . . implored the jurors not to think, "This is a wild beast, we must dispose of it," but to temper their justice with understanding. "Vacher was insane, he might still be."

WRITE BACK Choosing to Read Critically

Note that in the above excerpt from The Killer of Little Shepherds, Starr writes that each attorney interprets Vacher's actions through a "radically different lens." Break down each attorney's strategy by doing the following:

First, underline **evidence** that each attorney uses. For example, Ducher says that Vacher was a "violent child."

Second, circle any **interpretations** that the attorney forwards; for example, that Ducher was a "malicious" child. The examples provided here hinge on the fact that neither attorney disputes that Vacher was "violent"; however, the prosecutor wants to suggest that Vacher's violence was deliberate and evil (or "malicious"), rather than arising from self-defense or insanity.

Finally, write a paragraph in which you **explain each attorney's argument** in your own words.

Appeals to Pathos, Ethos, and Logos

The formula for how a lawyer argues a case in front of a jury serves as an example of the type of work you are doing in a thesis-driven or argumentative essay. You present your argument and then back up that argument with evidence, analysis, and discussion.

There are, of course, different kinds of evidence; statistics, for example, serve a different purpose than a first-person narrative. Additionally, there are different ways to present evidence; a bar graph, for example, serves a different purpose than an analogy. This section describes three different kinds of argument outlined by Greek philosopher Aristotle: pathos, or the appeal to emotion; ethos, or the appeal to authority; and logos, or the appeal to logic; and how you might use these appeals in your essays.

Pathos: The Appeal to Emotion

Have you ever seen one of those television commercials that present images of suffering in an attempt to get you to donate money to a cause? Ads for organizations that raise funds to fight animal abuse or charitable organizations that provide food or other necessities to combat poverty often use this mode. A close-up of a starving or beaten-down-looking dog behind a chain-link fence is designed to make you feel sad. The message or argument of the ad is "Isn't this terrible? *You should do something to make it better.*"

(In addition, one common argument in these ads is that what you might consider a little bit of money—"the cost of a cup of coffee"—could make a significant difference in another's life. This is an argument that depends on your feelings of empathy and guilt as well as comparison and logic: the cost will be small to you and it will help others immensely.)

Of course, the charity fundraising campaign is an extreme example of an appeal to emotion; many other uses of pathos are more subtle. Advertising in general often appeals to your emotions, whether it's fear that you'll be unattractive and unloved if you don't use a certain product, nostalgia for a time in your childhood or for "simpler times" in the past, or the implied promise that you'll somehow be happier if you eat at a certain restaurant or shop at a certain store.

Note how in the excerpt from *The Killer of Little Shepherds*, the attorney Charbonnier is noted for having a "sonorous voice" able to "communicate emotion." In addition, Charbonnier clearly appeals to the jury's emotions when he says that Vacher "is not a great criminal,

Choosing to Read Critically

Examples of Pathos

Conduct some research into a real-life high-profile case, such as the Casey Anthony trial, in which individuals felt passionately about the defendant's guilt or innocence. Locate the prosecution or the defense's closing argument. After reading or watching it, write an essay in which you use quotes in order to analyze the prosecution or defense's use of pathos.

but a poor, sick man." Ducher too uses emotionally charged language when he declares that Vacher is a "conscious, calculating predator."

Ethos: The Appeal to Character

An appeal that depends on ethos uses the writer or speaker's reputation to suggest that he or she is a valid source of information. For example, when your instructors explain concepts to you, you generally choose to trust that their information is sound. That these instructors have higher degrees and have been hired by the college or university you attend suggests to you that others within the academic world have evaluated their credentials and found them satisfactory. Thus, you trust your professors as authorities on their subjects.

We also often trust other "experts," whether they are accountants, lawyers, doctors, or (although often with more skepticism) journalists and politicians. Whenever someone who is an expert in her field gives us advice, she is implicitly relying on an appeal to ethos to have you believe her. If your doctor, for example, tells you that you have high blood pressure and prescribes a course of action that you should take, you probably wouldn't answer, "Well, what do you know? You only went to medical school."

However, the general wisdom that second opinions are often necessary thus speaks to an important part of appeals to ethos: experts aren't *always* right. That is, any student with a healthy skepticism of authority won't believe everything he hears, even if he hears it from politicians, professors, or other generally trustworthy sources.

Examples of appeals to ethos are all around us. In the world of advertising, you often see the appeal to ethos, as dentists recommend certain toothpastes and celebrities testify to the effectiveness of various products. In court cases, expert witnesses such as psychologists and doctors are often asked to testify. *The Killer of Little Shepherds* is

TIP BOX The Academic Peer
Review Process

Importantly, there are mechanisms in the academic world designed to make sure that valid information is distributed. Most scholarly work is put through some sort of *peer review* process, in which an author's peers provide feedback for and vet the author's work. (The peer review process is discussed further in Chapter 7). There are, however, people out there who might give themselves fancy and institutional-sounding names in order to suggest that they are part of a legitimate organization when, in fact, they are highly biased and perhaps uncredentialed. Your research experiences on the Internet have probably exposed you to some fake "professionals."

a book that largely traces how forensic scientists came to be regarded as expert witnesses in criminal cases as their field developed and as the larger public came to respect their training and knowledge.

In this textbook, you might look at the excerpt from Kelly Brownell and Katherine Battle Horgen's book *Food Fight* (in Chapter 10). Although you may not be familiar with Brownell's work, if you read the short biography before the selection, you'll discover that he is a well-respected researcher and author. Regardless of whether or not you agree with his argument, Brownell's academic position and multiple publications are evidence that he has the authority to discuss this topic. Notice that the short biographies before each selection serve to give you a little information about the author's relevant experience.

As you compose your essays, you will often draw on the work of others who have established their reputations in the area in which you're working. Perhaps most importantly, you should consider that

Choosing to Read Critically

Looking at Newspapers and Magazines

Pick up a newspaper or magazine that interests you and read four or five articles, circling all appeals to ethos that you can find. Note that magazines and newspapers often use interviews with and quotations from "experts," such as doctors, historians, nutritionists, and designers, as well as people who may not have credentials but are considered knowledgeable about the article's topic. Make a list of the "experts" and what their credentials are: are they affiliated with an institution of learning, a political organization, a hospital, a brand?

the point of many essay assignments is to encourage *you* to develop ethos or to become somewhat of an expert on a topic. Some essays will require you to draw on your own experiences and observations (for example, an essay on the current state of education in the United States) and others will ask you to conduct thorough research to demonstrate that you have the authority or expertise to comment on your topic (for example, explaining the development of laws securing access to education for individuals with disabilities).

Logos: The Appeal to Logic

An appeal to logic is an attempt to convince by outlining for your audience how your premises lead to certain conclusions. When you

---

TIP BOX Logical Fallacies

Many times, whether due to the heat of the moment when we're arguing or mistakes in thinking, our arguments fall prey to what are called *logical fallacies*. Fallacies can derail and sometimes ruin an argument. Here are a handful of examples:

Hasty Generalization: drawing a sweeping conclusion based on too little data

Example: *All of my experiences in math class were miserable. So, all math classes are horrible.*

Ad hominem: attacking the person

Example: *She couldn't be a good president because she is a bad dresser.*

Straw Man: setting up a weak oppositional position or misrepresenting what another is saying so that it's easy to dismiss the other position.

Example: *Someone else is arguing for more wheelchair-accessible entrances at school and his opponent argues, "He wants to discriminate against people who don't use wheelchairs."*

Slippery Slope: when one or two events will lead to disastrous conclusions

Example: *Smoking marijuana will result in smoking crack and homelessness.*

There are many more logical fallacies, and there are many excellent websites that provide thorough descriptions and discussions of fallacies. To see a good one, see the handout on fallacies available on the University of North Carolina at Chapel Hill's Writing Center's website: http://writingcenter.unc.edu/handouts/fallacies/

are composing a logical appeal, you use **evidence** (i.e., Vacher killed his victims deliberately and with "sangfroid" or calmness) to back up your **claim** (i.e., Vacher was not acting out of an insane or wild passion). There are a variety of kinds of evidence you can use to back up your claims, including definitions of key terms (designed to make sure your audience and you have the same meanings in mind as you present your argument), factual data and statistics, and quotations and citations.

For an example of an author who compellingly uses logic in order to advance her argument, see Anya Kamenetz's "Adapt or Decline" in Chapter 12. Kamenetz, using examples and facts, argues that American colleges are transforming. Near the end of the selection, Kamenetz describes four "trends" that are changing higher education; she then suggests how colleges must respond in order to survive.

Notice how in the courtroom example the lawyers use all three types of appeals, not just one. That is, a good lawyer wouldn't rely on just pathos or just ethos alone to make his case.

Considering Audience

You should carefully consider your audience when you are deciding what kinds of appeals to employ. As discussed in Chapter 1, different types of language and styles are appropriate in different writing situations. There may be very little room for pathos in many of your college-level essays, for example. However, all strong arguments incorporate logic and many balance all three of the above appeals.

Staying Aware of Counterarguments

It's also important to have a sense of your audience in order to anticipate possible objections to your ideas. If you have a strong thesis, it will certainly have counterarguments. For example, in the excerpt from Starr's *The Killer of Little Shepherds*, the attorneys are aware that the jurors might have their own interpretations of the evidence or their own preconceived notions about Vacher. In fact, Charbonnier at one point admits that Vacher committed murder "in an automatic fashion" (without great emotion or passion), thus acknowledging the counterargument that Vacher couldn't be insane if he remained so calm, but he asks the jury to see this as further evidence of Vacher's insanity.

As an essay writer, you want to be aware of what your audience might be thinking. Thus, if you're writing an essay that argues that people should decrease their consumption of meat, for example, you might anticipate a number of possible objections. Think of these objections not as flaws in your argument but as opportunities to demonstrate how thoroughly you have considered your topic. You might start a paragraph with a claim such as, "Although some people might object that red meat is an important source of many nutrients, such as iron, studies have shown that other sources for obtaining these substances might be healthier choices."

Emily Nussbaum in "Say Everything" (in Chapter 13) and Radley Balko in "Health Care Should Be a Personal Responsibility" (in Chapter 10) rely on the technique of counterargument, although in different ways. Nussbaum designs her discussion to logically respond to criticism about the "digital" generation's sense of celebrity and privacy. When older people claim that today's young people have no sense of privacy or shame, Nussbaum counters with her *"Charges"* to answer every claim. Balko starts by describing other's approaches to fighting obesity before announcing that these measures are ineffective and outlining his own approach.

Conclusion

Strong arguments often employ the three basic appeals: pathos (the appeal to emotion), ethos (the appeal to authority), and logos (the appeal to logic). Keep your audience in mind as you determine if and how you will use these appeals in your writing. Additionally, anticipate and address the objections that your readers are likely to have to your argument.

Follow-up Activity #1: Appeals in Advertising

Bring to class examples of appeals that depend on pathos or ethos. You might find a print advertisement, or you could write a description of a television ad that uses pathos. Alternately, you might discover the use of pathos in political speeches or opinion-editorials.

Follow-up Activity #2:
Developing Counterarguments

In pairs, come up with two or three counterarguments to the claim that social networking is beneficial for building strong relationships. Then, swap your counterarguments with another pair of students, who will respond to the objections. In responding, start by acknowledging the objector's position and then go on to demonstrate how it is not as significant as it might appear.

6 Chapter Six

From Paragraphs to Essays

Chapter Objectives

- Use first-hand experience and observation as evidence.
- Use sources beyond your experience as evidence.
- Create unified paragraphs using effective transitions.
- Compose strong introductions and conclusions.

>> Prereading Check-In

Evaluate yourself as a writer. Do you think you are a good writer? Why or why not? What are some of your strengths, and what are some of your weaknesses?

The previous chapter used the example of a courtroom procedural in order to demonstrate the importance of presenting and interpreting evidence for the construction of effective arguments. The centrality of interpretation or analysis is made clear when one considers that lawyers from opposing sides often use the same facts in order to arrive at contrary conclusions. Similarly, you will draw on and discuss diverse kinds of evidence as you compose essays. Building on what you probably already know about the basic form of an essay (introductory paragraph, body paragraphs, and conclusion), this chapter will present different techniques for further developing your paragraphing skills.

Building the Essay: Creating Strong Paragraphs

In general, a strong paragraph is a paragraph that develops one central point. That point should relate back to and develop your thesis statement. An effective way to highlight the central point that you will discuss is through the use of a **claim** early in the paragraph, perhaps as the paragraph's first sentence. The claim announces to your reader what it is you will be proposing and defending in that paragraph. An effective claim, then, is a proposition that you support by using evidence and analysis.

Your claim should thus be followed with support in the form of evidence. As suggested in Chapter 5, it is often not enough to simply state your evidence. Instead, you should analyze and interpret it for your audience. An attorney, for example, wouldn't just present evidence to a jury and expect the jury to know what to make of that evidence. Instead, an attorney offers an interpretation of that evidence (i.e., "The defendant's fingerprints on the murder weapon *mean that* the accused must have committed the crime").

Almost every paragraph in your essay should have a claim or, even more effectively, a transitional claim. In addition, it is helpful to identify and acknowledge counterarguments, or objections to your ideas, in your essay. This way, your position becomes clearer and potentially stronger. When you are acknowledging counterarguments, you may use sentences such as "Others argue _____. However, I contend that _____."

Here is a sample paragraph of how claims/evidence/counterarguments and analysis work. The student's task is to construct an argument about the role of gender stereotyping in the educational system, drawing on her own experiences and observations.

Claim:

A gender bias against females still exists in our school system.

Evidence:

When I was in sixth grade, I wanted to take the wood shop class that my brother had taken. I needed to get a form signed by the teacher, however, and when I went to see Mr. A, he informed me that he didn't think I would "enjoy the class" and that "most of the girls seemed to like Ms. B's classes better." Ms. B taught courses in time management, cooking, and "fabric arts."

Acknowledgment of counterargument:

I realize that this is just one example of gender bias and that Mr. A is just one teacher.

Discussion:

I think that my experience, however, was not exceptional. In fact, many other students I have spoken to say that they found themselves pushed—subtly or not—into classes and vocational programs that were clearly gender-coded. A problem with this is that I think I would have enjoyed wood shop much more than the fabric arts class I wound up taking. In addition, I probably would have gotten a better grade in the wood shop course. Finally, I might have even discovered a skill or an interest that would have shaped my career choice.

Transitional claim to begin the next paragraph:

In addition, recent research has shown that many teachers unconsciously promote traditional—and sexist—stereotypes.

WRITE BACK   Developing a Paragraph

Using your own experiences—or your imagination—write the paragraph that would develop the claim "The pressure to conform to traditional gender roles persists in upper-level education."

Here's another sample paragraph where the student's task is the same as the above: to address gender stereotyping in the educational system.

> At my high school, the boys' sports received lots of funding, while most of the girls' sports were notoriously underfunded. I played volleyball, and one year we had to buy our own uniforms and balls. Nobody ever asked the football team to do that. In fact, I think it's illegal. I excelled at volleyball, but I had to stop playing because I broke my wrist.

The above paragraph, as you probably noticed, does not follow the claim/evidence/counterargument/analysis pattern. In addition, the seemingly irrelevant remark about the student's wrist at the end of the paragraph demonstrates *how* and *why* it is so important to focus on making a single point in each paragraph. Sometimes your point might be complex or sometimes you will be forwarding more than one idea in a paragraph, but in general, you want to make sure your paragraphs have **unity**; that is, all the ideas are clearly related to each other.

Checklist   Strong Paragraphs

Although you will have some variety among your paragraphs, most of your paragraphs should meet the following criteria:

- The paragraph forwards one central point.
- The paragraph relates back to and supports the thesis statement.
- The paragraph includes a claim or transitional claim.
- The claim is supported with evidence and/or discussion.

WRITE BACK   Claim, Evidence, Analysis

Choose one of the following topics and write a two- to three-paragraph exploration of the issue, using your own experience and observations as evidence. Use the formula (claim, evidence, analysis) described above.

- Do the benefits of social networking sites (e.g., Facebook) outweigh the drawbacks?
- Should American teenagers care more about the environment and conservation?
- Is "difference" (any kind of your choosing, such as race, fashion choices, lifestyle choices) tolerated at your college?

Evidence and Analysis: Using Your Own Experiences and Observations

As discussed above, evidence and analysis are crucial to the development of robust, sophisticated, and well-organized paragraphs. There are many kinds of evidence that you can draw on when you compose an academic essay. Of course, audience will play a key role in how you select your evidence. Clearly understanding your assignment, as well as your professor's expectations, is crucial to your selection of evidence.

Some professors will invite you to write essays drawing on your own experiences and observations. The organizational formula of claim, evidence, and analysis can work nicely with this type of assignment. The first sample paragraph about gender roles is an example of an essay that advances an argument and backs up that argument with evidence drawn from the author's own experience.

Evidence and Analysis: Using Sources Beyond Your Own Experience

Facts, data, and quotes are some of the other kinds of evidence that appear frequently in academic writing. While summarizing, paraphrasing, and quoting is further discussed in Chapter 8, "The Research Paper," here are a few examples of how you would use evidence in various types of essays.

In a thesis-driven **position paper** (the kind of essay that you're often asked to write in a composition course), you advance an original argument, using outside sources, such as facts and quotes from experts, to back up your ideas.

Claim	The national driving age should be increased to 18.
Evidence	According to the Center for Disease Control, automobile accidents are the leading cause of death for teenagers. In addition, teenagers tend to engage in riskier behaviors than adults do, including talking and texting on cell phones while driving.
Analysis	This high rate of death suggests that teenagers under the age of 18 do not have the maturity to operate motor vehicles. Although not all teenagers make bad choices, these statistics suggest that we need to revise our ideas of who should be eligible for a driver's license.

In a **literary analysis**, you might be asked to forward a claim about a text. Quotations from the text would serve as evidence; your original interpretation would be based on your analysis of those quotes.

Claim	Shirley Jackson's short story "The Lottery" suggests that humans only care about injustice when they are the victims of that injustice.
Evidence	For example, the person chosen to be a human sacrifice, Tessie, has no problems with the tradition of the lottery until she finds out that she will be the one who is stoned to death. She screams, "It's not right! It's not fair!" as her fellow townspeople prepare to kill her.
Analysis	By describing Tessie as a willing participant when *someone else* will be the victim, Jackson highlights Tessie's hypocrisy. It is only "unfair" when she is the one who will be stoned.

In humanities classes, you may be asked to compose an essay in which you conduct research and present an **argument based on that research**. The following excerpt is taken from writer DeAnn Blanton's article "Women Soldiers of the Civil War." Note how the excerpt does or doesn't follow the claim, evidence, analysis formula discussed above.

It is an accepted convention that the Civil War was a man's fight. Images of women during that conflict center on self-sacrificing nurses, romantic spies, or brave ladies maintaining the home front in the absence of their men. The men, of course, marched off to war, lived in germ-ridden camps, engaged in heinous battle, languished in appalling prison camps, and died horribly, yet heroically. This conventional

WRITE BACK   Working Backward from Evidence

Alone or with a partner, create strong claims or the topic sentences for potentially strong paragraphs for the following pieces of evidence.

EXAMPLE #1

Evidence	There are more shopping malls than high schools in the United States, according to the authors of the book *Affluenza*.
Claim	Although Americans often say that education is a priority, our actions suggest the opposite.

EXERCISE #1

Evidence	According to Eric Weiner, Americans are "profoundly optimistic": "two-thirds of Americans say they are hopeful about the future."
Claim	

EXERCISE #2

Evidence	One of every seven low-income children is obese, according to the Center for Disease Control.
Claim	

picture of gender roles during the Civil War does not tell the entire story. Men were not the only ones to fight that war. Women bore arms and charged into battle, too. Like the men, there were women who lived in camps, suffered in prisons, and died for their respective causes.

Creating Unified Paragraphs

One way to create unity in your paragraphs, as well as in your essay overall, is to make sure that you are effectively using **transitions** and **transitional phrases**. A transition simply demonstrates the relationship or connection between your ideas. For example, a student might write a conclusion for an essay arguing that public schools should introduce uniforms: "**In conclusion**, there are three reasons that public schools should have uniform policies. **First**, uniforms equalize students in terms of economic class. **Second**, uniforms have been shown to improve overall behavior among students. **Most importantly,** uniforms prevent students from becoming distracted by each other's bodies and clothing during school hours."

Through the use of phrases such as "In conclusion" and the use of numbered points, such as "First" and "Second," the writer provides an obvious organizational structure for the reader. Further, the phrase "Most importantly" makes clear that the writer considers the last point his strongest (reflected, hopefully, in his discussions in the essay). These key words and phrases are the most basic types of transitions.

One-Word Transitions

There are a variety of transitions that you are probably already familiar with and which you use quite regularly. For example, words such as "however," "although," and "but" work to show relationships between ideas: they signal that although you made one point, you are going to amend or disagree with that point. Here's an example:

> "I am a city girl, *but* after reading *In Defense of Food: An Eater's Manifesto* (2008) by Michael Pollan, I am definitely going to plant a garden."

> "I am a city girl; *however,* after reading *In Defense of Food: An Eater's Manifesto* (2008) by Michael Pollan, I am definitely going to plant a garden."

> "*Although* I am a city girl, I am definitely going to plant a garden."

Especially if you haven't done so in the past, try using transitions deliberately and strategically (rather than intuitively). Below is a list of some frequently used transitions; in one of your next writing assignments, try to incorporate some of the transitions that you don't normally use.

TRANSITIONS THAT DEMONSTRATE CONTRAST

However	Although	In contrast
Whereas	But	Nevertheless
Regardless		

Example: "Although I hate writing, I love my English class."
Example: "The climb was difficult. Nevertheless, he made it to the top of the mountain."

TRANSITIONS THAT SHOW IDEAS BUILDING ON EACH OTHER

In addition	Also	Similarly
Further	Furthermore	Moreover

Example: "In addition to being a liar, Grady was a thief."
Example: "Parrots are intelligent. Furthermore, they are extremely social."

TRANSITIONS THAT SHOW CAUSALITY

As a result	Thus	For this reason
Therefore	Hence	Consequently

Example: "The data was destroyed. Therefore, the experiment had to be conducted again."
Example: "As a result of the accident, Jamie had to undergo rigorous physical therapy three times a week."

TRANSITIONS THAT SIGNAL ILLUSTRATION

For example	Specifically	For instance
In particular		

Example: "For example, this sentence shows how to use a transition that signals illustration."
Example: "Teachers don't expect many students to do well in math; specifically, they target girls as the weakest math students."

TRANSITIONS THAT SIGNAL SUMMARY AND/OR TIME

Finally	In short	In conclusion
Subsequently		

Example: "In short, transitions are valuable tools for writing."
Example: "Laura neglected to read the novel for class; she subsequently failed the test."

> **WRITE BACK**   Using Transitions
>
> *In order to show the relationship between the ideas in each of the sentences, insert a transition.*
>
> **Example:**
> The Internet gives us access to an abundance of information. Much of that information is shallow or even inaccurate.
>   The Internet gives us access to an abundance of information. However, much of that information is shallow or even inaccurate.
>
>   1. Many young people live in ignorance of our nation's history. They don't know anything about world literature.
>   2. Video games glamorize violence and cruelty. In the game *Grand Theft Auto*, players are encouraged to steal cars and to kill women.
>   3. Some people think video games are pure entertainment. Recent scholars have argued that these games are intellectually stimulating.

Transitional Phrases

In addition to using one-word transitions in and in between your sentences, *transitional phrases* can serve to both construct and signal larger moves in your essay. A **transitional phrase** or a **transitional claim** uses more than just one or two words in order to demonstrate how your ideas are building on each other. A transitional claim, more specifically, can sometimes do the work of summarizing the ideas you've already presented before describing how you will move on to your next point.

For example, imagine an essay arguing that schools should limit the use of computers.

Here's a schematic of the paper:

Paragraph 1: **Thesis:** Computers in schools disrupt, rather than facilitate learning.

Paragraph 2: **Claim:** Students use the Internet to socialize, not to study.

Paragraph 3: **Transitional Claim:** In addition to socializing, students use the Internet to cheat.

The first clause in Paragraph 3 ("In addition to socializing,") summarizes what the paragraph immediately preceding Paragraph 3 argued.

WRITE BACK   Transitional Claims Mad Libs®

Write three paragraphs on one of the following topics. Make sure that the second and third paragraphs start with clear transitional claims. For help developing transitional claims, see the examples below.

Topics:
- Why I chose to go to this college or university.
- What I think are the most difficult parts of being a student.
- How I prepare and write an essay.

Transitional claim examples:
- In addition to _____, I also think/do _____.
- Although I appreciate _____, I find _____ challenging.
- After I _____, I usually _____.
- While _____ is difficult, I find _____ worthwhile.

The second part of the clause ("students use the Internet to cheat") announces the point of the paragraph that will be written next. The rest of Paragraph 3 will go on to explain how students cheat and to provide evidence for that claim.

Writing Effective Introductions and Conclusions

While the previous section describes strategies for developing effective body paragraphs, this section deals with tackling some of the most challenging paragraphs to compose: introductions and conclusions. These paragraphs are so important because often how you introduce what you want to say and how you decide to conclude will determine your audience's receptiveness to and interest in your topic. Your introduction and conclusion are the first and last impression that your reader has of your work.

There are many ways to travel from an opening sentence to a thesis statement in an introductory paragraph. While many students rely on moving from general-to-specific statements, this section proposes that you might try the opposite—a specific-to-general approach.

Choosing a Specific and Strategic Opening

Many students start papers with statements such as:

"Throughout history, humans have used various technologies."

"Materialism is everywhere in today's society."

"People strive to be happy."

The above general statements are followed by sentences that become more and more specific until the author arrives at his or her thesis statement, or the sentence or sentences that sum up the essay's overall argument (see Chapter 4 for further discussion of thesis statements). For example, the sentence "Throughout history, humans have used various technologies" might lead to a thesis statement such as "Internet use has had a positive effect on our ability to interact with each other in real life."

These types of paragraphs move from the general idea ("throughout time," "everyone," "people") to the specific (the thesis statement: here's how a *specific* kind of technology, the Internet, affects a *specific* group of people, people today, in "real life"). While this can be a fine organization for your introductory paragraph, there are two potential pitfalls here. The first is that the general statement fails to "grab" your reader; the first impression you make is that your paper will be obvious or boring. The second pitfall is that sometimes generalizations go on for too long and you wind up wasting valuable space in your essay as you continue pointing out things your reader already knows (i.e., humans use technologies; some inventions are more helpful or beneficial than others).

If the movement from general to specific is the "default" approach you use in introductions, try another of the strategies described below. If, after having tried other types of first paragraphs, you feel that the general-to-specific mode is still the best for you, that's fine. You may have really mastered that mode. However, this is yet another opportunity for you to explore new ways of expressing yourself in writing and to hone your skills, rather than falling back on old habits.

The Opening Anecdote

People tend to love a good story. For this reason, an anecdote is often an effective way to engage your reader, not only for argumentative papers, but also for "statement of intent" essays (the kind you write when you apply to colleges or graduate school). An anecdote is a brief but meaningful story. Your anecdote, or short story, should be at most a paragraph long and should serve *to bring into focus the issue you are going to explore in the essay.* The most effective way to incorporate an anecdote is to jump right into the story, make the transition into your thesis, and then present your thesis statement.

Below is an introductory paragraph that makes use of an opening anecdote based on a student-writer's experiences working at an animal shelter. Notice how the writer jumps right in; he doesn't start "setting up" the story. Instead, he begins by describing a dog he encountered. Then, near the end of the paragraph, notice the transitional sentence. The writer is moving from describing his experience to saying what this experience demonstrates. This transition does a nice job of setting up the thesis statement, which is the sentence in bold.

EXAMPLE 1

Rocka was a fifty-pound pit bull-mix with huge brown eyes. She had been left chained up to a fence in a shopping center, and she was scarred and scared. Even though she was traumatized, she was clearly eager for human attention and affection. She really could have made a great pet for someone. Unfortunately, Rocka was "put down" or euthanized after a few weeks at the shelter. The problem is, Rocka's story is not unique. And every day, innocent animals are dying because of human irresponsibility. **In order to truly deal with this terrible situation, we need better enforcement of animal registration, new policies for spaying and neutering pets, and stricter penalties for animal abuse.**

An opening anecdote doesn't have to be a personal story. Instead, as the second example suggests, it could be an example from history, from current events, or from literature.

EXAMPLE 2

A scene in Morgan Spurlock's 2004 documentary *Supersize Me* shows junior high school kids in their school cafeteria, selecting soda and French fries for lunch. Spurlock questions the adults supervising the kids, who assure him that the kids will eat other, healthy foods as well. But when Spurlock follows up, he finds that the children, when given the choice, will only eat junk food. This scene suggests that our schools are themselves promoting unhealthy lifestyles. **If we are ever to be successful in getting young people to seek alternatives for fast food, we must make sure that fruits, vegetables, and healthy food choices are available to children in our school cafeterias.**

WRITE BACK   Opening with a Story

Construct an opening anecdote for the best thesis statement you developed with your group in the "Thesis Statement Telephone" exercise from Chapter 4. (This time, however, you'll be working alone. For the purposes of this exercise, if your instructor permits, you are free to make up a story (i.e., a hypothetical example) or even use a story you've seen represented on television or in a movie.

Notice that the last sentence or two sentences of each introduction is the thesis statement. While many professional writers, including those represented in this anthology, don't always make their theses so clear, it's important that your readers—your instructor and your peers—can clearly and easily identify your thesis statement. Not only does this make it easier for others to follow your argument, but it also provides the structure for your paper.

The Crystallizing Quotation and the Startling Statistic

Like the opening anecdote, the crystallizing quotation should serve to bring into focus the primary points of your argument. It is often a good idea to begin with a quotation from an author whose work you will continue to explore in the essay. As with the opening anecdote, it is often effective to present the quotation or the context for the quotation right away, bridge the quotation and your thesis statement with a transitional sentence, and then announce your thesis. See if you can identify each of these parts of the following paragraph examples.

TIP BOX   Finding an Appropriate Quotation

Warning: Take pains to make sure that your quotation is truly relevant. Too often students grab a quotation (after a quick Google search for "important quotes") that sounds smart, but really has nothing to do with the essay, is basically a cliché, or is too general a statement to allow you to develop your ideas.

EXAMPLE 1

Mahatma Gandhi famously urged people to "be the change you want to see in the world." His words suggest that it isn't enough just to sit passively by or even complain about problems we see in the world. Instead, we each have a duty to change ourselves and our immediate or local environments. Gandhi's words should inspire us to take action when it comes to pollution. Instead of expecting the government to take control and make changes, individuals have to show that they care about the environment through the choices they make.

The following is an effective use of a quotation to set up a literary analysis paper.

EXAMPLE 2

In a pivotal moment in Frederick Douglass's narrative, he writes, "You have seen how a man is made a slave; you shall see how a slave is made a man." Douglass's contention, that his writing will show the reader how social systems affect human beings, is explored throughout his text. In this essay, I will argue that Douglass's text performs what it describes; that is, that the experience of reading Douglass's book should itself effect a change in the reader.

The following is an effective use of a fact or statistic.

EXAMPLE 3

According to the Surgeon General's report of 2003, nearly two out of every three Americans are overweight or obese. One out of every eight deaths in America is caused by an illness directly

WRITE BACK   Identify the Internal Organization

After looking at each of the above introductory paragraphs, figure out how it works. Underline the "specific" element that the writer includes in order to grab his or her reader. Circle the transitional sentence. Then, put a star next to the thesis statement.

After identifying how each paragraph is constructed, write a paragraph explaining which paragraph you find the most effective and why. Consider: if you had to read the entire paper based on one of the intros, which one would you choose? Defend your choice.

related to excess weight and obesity. These statistics suggest
that we are in a health crisis. In this essay I will argue that it is
time for all of us to take drastic measures to combat obesity:
we must cut out fast foods, exercise portion control, and monitor when and how we eat.

As you may have noted, the opening anecdote, the crystallizing quotation, and the startling statistic all proceed from a narrow focus and
allow you to move into your general statement about the text or issue
you will be discussing.

Writing Conclusions: Ending Your Discussion Thoughtfully

As mentioned in Chapter 4, sometimes students turn in essays only to
have the instructor comment that the conclusion should have been the
introduction. This might be because we often don't really know what
we're arguing until we've finished analyzing all of the data and come to
the end of our essay.

You may find conclusions difficult to write. Of course, you don't
want to simply restate your introduction. Not only does this look
amateurish, but if you're developing a strong introduction (using one
of the strategies described above, such as an opening anecdote), it
wouldn't make sense to simply repeat it at the end of the essay. You
do, however, want to restate your central points. Some instructors
also want to see you looking forward or commenting on questions
that remain or research that needs to be done on your topic; these
devices are good to use, as long as you don't present ideas that are so
compelling that your instructor wonders why you didn't pursue these
issues instead.

In a paper that calls for more governmental attention to potential
toxins in everyday products, the following conclusion (using a "crystallizing quotation") might be effective:

> In her landmark book *Silent Spring* (1962), Rachel Carson writes
> that we have to start paying attention to the potential consequences
> of exposure to chemicals: "Like the constant dripping of water that
> in turn wears away the hardest stone, this birth-to-death contact with
> dangerous chemicals may in the end prove disastrous. Each of these
> recurrent exposures, no matter how slight, contributes to the progres-
> sive buildup of chemicals in our bodies and so to cumulative poison-
> ing." Although written almost fifty years ago, Carson's warning is

relevant today because it brings into focus the ways in which we still put ourselves in contact with various chemicals. We need our government to take firm action in terms of the regulation of toxins in our everyday products.

Here's another example of a conclusion that uses a quotation.

In *In Defense of Food: An Eater's Manifesto* (2008), Michael Pollan makes a seemingly simple recommendation: "Eat food. Not too much. Mostly plants." Pollan's advice seems common sense, but in this age of hyper-processed foods, his words can serve as a reminder of what the ultimate purpose of food is: to sustain us. By eating "lower down on the food chain," more Americans can save money, avoid obesity, and live healthier and longer lives.

Similarly, you may choose to introduce a closing anecdote in your conclusion, a story that brings into focus the points you've been trying to drive home.

Last year, I received an email from a kid I went to kindergarten with. I was excited at first, and we made all sorts of plans to get together sometime when we were both home from college. Gradually, however, the frequency of our emails decreased. Finally, they stopped altogether. We never got together as we had planned. The correspondence was fun, but shallow. My experience demonstrates the principles that I have been attempting to prove throughout this essay. While much-celebrated for their capacity to "connect" us to other people around the world, most new technologies promote a truly shallow kind of "connection." As entertainment, the collecting of casual acquaintances may be all fun and games. However, I argue that these technologies, under the guise of being democratizing and unifying, are actually harmful to us in that they keep us from developing meaningful political and emotional relationships with others.

Conclusion

Using a claim, evidence, and analysis formula may assist you in the organization of ideas in your paragraphs. Transitions and transitional claims provide unity and signal to your readers where you've been and where you are going next. In addition, introductions and conclusions need not be tedious exercises in saying absolutely nothing. Instead, introductions, in particular, provide you with an opportunity to truly engage your reader. Using techniques such as the opening anecdote or startling statistic will enable you to start your essays specifically, rather than with a general statement.

Follow-up Activity #1:
Introduction Scavenger Hunt

By drawing on articles you've already been assigned or by flipping through the second half of this book, find two or three selections that use any or all of the strategies described above in either their introductions or conclusions. For each article, write a paragraph identifying the strategy used and explain whether or not you found that particular opening or closing effective.

Follow-up Activity #2:
Using Transitions Effectively

The following is the first draft of a short essay on cell phones and teen-agers. After an in-class workshop, the students in the writer's group informed her that she needed to provide more transitional claims to set up her paragraphs. Please provide transitional claims where indicated in order to demonstrate how the paragraphs are building on each other. One way to approach this exercise is to create a reverse outline before you begin—figure out the central point of each paragraph and write it next to that paragraph. Then, when possible, write a transitional claim that accomplishes two goals: telling the reader what the author said in the previous paragraph and telling the reader what the author will argue in the next paragraph. Your transition will demonstrate the relationship between these two parts.

Chynna G.

First Draft Cell Phone Essay

Thesis: Only people over the age of 18 should be allowed to own and use cell phones.

   Paragraph 1: The most important reason that we should be limiting cell phone use among young people is because we still aren't com-pletely clear about what the long-term health effects of cell phone use are. In her article, "Cell Phones and Brain Cancer: The Real Story," Devra Davis reports on the finding of the World Health Organization's Interphone Study: "top users of cell phones had a doubled risk of malignant tumors of the brain." Cell phones might cause cancer. Do we really want to put young people, who are famous for using their phones all the time, at risk?

Paragraph 2: _____. I have observed many of my peers texting and talking on the phone while they are driving, even though it's illegal. For example, my sister was recently texting and driving when she rear-ended the car in front of her. Although she was not seriously hurt, she could have been. The point is that these practices are dangerous, but young people do them anyway.

Paragraph 3: _____. I have observed my peers texting during class when they should be paying attention. Not only is this behavior rude, but it also compromises their educations. They are playing with their gadgets when they should be concentrating. Who can blame us? Texting is addictive! I don't think this makes us bad people; I just think most of us are not mature enough to handle having a technology that is so distracting.

Conclusion: _____. Cell phones are potentially harmful to our health and are the cause of accidents and other distractions.

Works Cited

Davis, Devra. "Cell Phones and Brain Cancer: The Real Story."
    www.huffingtonpost.com 22 May 2010. Web. 27 June 2010.

7 Chapter Seven

The Revision Process:
Looking Back, Looking Ahead, Looking Again

Chapter Objectives

- Explain the process and methods for revision.
- Distinguish between editing and global revision.
- Select and apply a revision approach using a revision checklist.
- Engage in peer review and use constructive criticism to enhance your writing.

>> **Prereading Check-In**

Describe an activity that you have worked hard on in the past, such as an artistic creation, an athletic goal, or a role for a play. Discuss your process and what you did in order to improve your skills or the piece you were working on. Did you find that revision, changing the way you were doing something or even starting over from scratch, was ever helpful?

What Is Revision?

The word "revision" means to look again or to re-see. This chapter discusses why revision is important and offers some strategies for reviewing your work with the goal of improving your writing. In addition, this chapter discusses peer review as an activity that many writers find extremely helpful when they revise their work.

Why Revise?

If you ask professional writers about their processes, you'll find that many of them rigorously revise their work. Some authors even say that revision is the most important aspect of writing. Authors who return to their writing again and again work hard so that their audience doesn't have to. In other words, good writers recognize that it's *up to them* to make their ideas and arguments clear and compelling for their readers.

There are lots of reasons to revise your writing, whether that writing is an email message, a resume, a blog entry, an in-class exam, or an essay. Often, we don't say exactly what we need or want to say the first time around. Even when speaking, we often "revise" by using phrases such as "what I really meant was," and "but what I'm saying is," and "to make a long story short."

The task of revising more "high stakes" items, such as cover letters, tests, essays, and research papers, however, means that you must continue to give your topic and your writing sustained attention even after you have produced what you might consider a pretty good draft. Looking at your essay a second, third, fourth, or fifth time can yield excellent results, in that you can push yourself to continue developing your ideas and refining your language. This kind of close scrutiny to your work is fundamental to making you a stronger writer and thinker.

Choosing Your Revision Approach

Although writing instructors tend to favor certain scenarios for successful revision, the chart below sums up the pros and cons of different revision situations and techniques. One or more of the following scenarios may appeal to you.

Revision Scenarios	Pros	Cons
Revising Your Work by Yourself	You know your writing better than anyone else. You know what the assignment calls for. Unless you do not credit your sources adequately, you run little risk of plagiarism.	You may become frustrated because you cannot really tell where you need to revise. Sometimes, you aren't really even reading your essay; you're just looking at it again and again. You may think you're revising when you are really editing (fixing typos and punctuation errors).
Revising Your Work with Help from a Friend or Family Member	Working with someone you know and love can be very comfortable and can produce some terrific revisions. Your friend or family member might be able to ask questions and make suggestions that will bring out your best ideas.	There is a danger that your collaborator may shape the revision more than he or she should, and you may find yourself using his or her ideas or vocabulary—a form of plagiarism. Another danger is that, ironically, people who love you may become impatient or may criticize your work more harshly than others, leading to many arguments around the kitchen table.

Revision Scenarios	Pros	Cons
Revising Your Work Using Class Peer Review	Your draft receives detailed criticism and commentary from multiple readers. In addition, other students may have a different, or better, sense of the assignment and whether or not your work fulfills it. You are not obliged to make changes according to your group's assessments; however, you will probably gain a better idea of what is working and what is not working in your essay.	If you are shy or uncomfortable about your draft, peer review can be tough going. Feedback from a bunch of people done in a short time may be overwhelming. Finally, not all of the comments you receive will be helpful.
Revising Your Work Using Your College's Writing Center/ Writing Workshop (WC/WW)	Typically, WC/WW tutors are specialists in grammar/expository writing/composition practice and theory. They bring a wealth of knowledge and sure-fire techniques to the tutoring session. He or she will ignore minor or even major grammatical errors, as he or she will be more interested in helping you to "look again" at what you have said and to "look ahead" at what you ultimately wish to say.	If you are interested in editing rather than revising, you may be disappointed: the tutor almost certainly will focus on a global revision (see below). You might feel frustrated if you expect the tutor to provide free proofreading services.
Revising Your Work Using Your College's OWL (On-Line Writing Lab or Tutoring Service)	If you have difficulty getting to campus or feel uncomfortable about asking for help face-to-face, your college's OWL may allow you to submit your draft as an email attachment. You can then engage in a short-term email discussion of the revision of your paper.	As most OWLs require that you send a paper in a few days before you want it back with commentary, procrastinators probably won't be able to avail themselves of this service. The personal and intimate aspects of face-to-face tutoring will not be featured during OWL communication.

Editing Versus Global Revision

Many students confuse the practice of revision with the practice of editing, which is going through a paper fixing awkward phrases and correcting typos and grammar errors. While it is extremely important to edit or proofread your work, true revision allows for dramatic changes. A "global revision" can only take place when you look at your essay as a whole. Revising a paper may mean shifting your focus, rewriting your thesis statement, reorganizing your points and/or your paragraphs, strengthening your claims and/or analysis, and generally reconsidering your project as a whole. It might mean a complete transformation of your draft.

Revision Steps

After you've completed a first draft, you may want to set it aside for a day or two (if you have that kind of time) in order to give yourself a little distance from your work. Once you're ready to revise, you might start by rereading the assignment to make sure that you are fulfilling the requirements and meeting your professor's expectations.

The next step, especially if you've taken some time off from the essay, is to freewrite about your paper. Write down what you think you're communicating in the essay and how you go about proving your points. Writing about your composition, about your process and plans, can be very effective at this point: You might discover that you thought you were focused on or making an argument about one topic, but that the paper is really focused on something else, or you might find the needed phrasing for a point that you were having difficulty articulating.

As your thesis statement drives your essay, you ought to scrutinize that next. Ask yourself if your thesis statement is truly representative of the point you are trying to make in the paper. If it's not, be prepared to give it a makeover. As mentioned in earlier chapters, sometimes the working thesis you've developed no longer matches the rest of the paper. If this is the case, you should probably reconsider and revise your thesis statement.

Another helpful strategy to make sure that your thesis statement works and that the progression of your claims flows, reads well, and holds up is to compose a reverse outline of your work. When creating a reverse outline, you figure out the central point of each paragraph and write that point down, either beside the paragraph or in outline form. Then, you look over all of your major points and how they build

---

Checklist Revision Steps

You may find it helpful to follow these steps when you begin revising an essay.

1. Take some time off—a day or two—from working on the essay.
2. Reread the assignment; reread your essay to see if you are fulfilling the assignment.
3. Freewrite on the progress of your essay.
4. Reconsider and, if necessary, revise your thesis statement.
5. Compose a reverse outline of the essay.
6. Make necessary changes, which may include changing the thesis statement, reorganizing paragraphs, using evidence more effectively or doing more research, and rethinking the introduction.
7. Repeat.

---

on each other. Is there a logical progression from one idea to the next? Should you revise the order in which you present your evidence?

The reverse outline can also help you to see if you need to continue developing your paragraphs. You might need to further discuss or expand on the evidence you've included, or you might need to conduct more research to find more or stronger evidence to support your claims.

Wide Awake to Your Own Work: Staying Open to Change

Here's an analogy often used to describe the practice of revision: It's like redecorating a house. Let's say you buy a new couch for your home; suddenly, the walls seem kind of dingy, and you realize they need to be repainted. So you paint the walls; suddenly, you realize the carpet doesn't match anything anymore. So you change the carpet; the next thing you know, you have to get new curtains because they don't suit the new decor. After a lot of work, every piece in your house is coordinated and each contributes to a whole.

While revision doesn't have to be never-ending (thank goodness for due dates!), this analogy should bring into focus the ways in which changing one part of your paper can have an effect on another part of your paper. If you change your thesis statement, you may suddenly need to refine your claims. Refining your claims might make some reorganization necessary. Don't get discouraged. As you revise, be open to making large or "global" changes. Unlike redecorating a room or a home, you can always save an early version of your draft on your computer or in a USB, so changes shouldn't be too difficult to reverse if you find you want to go back to the way things were. In addition, noticing these larger concerns in your own work means that you are becoming a sharper reader and a stronger writer.

Peer Review and Constructive Criticism

If you are not used to revising your work or find revising on your own difficult, working with another person or persons can produce wonderful results in a shorter period of time than you would think. Peer review, also called a workshop, is an important component of many composition classes. During peer reviews, which usually take place during class time, a group of students reads each other's papers. Instructors might ask students to work in pairs or in groups of three or four. Engaging in peer review as a writer, you can potentially find out if you are expressing your ideas clearly and effectively since your classmates will tell you what they think about your paper. As a reader, you can see how your classmates approach writing and, through identifying the strengths and weaknesses in their papers, you might be better able to see your own strengths and weaknesses.

Practically, peer review functions as a way to get others' feedback so that you can revise fruitfully. When it's time for your paper to be under review, it is important for you to solicit specific comments from your group. Often, especially when students don't know each other very well, they fall back on comments such as "This is really good" or they just pay attention to grammar, editing when they could be attending to global issues. For peer review to be most effective, however, all students in the group must be serious in their roles as critics, focused on each essay under consideration, and tactful in phrasing their remarks.

Conclusion

Revision is a key component of successful writing, and this chapter describes several options that you have when it comes time to revise your essay. Whether you work alone, participate in a peer review workshop, or consult a professional about your writing, your choice to revise will doubtless have a positive effect on your work and on your development as a writer.

Follow-up Activity #1:
Peer Review

Photocopy the following Peer Review Worksheet for each member of the group. A scribe will be assigned for each writer. This means that if A's paper is under review, B will take notes on the worksheet. When B's paper is under review, C will take notes on the worksheet. At the end of the session, each student will take home the worksheet completed by their group.

Note: Although only one student will fill out the worksheet, the information that is recorded should come from all students in the group. That is, use the group's comments to provide the feedback that is recorded on the sheet.

Sample Peer Review Worksheet   For a Thesis-Driven Essay

Peer review can work in pairs or in groups of three or four students. For this peer review session, the author should read her paper out loud to the group. (If the author is uncomfortable reading aloud, another member of the group may read it for her.)

As the author is reading, all students in the group should have copies of the essay under discussion in front of them and should mark areas of the essay that they want to further discuss with the author. After the author reads the essay aloud, students next spend time on each of the following directives.

1. Underline the thesis statement. The thesis should be specific, argumentative, and compelling. The group should discuss possible counterarguments and record one or two below. If the group cannot come up with counterarguments, then perhaps the thesis isn't advancing a clear argument. In that case, the group should discuss with the author what they think she is arguing in the paper and should provide suggestions for improving the thesis.

2. After you discuss the thesis statement, look at the first sentence of each paragraph. Is that first sentence a claim or a transitional claim? Every paragraph should have one central point and that point should relate back to and support the thesis statement. Provide suggestions for helping the author to strengthen her claims.

3. Discuss the types of evidence that the author includes. Is the evidence compelling? Can the group make any suggestions for more effective use or placement of the evidence?

4. Discuss and record, for the author, the best thing about the paper. What is really working here?

5. Discuss and record one aspect of the essay that the author should continue working on.

6. Review the introduction. Provide suggestions for an alternative opening. The author doesn't have to use it; just make sure that the author is aware that there are other ways to start the paper.

Follow-up Activity #2:
Review a Sample Paper

The following sample paper, about obesity in America, offers you an opportunity to suggest revisions for a hypothetical student. Applying the six peer review topics described in the worksheet above, suggest ways in which this student could revise his paper.

L. Winston

Education is the Key to Avoid Obesity

Everybody likes to eat. Maybe some of us like to eat too much. This has resulted in an obesity problem in the United States. In "Health Care Should Be a Personal Responsibility," Radley Balko argues that the government should play no role in curtailing the current obesity epidemic. While Balko goes perhaps too far, his point that we need to emphasize individual responsibility has merits. Americans need to drastically change their eating habits. But this will only happen if individuals are made even more aware of what exactly they are eating, as well as the health and economic effects of obesity. I propose an intensive campaign to better educate eaters and to empower individuals in order to combat the recent increase in obesity.

While most people are somewhat aware that it isn't healthy to eat too much and almost everyone knows that fat is vilified in this country, these factors have not led to a decrease in obesity. And I recognize how it might be easy for people to fall into the trap of obesity. When I was a kid, my mom rarely cooked. She was raising us as a single parent, she worked full time, and she wasn't ever really interested in cooking to begin with. So, most nights, she would order in or take us to McDonald's or just heat up a frozen dinner. When I got older, my brother and I usually picked up our own dinner on the way home from school, and this meant pizza, hot dogs, or some other kind of fast food. While I never got "obese" (probably because I played sports), I did pack on the pounds. Now that I'm in college, I eat really differently, and I can see—and feel—the difference. I don't automatically feel like falling asleep after I've had a meal, for one thing. Overall, I have more energy, my skin is clearer, and I think I'm a healthy weight.

But I didn't just wake up one day and suddenly know how to eat right. Instead, most of the changes I made in my diet were the result of taking a nutrition class during my first semester. Not only did that class change the course of my career (I now want to go into the field of nutrition), but it also really changed the way I looked at food. Instead of seeing food as just something tasty that you cram down your throat until you feel sick a few times a day, I now see food as fuel. I understand that my body needs certain things in order to function at its maximum potential. While I still indulge in a McDonald's hamburger or a donut from Dunkin Donuts sometimes, I understand these snacks as treats or desserts, rather than seeing them as meals.

I think that all people should be given the kind of education I received in that nutrition class and at a much earlier age. In Paul Krugman's article "Free to Choose Obesity?" he says that "we need to put aside our anti-government prejudices and realize that the history of government interventions on behalf of public health, from the construction of sewer systems to the campaign against smoking, is one of consistent, life-enhancing success. Obesity is America's fastest-growing health problem; let's do something about it." Krugman basically argues the opposite position from Balko's. He's saying that we need the government to get involved. And we do. I think that we need to make sure that not only physical education is mandatory at all of our elementary schools, but that from a young age children are taught about proper eating habits. Physical education classes have already been cut, because the government put an emphasis on test scores and, as a result, schools felt like they had to cut something. Let's refocus and put the emphasis back on health.

Some states have already started to do this. Schools in Georgia now use a "School Health Index" in order to see how well schools are dealing with subjects like nutrition ("State Uses Many Strategies"). In addition, "Hundreds of bills introduced in 40 states attempt to create a healthier, more active school environment for children and adolescents. The issue of foods and beverages sold in competition with school breakfast and lunch programs continues to be a popular avenue for state legislators to address this issue" (Plaza).

Some might argue that it is the parent's responsibility to teach their kids what to eat. Frankly, that just hasn't been working. Parents haven't been doing it. If the current rates of obesity mean anything at all, it means that parents don't even know how to feed themselves. But I don't want to simply blame parents. I want the current conversation to move beyond discussion of what we *can't* do and start focusing on what we can do. And what we can do is to start educating children about dietary choices.

Works Cited

Balko, Radley. "Health Care Should Be a Personal Responsibility." *Wide Awake: Thinking, Reading, and Writing Critically* Ed. Sara Hosey. New York: Pearson Longman, 2012. 124–126.

Krugman, Paul. "Free to Choose Obesity?" *The New York Times.* 8 July 2005. Nytimes.com. Web. 28 September 2009.

Plaza, Carla I. "State's Public Health Initiative Address Nutrition, Obesity, and Physical Education." 1 September 2004. *Allbusiness.com.* Web. 29 September 2009.

"State Uses Many Strategies to Fight Obesity." *Georgia Department of Human Services.* 26 August 2005. www.dhr.georgia.gov. Web. 27 September 2009.

Chapter Eight

Research and Writing

- Gather, evaluate, and select sources for your paper.
- Distinguish between scholarly and popular sources.
- Identify different kinds of evidence and their uses.
- Clarify the different types of plagiarism in order to avoid common mistakes.
- Successfully incorporate sources into your work using summary, paraphrase, and quotation.
- Cite sources accurately in text and on your works cited page.
- Document and cite your sources.

》Prereading Check-In

Have you used sources from the library or the Internet to write essays in the past? Describe your experience with research. What kinds of sources do you usually use, and how do you find them?

Finding and Incorporating Sources

As suggested in Chapter 6, "From Paragraphs to Essays," the kinds of sources you'll incorporate will depend on whether or not your assignment calls for you to use your own experiences and knowledge and/or outside or academic sources. This chapter focuses on assignments that ask you to incorporate others' work in order to demonstrate that you have done research and that you have a deep understanding of the important debates surrounding your topic.

The sources you choose to include in your essays will be determined primarily by what skills your instructor would like to see you practice and demonstrate as well as by the parameters of the assignment. This chapter focuses on using print and electronic sources. However, personal interviews and surveys, as well as other kinds of independent research can also be effective strategies for gathering data for analysis.

> **TIP BOX** Primary and Secondary
>   Sources
>
> When you write research papers for humanities classes, you'll often draw on
> primary and secondary sources. A **primary source** is an original source, such
> as a work of literature or a painting or an interview that you conducted that
> you will discuss and/or analyze. For example, if you were writing an essay on
> Abraham Lincoln's Gettysburg Address, you would certainly read the original
> speech; the Gettysburg Address is your primary source. If you also consulted
> Garry Wills' excellent study of the Gettysburg Address, *Lincoln at Gettysburg*,
> Wills' book is then considered a **secondary source**. A secondary source com-
> ments on another text.

Gathering, Evaluating, and Selecting Sources

One of the crucial moves in academic writing is to enlighten yourself
about current conversations concerning your topic so that you have
something meaningful to contribute. Thus, in order to develop your
own well-considered position, it is crucial that you become aware that
the topic you have chosen has probably prompted *many* conversations
and controversies. Your aim is to enter and contribute to this conversation. Research within your topic will broaden your knowledge and
make you aware of others' positions.

Of course, there is an abundance of information available online
these days. Much of that information is valuable; much of it is useless.
While you may be quite Internet-savvy, you still might want to take advantage of one of your college's most valuable resources: the librarian.
Your college librarian is an expert on locating credible sources and will
most likely be more than happy to assist you.

Whether or not you consult the librarian, many of you will probably
start your research on the Internet. The Internet can be extremely useful in providing you with an overview of your topic. Beware, however.
Using a search engine is just the beginning of your research, not the
end. While using Google or Yahoo can give you a sense of the information, perspectives, and arguments surrounding your topic, much more
specialized digging will result in a higher quality of research. After you
provide yourself with an overview of what's on the Internet, you should
use that information in order to find credible and, if necessary, scholarly sources.

TIP BOX Wikipedia

Wikipedia and other online reference materials, such as Dictionary.com, can be useful tools at the beginning stages of your research because they can provide definitions and overviews of some of the big issues affecting your topic. However, Wikipedia is by no means the place where you end your research. Wikipedia, as its very name announces, is a form of an encyclopedia, which is a type of reference material that is designed to allow readers to get the basic information they need quickly. Encyclopedias, because they are general and superficial, are not deemed appropriate sources for college papers. Be aware that many college professors will not accept any use of Wikipedia.

Selecting Sources: Popular and Scholarly

Many instructors will want you to use scholarly sources, including books and journals, while others will invite you to use popular sources, such as websites and magazines. The main difference between scholarly and popular sources is that scholarly sources are **peer reviewed,** meaning that, before an article is published, a number of a scholar's peers, or other scholars, have agreed that the article is worthwhile and that its findings are valid. The peer review process is designed to make sure that high-quality, credible publications are produced. In addition to being peer-reviewed, scholarly articles are often longer than popular articles; they usually don't have photographs or other images, and they almost always display authorship (provide the author's name). They often appear in books that are collections of articles by various authors or in publications that have the word "journal" somewhere in the title, such as *The Journal of Literary and Cultural Disability* or *The American Studies Journal.* When you are searching a library database, there is often a "Scholarly" or "Peer Reviewed" box that you can check in order to limit your results to scholarly sources.

Popular articles, on the other hand, are articles on personal blogs, in newspapers, or in mainstream magazines or websites such as *Newsweek* or *Rolling Stone.* A popular article may or may not feature the author's name and is written for a more general audience than a scholarly article.

TIP BOX Finding Scholarly Articles for Free

You'll find a mix of scholarly and popular sources on the Internet, although there are probably more popular sources available for free than there are scholarly. One strategy for finding scholarly articles is to use the "Google Scholar" option under "Advanced Search" in Google. Once you enter a search term, the results list will only include scholarly sources. However, many of the hits you receive will be unavailable to you unless you pay to subscribe to a specific journal or database. At this point, you should consult your college library's website to see if your college already has access to this journal or database, and you can find the article (for free) there. (A side note: Libraries subscribe to all sorts of expensive databases; take advantage of your access to them while you're in school!)

Once you have a few sources that you think are useful, consult their bibliographies in order to find even more possibly valuable sources. One strategy for conducting research is to collect as much information as possible before you start narrowing down and selecting which sources are the most relevant for your purposes.

Evaluating Online Sources

Many academic or scholarly journals are now available online. Further, there are many authoritative websites that might prove relevant and valuable to you in your research. In order to determine if a website is credible, you should look at a few key indicators. First of all, does the website or the article on the website have an author? (Anonymously written articles are often less reliable than those to which authors have attached their names.) If so, you may take a minute to Google the author in order to see his or her professional affiliations and experience. Second, when was the site last updated? (In general, you want to look for the most current information available.) Third, can you figure out who the site's audience is by looking at the content? In addition, can you figure out what the purpose of the site is? For example, an article on TMZ.com is designed, generally, to entertain and to provide celebrity gossip (and is perhaps not the most reliable—or relevant—source of information). An article on moveon.org might clearly have a politically left-leaning bias, while an article on the drudgereport.com might clearly have a politically right-leaning bias. These sites may provide information that is relevant and credible, but it might be important for you to acknowledge their political disposition if you were to cite them in a paper.

Finally, a website's URL can give you an indication of what kind of source it is. Websites ending in .gov, .mil., .org, and .edu are run by nonprofit organizations and are generally trustworthy. Websites ending in .com are commercial sites and, while they may have some very good information, you should still look at them carefully.

Constructing Your Research Essay
Different Kinds of Evidence

Facts and statistics are often important components of research essays. This kind of information can be found in many different sources, such as articles and books as well as government and institutional websites. Thus you might use a government website in order to find demographic information for your topic (for example, how many people with disabilities are living in the United States) or for information about government programs (the "No Child Left Behind Act," for example). Argumentative pieces, like many of those in the anthology section of this textbook, also often include useful facts and statistics. See, for example, the excerpt from Mark Bauerlein's *The Dumbest Generation* (Chapter 13) or G. E. Zuriff's article "Personality Disorders Should Not Be Accommodated in the Workplace" (Chapter 9).

Often, when you are using an argumentative piece or an article that takes a clear position, you will want to choose one of three strategies for incorporating the source. First, you could *agree* with the author whose ideas you include, thus using that author's ideas to support your own ideas. Second, you could *disagree* with an author whose ideas you include. That is, you present another author's ideas and then take apart those ideas, demonstrating how they're wrong in order to put forward your own, correct, ideas. Finally, you could agree with the author's argument but *qualify* that agreement, which means that, while you see some valid points, you also want to build on what you perceive as the shortcomings of the work. An example of a sentence in which you agree with qualifications is "Although X advances many good points about the topic, her study neglects _____ aspects. In this essay, I will argue that _____ aspects reveal . . . ."

It is crucial that you make clear when you are drawing on and responding to another author's ideas. The next section discusses the dangers of failing to attribute or to cite correctly.

Avoiding Plagiarism

Plagiarism is a complicated issue, but simply defined, it is using another person's work without giving that person credit. This includes:

- buying or copying an essay from another person or from the Internet;
- allowing another person to write your paper;
- using someone else's ideas without giving that person credit;
- failing to use quotation marks or providing a citation when appropriate.

For more information about plagiarism, please see the fine website, plagiarism.org. In addition, you should always speak to your instructor if you have any questions about whether or not what you are using or how you are using a source is potentially plagiarism.

All authors have to be careful to make sure that it is always clear to their readers which ideas are their original ideas and which ideas come from other sources. The next section reviews valuable techniques for including secondary sources without falling prey to plagiarism.

Summarizing, Paraphrasing, and Quoting

Once you've located and selected the sources that you will use in your essay, the next step is to figure out which information you will incorporate and how you will incorporate it. *Summarizing, paraphrasing,* and *quoting* are key skills that you'll need to develop in order to write successful college papers.

A **summary** provides an overview of a text, a **quotation** focuses on a very specific part of the text, such as a word or phrase, and a **paraphrase**, which exists somewhere in between summary and quotation, focuses on a section of a text, such as a paragraph.

Here are some examples of each technique, using a movie as a primary source. (While in general, you will be summarizing, paraphrasing, and quoting from written material for your essays, the *Star Wars* example is meant to demonstrate the *scope* of the technique.) Explanations of the examples, as well as more extensive discussions of each term, follow below.

Summary:

George Lucas's *Star Wars* (1977) is a futuristic film that
tells the story of Luke Skywalker, who becomes an unwit-
ting hero in the war against the evil empire that rules his
galaxy. Skywalker starts off as a young would-be pilot who
is stuck on his uncle's farm. After his family is slaughtered,
Skywalker sets off to rescue a beautiful princess from the
villain, Darth Vader. Although Vader escapes, Skywalker succeeds in rescuing the princess and dealing a crucial blow to
the empire.

Paraphrase:

At one point, Luke and the other rebels escape from an on-
coming military force by diving down a chute that leads into
a garbage compactor. Not only is there a dangerous snake-
like creature inhabiting the compactor, but the walls slowly
begin to close in on the rebels, threatening to crush them. At
the last minute, Luke makes radio contact with his faithful
droid who is able to stop the compactor walls from killing the
rebels.

Quotation:

Obi-Wan Kenobi says, "Use the force, Luke."

As you can see from the above examples, the summary has the largest
scope: It provides an overarching view of what happens in the movie.
There are some specifics, but the summary's primary purpose is to
give you a sense of the "bigger picture." In a summary of a written
work, you want to provide the overall point of the piece, including the
author's thesis and important supporting points.

The paraphrase, on the other hand, focuses in on and provides
an overview of a specific scene in the film. Its scope, then, is significantly smaller than that of the summary. The paraphrase doesn't use
any quotations; instead, the writer uses her own words to describe
the thrust of the scene. In writing a paraphrase of a piece of written work, you would focus in on a paragraph or two in order to
describe, *in your own words*, the author's point or points in those
paragraphs.

The scope of the quotation is quite narrow. The quotation, as you
can see, uses exact words from the film. Using the source's exact
words is also how you quote from written material. Effective quoting is
discussed further below.

Composing a Formal Summary

While most written assignments in composition class do not call for *formal summary*, it is helpful to know how to construct one. Mastering the summary will certainly help you in your future writing because it facilitates your reading comprehension and is a tool for integrating others' ideas into your essays.

The first sentence of the formal summary provides the author's name, the title of the work you are summarizing, and a brief articulation of the author's thesis. (If it is possible to do so, you may use a quotation from the text in order to express the author's thesis.) The sentences that follow should provide the major points of the article or essay. One way to identify the major points is to make up an outline of the text and then to create your summary from that outline.

> First Sentence = Author + "Title" + Author's Thesis

While the length of a summary might vary according to the length of the source you are summarizing, summaries should be *brief*. Unless you are writing a very long article or even a book-length study, you should probably try to keep your summaries down to a paragraph or two.

Additionally, you want to make certain that, in your summary, you do not inadvertently misrepresent the author's ideas. Your commentary should not appear in the summary; instead, the summary should provide an unbiased description of the author's point or points.

Here's an example of a summary of an article from this textbook:

> In "An Introduction to Universal Design," Graham Pullin claims that architectural designs that "work for disabled and non-disabled people alike" have not really caught on yet, but that they should (83). Pullin describes some successful universal design projects, such as the curb cut, and suggests that we'll be seeing more universal design as populations age and more and more people become disabled.

WRITE BACK   Summary

Compose a formal summary of Laura Wray and Constance Flanagan's "An Inconvenient Truth About Youth" (in Chapter 11).

Note that the summary begins by identifying the title and author of the piece, as well as the specific thesis statement.

Effective and Successful Paraphrasing

Similar to the summary, the paraphrase is a tool for describing another's ideas (and again, is not a forum for you to voice your own opinions). While it is important to respond to the sources you include in your essays, you want to make clear when you are articulating another's ideas and when you are commenting on them.

Paraphrases are particularly tricky because you might unwittingly find yourself repeating an author's words without meaning to. However, as you know already, this is plagiarism. Keep in mind this basic rule: If you're using more than two or three significant words from another's work, you should use quotation marks and give that author credit. Additionally, if an author uses a specific and unique word (as though he or she is coining it or using it in a new way), that should also go in quotation marks. For example, in Chapter 9, Eli Clare uses the term "supercrip"; if you were to use this term in your essay, you should put it in quotation marks.

Here's an example of a passage taken from Garry Wills' *Lincoln at Gettysburg*. The paragraph is followed by a successful paraphrase. Please note how the paraphrase does not use the exact language or structure that Wills' passage uses. The point of the paraphrase is that you want to communicate some important ideas, but you don't want to quote the whole passage.

Immediately before this passage, Wills recounts some of the myths surrounding Lincoln's composition of the Gettysburg Address, including the one that Lincoln wrote out his speech on an envelope just before arriving at Gettysburg. Wills writes:

> These mythical accounts are badly out of character for Lincoln, who composed his speeches thoughtfully. His law partner, William Herndon, observing Lincoln's careful preparations of cases, records that he was a slow writer, who liked to sort out his points and tighten his logic and his phrasing. That is the process vouched for in every other case of Lincoln's memorable public statements. It is impossible to imagine him leaving his speech at Gettysburg to the last moment. He knew he would be busy on the train and at the site—important political guests were with him from his departure, and more joined him in Baltimore, full of talk about the war, elections, and policy. At Gettysburg he would be entertained at David Wills' house, with Everett and other important guests. State

delegations would want a word with him. He hoped for a quick tour of the battle site (a hope fulfilled early on the nineteenth). He could not count on any time for the concentration he required when weighing his words.

Here's a paraphrase of the above passage:

Wills debunks the myth that Lincoln jotted down his speech imme-diately before the ceremony at Gettysburg, pointing out that Lincoln was occupied with meetings and discussions in the hours preceding his arrival. Even more importantly, Lincoln was a deliberate writer who took his time composing. Thus, it would not have been consis-tent with his earlier behavior for Lincoln to have left his writing of the speech until the last minute (28).

You'll notice in the paraphrase that the writer does not include every detail that Wills does; he leaves out, for example, the place where Lincoln was staying and the fact that Lincoln visited the battlefield the day after his arrival. In addition, note that the order of the ideas is dif-ferent in the paraphrase than it is in the original.

There are two more elements of the paraphrase that you should note. The first is that the author of the paraphrase makes clear that he is describing someone else's ideas; he attributes the ideas to Wills within the paragraph itself. It is often appropriate and effective to foreground the sources and authors that you are using in your essay. However, this isn't always necessary; in fact, the paraphrase could have started with the words, "Lincoln did not jot down his speech on an envelope as some of the stories suggest."

The second important element to notice is that the paraphrase concludes with the page number that the original passage can be found on. Citation is discussed below. However, you should know that you must provide citations (page numbers or other source information) for paraphrases.

WRITE BACK   Paraphrase

After reading the entire article, paraphrase paragraphs six and seven of Vicki Haddock's article "The Happiness Quotient: Do High Expectations and a Plethora of Choices Make Modern Women Miserable?" (Chapter 14). (Paragraph six begins "Yet the paradox . . .").

Effective and Successful Quoting

Quotation is using another's exact language and attributing it appropriately. There are a number of reasons to use quotations rather than paraphrases. First, an author may have articulated an idea in beautiful or extremely effective language. Another reason to include a quotation is because you plan to analyze it (this works both in literary analysis essays, as well as in essays in which you want to pick apart another's ideas or writing).

Quotations should not be dropped into your paragraphs as free-standing sentences. Instead, quotations should be embedded in your sentences. This means that a quotation should be either preceded by or followed by your own words. Here's a list of some phrases that may be helpful to you when you are setting up your quotations:

According to	Author claims
Author contends	Author suggests
Author writes	Author implies
Author states	Author describes

Each of the above phrases draws attention to the fact that you are using another author's ideas.

Here are some examples of quotations. The first example, taken from Tom Vanderbilt's book, *Traffic: Why We Drive the Way We Do (and What It Says About Us)*, demonstrates how a quotation should be incorporated in a sentence; the second two examples demonstrate how to use the above phrases when you are quoting.

> **It's difficult to be aware of ourselves as drivers because** "our vehicle becomes our self" (Vanderbilt 24).

> **Vanderbilt contends** that it's difficult to be aware of ourselves as drivers because "our vehicle becomes our self" (24).

> "Our vehicle becomes our self," **according to Vanderbilt** (24).

The words in bold are the set-up or signal words that frame the quotation. You may also have noted that the first example is followed by the author's name and the number of the page on which the quotation may be found, whereas the second and third examples only provide the page number. This is because the second and third examples name the author in the sentence itself, so the reader already knows which source is being used.

WRITE BACK Quoting

Drawing on the information provided above, please provide the signal phrases or frames for the following quotations:

_____, "Even in the best schools a close examination of curriculum and its sequences turns up a lack of coherence, full of internal contradictions" (Gatto 175).

"The most important day I remember in all my life is the one on which my teacher, Anne Mansfield Sullivan, came to me,"_____ (Keller 77).

Citing Your Sources

There are three major citation styles used in academic writing: MLA, APA, and Chicago. Because it is the most often used in the humanities, we will confine our overview to MLA style. However, professors in other courses may ask you to use the other styles and, as suggested below, there are many wonderful websites that provide the information you'll need to display sources according to the style required.

The basic idea behind citing sources is that you give credit where credit is due. Thus, if you write a wonderful book on the history of bicycles and someone else wants to incorporate your ideas in his or her own piece about bicycles, that someone else must make clear when he or she is using your ideas.

This text does not provide an exhaustive list of rules and examples for citation because this information is easily accessible on the Internet. Many colleges and universities (perhaps even your own) have excellent online writing resources that provide information on citing and documentation. Most importantly, you should know that you don't have to memorize documentation styles (although you might find this happening anyway). Instead, you just need to know where to look for information. A quick Google search will yield many helpful results. Purdue University's online writing lab (*http://owl.english.purdue.edu*) and the University of Wisconsin-Madison's Writing Center website (*http://www.writing.wisc.edu*) are particularly strong resources. Of course, if you find documentation overwhelming and confusing, your college librarian will probably be happy to assist you.

In-text Citation: Making Your Sources Visible

In-text citation is basically the practice of making clear to your reader where you are getting your quotations and information from. After you incorporate an idea or quotation, provide the author's last name and the page number that the information can be found on in parentheses: (Author #). The following two examples illustrate how in-text citations can be incorporated seamlessly into your own sentences:

> Lincoln's voice had more "carrying power" than Everett's (Wills 36).
>
> According to Wills, Lincoln's voice had "carrying power" (36).

You may note that both the author and the page number are provided in the first example. In the second example, only the page number is provided in the parentheses. This is because, as with the Vanderbilt example, the second sentence invokes or names the author in the sentence itself, so it isn't necessary to put his name in the parentheses. The idea underpinning citation is that you make it very easy for your reader to see where you're getting your information. If your reader is intrigued by what you quote from Wills' book, she would not only have the page number for the quotation, but she could consult your works cited page in order to get the full information about Wills' book.

See below for a discussion of situations in which you don't have an author name or a page number to include in your in-text citation.

Your Works Cited Page

A works cited page is exactly what its title declares it to be: a page on which you will list all of the works (articles, books, or other texts) that you cited (used) in your essay. There are some specific formatting rules for your works cited page. First, the words "works cited" should be at the top center of the page. Second, list each of your sources in alphabetical order of each author's last name. Here's an example of how the list on a works cited page should look:

Works Cited

Schwartz, Barry. "Collective Memory and History: How Abraham Lincoln Became a

Symbol of Racial Equality." *The Sociological Quarterly* 38.3 (Summer 1997):

469–496.

Wills, Garry. *Lincoln at Gettysburg: The Words that Remade America.* New York: Simon

     and Schuster, 1992.

Note how the first line of each entry is flush left, but the second (and any subsequent lines in the entry) is indented once. This way, it's easy for a reader to scan a works cited page to find a particular author.

     Here are a few examples of basic entries.

- The basic format for a **journal** entry:
  Last name, First name. "Title of Article." *Title of Journal* Volume Number

  (Date of Publication): Page numbers.

- Here is the basic format for a works cited entry that is a **book**:
  Last name, First Name. *Title of Book.* Place of Publication: Publisher, Year.

- Here is the basic format for citing an **electronic source:**
  Author. "Article Title." *Site Title.* Date posted. Name of institution that

  maintains site. Access date.

An example might look like this:

Begley, Sharon. "Are We Taking the Wrong Approach to Curing Alzheimer's?"

Newsweek.com. 16 July 2009. Web. 17 July 2009.

A few notes:

- When an article doesn't have pages, you can't include the page number in your in-text citation. For example, the in-text citation for a quote from Begley's article might look like this:

  In "Are We Taking the Wrong Approach to Curing Alzheimer's?", Sharon Begley writes that "plaque-clearing drugs may be not only useless against Alzheimer's, but possibly dangerous."

Or this:

  In fact, "plaque-clearing drugs may be not only useless against Alzheimer's, but possibly dangerous" (Begley).

- Note that if a website doesn't have a publication date, you write *n.d.*

- When an article or website has no author listed, use the title in your in-text citation in the place of the author's name on the works cited page. You should shorten the title when you cite it in the text. Thus, the title "New Oil Numbers Mean More Environmental Damage" would appear like this as an in-text citation: ("New Oil").

Conclusion

Use sources in order to demonstrate that you have a deep understanding of your topic and that you are equipped to contribute to the conversation. Summarizing, paraphrasing, and quoting are methods for incorporating others' works. It is necessary to properly cite your sources so that you can easily and clearly give others credit; you don't have to memorize citation styles, but you do need to know where to look for helpful information.

Follow-up Activity #1: Evaluating Websites

Research and print out an example of a website that might first seem to be legitimate, but under close scrutiny reveals itself as not credible. (A particularly horrifying example is one website that pretends to provide history and information about Martin Luther King Jr., but which is actually run by a hate group. We won't provide the address, but you can probably find it if you need the example to be illustrated for you.) Alternately, find a website that has a clear audience and purpose, print out a page or two and share your results with the class.

Follow-up Activity #2: Researching a Monetary Unit

Write a research paper about the various symbols that appear on the U.S. dollar bill (or another currency). Like the analysis of a dollar bill that appears in Chapter 2, this essay should advance an argument about the meaning of the symbols, but this argument should be backed up with quotations, paraphrases, and summaries from authoritative sources.

 **Chapter Nine**

Disability Studies:
Questioning "Normal"

>> **Prereading Check-In**

1. Do you have or have you ever had a physical condition that made everyday activities difficult for you? Has anyone you love been affected by a disability or impairment? (If your answer is "no" to the previous two questions, consider answering the next Prereading Check-In question).

2. Within the disability community, some have taken to calling people without disability "temporarily abled." This term is meant to suggest that if a person lives long enough, he or she is likely to be disabled at some point (for example, to need a prosthetic device, like glasses, a wheelchair, or a pacemaker). What do you think of this term? How does the term "temporarily abled" ask people to think differently about disability?

Until recently, disability was a topic that was not generally studied in academic settings beyond the fields of biology and medicine. However, disability or impairment is a condition that is quite common and familiar to many of us; the U.S. Census Bureau reports that almost 50 million Americans have some sort of impairment. In recent decades, people with disabilities and their allies have been speaking up about their experiences, calling attention to the idea that having a disability does not make a person "inferior" or "abnormal" and working hard to make sure that they have recognition and rights in our culture. In addition, while there are certainly people who suffer due to disabilities, some writers and activists think that it is important to emphasize that there are many individuals with disabilities who are quite content, even if their bodies don't conform to conventional ideals. Further, there are those who argue that disability itself poses fewer problems than social prejudices and lack of accommodations. For example, an accomplished musician who happens to use a wheelchair becomes disabled as she attempts to use inaccessible stations in the New York City subway system, and a brilliant student who happens to have cerebral palsy may not be able to do his best work in a classroom without an aide, scribe, or laptop.

Often, accommodations can be simple and can improve everyone's experiences. Recently, disability activists have called for the use of "universal design" in various areas of public life, such as architecture and education. Universal design means design that all people can use. For example, more people can easily use a ramp than can use a staircase. Yet universal design often asks people to remake their world—the tools they use to travel, to communicate, to cook, and to learn and educate, among other things—in new and sometimes unfamiliar ways. Further, critics of changes to accommodate those with disabilities might suggest that the ways we measure whether or not an individual needs accommodation are problematic and that the costs of accommodation—be they economic, practical, or social—may sometimes be too high.

Bringing together multiple voices and perspectives on disability, this chapter investigates the idea of "normalcy" in addition to challenging many of the stereotypes surrounding disability. Whether or not you are an individual with a disability, these readings ask you to consider your relationship to your body and your "built environment," what it means to be "normal" and how that category might be constructed, and what it means to truly value difference and diversity in our culture.

Helen Keller, from *The Story of My Life*

> **>> Prereading Check-In**
>
> **1.** Describe an "aha!" moment that you've had. What didn't you understand, and what helped your comprehension? How did you feel after you "got it"?
>
> **2.** Are you familiar with the author and activist Helen Keller? Write down what you already know about her.

Helen Keller *(1880–1968), who was almost two years old when she became deaf and blind as the result of childhood illness, was a famous writer and political activist who toured the globe giving lectures. Keller's life story was made into a play and movie titled* The Miracle Worker *(1962). In this excerpt from Keller's autobiography* The Story of My Life *(1905), she describes the arrival of her tutor, Anne Sullivan, and how Sullivan helped her to acquire language (at first by teaching her to read and spell out letters with her hands). Keller uses vivid sensory descriptions and figurative language to convey her feelings and experiences before and after Sullivan teaches her to communicate through touch.*

From *The Story of My Life*

The most important day I remember in all my life is the one on which my teacher, Anne Mansfield Sullivan, came to me. I am filled with wonder when I consider the immeasurable contrasts between the two lives which it connects. It was the third of March, 1887, three months before I was seven years old.

On the afternoon of that eventful day, I stood on the porch, dumb, expectant. I guessed vaguely from my mother's signs and from the hurrying to and fro in the house that something unusual was about to happen, so I went to the door and waited on the steps. The afternoon sun penetrated the mass of honeysuckle that covered the porch, and fell on my upturned face. My fingers lingered almost unconsciously on the familiar leaves and blossoms which had just come forth to greet the sweet southern spring. I did not know what the future held of marvel or surprise for me. Anger and bitterness had preyed upon me continually for weeks and a deep languor had succeeded this passionate struggle.

Have you ever been at sea in a dense fog, when it seemed as if a tangible white darkness shut you in, and the great ship, tense and anxious, groped her way toward the shore with plummet and sounding-line, and you waited with beating heart for something to happen? I was like that ship before my education began, only I was without compass or sounding-line, and had no way of knowing how near the harbour was. "Light! give me light!" was the wordless cry of my soul, and the light of love shone on me in that very hour.

I felt approaching footsteps. I stretched out my hand as I supposed to my mother. Some one took it, and I was caught up and held close in the arms of her who had come to reveal all things to me, and, more than all things else, to love me.

The morning after my teacher came she led me into her room and gave me a doll....When I had played with it a little while, Miss Sullivan slowly spelled into my hand the word "d-o-l-l." I was at once interested in this finger play and tried to imitate it. When I finally succeeded in making the letters correctly I was flushed with childish pleasure and pride. Running downstairs to my mother I held up my hand and made the letters for doll. I did not know that I was spelling a word or even that words existed; I was simply making my fingers go in monkey-like imitation. In the days that followed I learned to spell in this uncomprehending way a great many words, among them *pin*, *hat*, *cup* and a few verbs like *sit*, *stand*, and *walk*. But my teacher had been with me several weeks before I understood that everything has a name.

One day, while I was playing with my new doll, Miss Sullivan put my big rag doll into my lap also, spelled, "d-o-l-l" and tried to make me understand that "d-o-l-l" applied to both. Earlier in the day we had had a tussle over the words "m-u-g" and "w-a-t-e-r." Miss Sullivan had tried to impress upon me that "m-u-g" is *mug* and that "w-a-t-e-r" is *water*, but I persisted in confounding the two. In despair she had dropped the subject for the time, only to renew it at the first opportunity. I became impatient at her repeated attempts and, seizing the new doll, I dashed it upon the floor. I was keenly delighted when I felt the fragments of the broken doll at my feet. Neither sorrow nor regret followed my passionate outburst. I had not loved the doll. In the still, dark world in which I lived there was no strong sentiment or tenderness. I felt my teacher sweep the fragments to one side of the hearth and I had a sense of satisfaction that the cause of my discomfort was removed. She brought me my hat, and I knew I was going out into the warm sunshine. This thought, if a wordless sensation may be called a thought, made me hop and skip with pleasure.

We walked down the path to the well-house, attracted by the fragrance of the honeysuckle with which it was covered. Someone was drawing water and my teacher placed my hand under the spout. As the cool stream gushed over one hand she spelled into the other the word *water*, first slowly, then rapidly. I stood still, my whole attention fixed upon the motions of her fingers. Suddenly I felt a misty consciousness as of something forgotten—a thrill of returning thought; and somehow the mystery of language was revealed to me. I knew then that "w-a-t-e-r" meant the wonderful cool something that was flowing over my hand. That living word awakened my soul, gave it light, hope, joy, set it free! There were barriers still, it is true, but barriers that could in time be swept away.

I left the well-house eager to learn. Everything had a name, and each name gave birth to a new thought. As we returned to the house every object which I touched seemed to quiver with life. That was because I saw everything with the strange, new sight that had come to me. On entering the door I remembered the doll I had broken. I felt my way to the hearth and picked up the pieces. I tried vainly to put them together. Then my eyes filled with tears; for the first time I realized what I had done, and for the first time I felt repentance and sorrow.

I learned a great many new words that day. I do not remember what they all were; but I do know that *mother, father, sister, teacher* were among them—words that were to make the world blossom for me, "like Aaron's rod, with flowers." It would have been difficult to find a happier child than I was as I lay in my crib at the close of that eventful day and lived over the joys it had brought me, and for the first time I longed for a new day to come.

Choosing to Read Critically Questions

1. In this passage, Keller suggests that language plays a crucial role in personal development. She writes that language made "the world blossom." Describe how language acquisition changes Helen.

2. Why and how do Helen's feelings about the doll change?

3. Keller uses the metaphor of being at sea in a "dense fog" without a compass or "sounding-line" in paragraph 3. Look up these terms, and write a paragraph explaining the significance of the metaphor. What does it tell you about how young Helen feels? Why does Keller use this metaphor? Do you find it effective? (Be sure to look up any terms you might not be familiar with.)

4. Why, do you think, did Keller write her autobiography? You might also consider that *My Life* has had enduring popularity and has been made into a play and movie. What, do you think, do audiences find appealing about this story?

Choosing to Respond Questions

1. Compare your perspective on education to Keller's. Keller's teacher enabled Keller to more effectively participate in the world. Do you feel that your teachers played a similar role?

2. Keller's accomplishments have made her a hero to many disabled and nondisabled people alike. What, do you think, a modern reader can take away from Keller's story? What part or parts of the narrative do you find most relevant for a reader today?

Wide Awake to Connections Questions

1. Read the entirety of Keller's book *My Life* or watch the film adaptation, *The Miracle Worker,* and write an essay in which you discuss how and why the above excerpt is so important to Keller's larger story. How, for example, does the film treat the scene? How are audiences supposed to feel? Do you like Keller's work or the film version better? Why?

2. Read Greek philosopher Plato's "Allegory of the Cave" (which can be found in Chapter 12 of this book, "American Education"). Both Plato and Keller use metaphor in order to describe what it is like to become enlightened or to learn a truth about the larger world. Write an essay in which you compare and contrast the ideas and imagery that you find in each text.

Graham Pullin, "An Introduction to Universal Design"

>> **Prereading Check-In**

1. Describe a time in your life when you became aware of the limitations of your body. (An example might include not being able to read something at a distance or not being able to squeeze into an airplane seat.) What happened, and how did you feel about it?

2. Do you think that your campus is accessible for all people? Think about a particular building where you spend a lot of time and describe it. Would it be easy to navigate that building if you were in a wheelchair or on crutches?

Graham Pullin *is a designer who works with designs for both the disabled and the nondisabled communities. He teaches at the Duncan of Jordanstone College of Art and Design at the University of Dundee in Scotland and has written the book* Design Meets Disability *(2009). The following article appeared in the March 2009 issue of* Dwell, *a design magazine. In it, Pullin describes some of the principles of* *"universal design" and suggests that we should all embrace design "for the whole population."*

An Introduction to Universal Design

Mention universal design and see your companions' eyes start glazing over. Though formally flashy chairs and posh penthouses may reside at the sexier end of the design world, universal design actually affects us all. So pay attention and prepare to learn something—your less hale days aren't far off; none of ours is.

The term "universal design" is attributed to the architect Ronald Mace, and although its scope has always been broader, its focus has tended to be on the built environment. Those using the term often define it as design "for the whole population," with the notion being that a design should work for disabled and nondisabled people alike. And what idealistic follower of design's evolution would balk at this humanitarian quest? The very term evokes the jet-setting glamour of the late 1950s: a global consultancy with its HQ on Madison Avenue, perhaps, sharing offices with the sharp-suited ad execs from *Mad Men*, of James Bond's cover job with Universal Exports. Yet at the moment, the subject seems neither all that glamorous nor, well, universal.

The classic example of universal design is the curb cut. Initially installed to help wheelchair users navigate from street to sidewalk, these unobtrusive bits of public design turn out to be just as useful for parents with prams and travelers lugging wheeled suitcases. The higher aspiration is full social participation. But as useful as universal design can be, something like a wheelchair ramp sited in an ill-lit side entrance does little to ease the stigma people with disabilities face each day.

Certain objects that exemplify universal design have crept into the wider culture. Certainly Braille on elevator buttons or an induction loop at a bank teller's window fit the bill, and one even finds universal design that doesn't wear its "I'm meant for the disabled" badge quite so prominently. The OXO Good Grips potato peeler is easier to use if you have reduced dexterity or weak grip strength, but it is a popular choice for any kitchen.

Perhaps the most common approach, a rough principle of universal design, is to make information about an object or a building available through several senses at once. So pedestrian crossings displaying "WALK" also make noises to help those with visual impairments.

Naturally, other people can benefit too—for example, subtitles on the TV intended for the hard of hearing can aid nonnative speakers in learning a language or those trapped in the airport to get their daily dose of news.

In the 1970s, much of the political pressure exerted for disability rights came from groups such as the Eastern Paralyzed Veterans Association—often young, otherwise active Americans who found themselves excluded from public life as much by their surroundings as by their wartime injuries. This led to the Americans with Disabilities Act of 1990, which outlaws discrimination based on disability, including inaccessible places, information, and communication. But at the same time, this lineage—and even the wheelchair icon itself—can help to perpetuate the stereotype of people with disabilities as young men in wheelchairs.

In the 21st century, demographic changes are altering our perspectives. As lifestyles and modern medicine keep us alive longer, and fewer disabling conditions prove fatal, more and more of us will eventually become disabled. Not the spandex-jacket-and-rocket-pack future the 1950s promised—but culturally, we'll be healthier, at once grayer and more multicolored, more diverse. It will no longer be possible to marginalize universal design: When more of us have a "disability" than not, universal design will indeed become universal.

Choosing to Read Critically Questions

1. In your own words, explain what "universal design" is. In addition, what does Pullin mean by "full social participation"?
2. Summarize the development of the disability rights movement, as outlined in the article's final two paragraphs.
3. This article appeared in *Dwell,* a design magazine. Describe the article's primary audience and Pullin's purpose in writing.
4. Pullin argues that universal design will become more prevalent in coming years. What is his rationale for this? Do you find his ideas compelling?

Choosing to Respond Questions

1. What do you think of the idea of "universal design"? Would you like to see more universal design on your campus and in other public places?
2. Design an accessible college campus. You may do this using visual aids that demonstrate the ways in which your campus will be accessible to all people. Write up a description of your campus to accompany your drawings or renderings.

Wide Awake to Connections Questions

1. Recently, some educators have been calling for universal design in teaching approaches. Conduct some Internet research, and summarize the main principles of universal design in education.

2. Psychologist Ed Diener has reported that individuals with disabilities are, in general, pretty happy. (See Diener's book *Happiness: Unlocking the Mysteries of Psychological Wealth*, 2011, for more information.) Does this finding surprise you? Drawing on one or two articles from this section, as well as one or two articles from Chapter 14, write an essay in which you discuss the possible relationships between happiness and physical dis/ability. You might consider interviewing someone with a disability, reading more about the research on happiness and disability, and/ or using Pullin's article in order to address how one's physical environment impacts one's happiness.

Winstone Zulu, "I Had Polio. I Also Have Sex."

❯❯ Prereading Check-In

1. What, do you think, are some common myths or stereotypes about individuals with disabilities? List two or three. (This question is not meant to simply rehash offensive stereotypes, but to raise awareness of some of the stereotypes that persist today.)

2. Write down your thoughts about sexual education for teenagers and adults. Do you think sex ed should be taught in school, by parents, by both, or by neither? Give some reasons for your opinion.

The coordinator of Health Triangle Zambia, **Winstone Zulu** *(b. 1964) is an HIV-positive survivor of tuberculosis. Zulu was the first Zambian to publicly disclose his HIV status and is a globally recognized activist fighting to raise awareness about and fight the spread of tuberculosis. The following piece first appeared in the* New York Times. *In it, Zulu explains a common misconception about individuals with disabilities—and its potentially harmful consequences.*

"I Had Polio. I Also Have Sex."

I spoke at an AIDS conference not long ago, and after the talk, someone asked me how I had contracted HIV "Well," I replied, "sexually." Staring at my crutches, which I have used since I got polio as a child, she exclaimed, "But how?"

The assumption that all disabilities—of hands, feet, hearing, sight—somehow also affect the ability and desire to have sex is common. It would be comic if it didn't have such serious consequences: people with disabilities are rarely exposed to sex education and are almost never considered in need of information about HIV and treatment for it.

As a result, although people with disabilities are just as likely to be sexually active as people without, our HIV infection rate is up to three times higher.

In Africa, children with disabilities are less likely to receive sexual health education, both because they are less likely to be enrolled in school, and because those who attend are sometimes removed from sexual health classes. Due to the widespread belief that we are asexual, we are often left out of family planning programs, despite the fact that many of us want children or are parents already.

The blind can't read HIV prevention posters; the deaf can't hear radio campaigns. Vague messages are not understood by those with intellectual disabilities. Places where condoms and education materials are available are often physically inaccessible.

People with disabilities are often among the poorest of the poor, and can't afford health care services. But even those with access to health care often experience discrimination and loss of privacy in health centers. Consider my hearing-impaired friends, who have to bring a family member to interpret if they want to get tested for HIV In many places, people face being evicted or ostracized if family members learn they have HIV The lack of confidentiality is a big deterrent to testing and treatment.

Worst of all, when drugs and services must be rationed, our lives are sometimes valued less than others. I have heard of cases where people with disabilities are given a lower priority for life-saving antiretrovirals.

[Recently] world leaders met at the United Nations to discuss efforts to fight HIV Despite pledges for universal access to prevention, treatment and care, some people—children and heterosexuals—always get more attention in these meetings than others—sex workers, drug users, gays and lesbians and people with disabilities.

We must no longer be overlooked because of false assumptions about our sexuality. People with disabilities can and do have sex. I know from my own experience. We need to be a part of the fight against HIV, too.

Choosing to Read Critically Questions

1. In your own words, summarize the stereotype Zulu identifies as well as the consequences of that stereotype.
2. Explain how and why some individuals with disabilities may not be getting important information about HIV prevention.
3. What was your first reaction to Zulu's title? Do you find it effective?
4. What do you think of Zulu's opening anecdote—the description of his encounter with another individual at a conference? Do you think it was a compelling way to start his article? Why or why not?

Choosing to Respond Questions

1. Using Zulu's discussion as a springboard, interrogate some other assumptions about disability. Does this article make you aware of other stereotypes that you or other people might have uncritically held?
2. Have you seen any depictions of disability on television or in the movies recently? With a group of students, brainstorm a list of disabled characters in popular culture. Do these depictions prove Zulu's point that disabled individuals are often stereotyped as asexual, or do they suggest that attitudes toward disability are changing? Present your findings to the class.

Wide Awake to Connections Questions

1. Zulu's activism is primarily focused in Africa. Choosing a country or area outside of the United States that is of interest to you (it may be a region you have visited or that you have family in), conduct some research about the situation of individuals with disabilities in that nation.
2. Zulu's article brings into focus a problem that stems from a lack of information and education. Building on the concerns he presents here, as well as one or two articles from Chapter 13, "Social Networking," discuss the possibilities of using the Internet and other communication technologies for spreading information. How might technologies be used to solve some of these problems? In addition, what are the limitations of these technologies?

G. E. Zuriff, "Personality Disorders Should Not Be Accommodated in the Workplace"

>> **Prereading Check-In**

1. To what extent do you think that people with "invisible" disabilities—that is, psychological, mental, or emotional disabilities—should be accommodated in school and in workplaces? Explain what kinds of accommodations you do or don't agree with.

2. What have you heard about the Americans with Disabilities Act? Alternately, write down what you think the law requires schools and employers to do in order to accommodate individuals with disabilities.

G. E. Zuriff *(b. 1943) is a professor of psychology and a clinical psychologist affiliated with Wheaton College and the Massachusetts Institute of Technology. Zuriff has written on subjects including learning disabilities and diversity in schools. The following excerpt from Zuriff's article "Medicalizing Character," which originally appeared in 1996 in* The Public Interest, *critiques the scope of the ADA and, in particular, how mental illnesses are defined and treated in our society.*

"Personality Disorders Should Not Be Accommodated in the Workplace"

Hailed as "the most far-reaching legislation ever enacted against discrimination of people with disabilities," the Americans with Disabilities Act (ADA) extends the civil-rights protections of individuals with disabilities to employment, public accommodations, transportation, government services, and telecommunications. Not only is discrimination outlawed but businesses and public facilities must make "reasonable" changes to accommodate disabilities, unless "undue hardship" would result.

When most Americans think of the ADA, they imagine people in wheelchairs or with visual impairments working productively, attending college for the first time, or using accessible buses, all because the law now requires that their special needs be met. However, within disability laws are provisions going beyond these inspirational images and threatening to undermine our culture's already fragile sense of personal responsibility.

Not surprisingly, the ADA's definition of a disability includes a variety of physical disorders, but it is less well known that the definition also includes "mental impairment that substantially limits one or more major life activities." In fact, during the first 15 months of the ADA, nearly 10 percent of all violation complaints concerned mental disabilities, second only to back problems. Unfortunately, however, "mental impairment" is not well defined within either the ADA or psychiatry.

Defining Disorders

Federal regulations attempt to clarify by stating that "mental impairment means any mental or psychological disorder such as mental retardation, organic brain syndrome, emotional or mental illness." Yet no regulation specifies what constitutes an emotional or mental illness. Nevertheless, when we look at the legislative history of the ADA, the opinions of experts in the field, and ADA court cases, we find a consensus that the *Diagnostic and Statistical Manual of Mental Disorders* (DSM), first published by the American Psychiatric Association in 1952 and now in its fourth edition, is the definitive guide. This tome provides the official names, descriptions, and diagnostic criteria for hundreds of psychological disorders.

Perusing the DSM is an eye opener. Of course, we find mental retardation (five varieties) and schizophrenia (also in five varieties), but we also encounter oppositional defiant disorder, anxiety disorders (11 types), and mood disorders (17 types). Most disturbing in their practical and moral implications are the 11 categories of "personality disorders." For example, the "narcissistic personality disorder" consists of "a pervasive pattern of grandiosity (in fantasy or behavior), need for admiration, and lack of empathy . . . present in a variety of contexts, as indicated by five (or more) of the following." What follows is a list of nine personality traits, including that the person has a grandiose sense of self-importance, believes that he is "special," requires excessive admiration, takes advantage of others, lacks empathy, is envious of others, and shows arrogant attitudes. For the "obsessive-compulsive personality disorder," we find "a pervasive pattern of preoccupation with orderliness, perfectionism, and mental and interpersonal control, at the expense of flexibility, openness, and efficiency." The person disabled by an "avoidant personality disorder" shows "a pervasive pattern of social inhibition, feelings of inadequacy, and hypersensitivity to negative evaluation."

What were in earlier times considered to be faults of mind and flaws of character are today regarded as "psychological disorders," which are, moreover, covered by the ADA. If an employee can show, for example, that an inability to relate well to co-workers is a direct result of a narcissistic personality disorder, then the employer is not only forbidden to dismiss the worker but must also make reasonable accommodations for this "disability."

Frightening Implications

The social implications of treating personality disorders on a par with physical disabilities are momentous. First, we do not know how many people meet the DSM diagnostic criteria and can, therefore, demand legal accommodation. The DSM estimates the prevalence of each of its personality-disorder categories at about 2 percent of the population, creating the potential for 10 million to 20 million Americans requiring accommodations in work, school, and public facilities because of their personalities.

If the experience with the Individuals with Disabilities Education Act (IDEA) is any indication, we are in for a frightening future. Once a diagnosis of the psychological disorder "learning disability" became an admission ticket to a variety of entitlements and civil rights under IDEA, the number of diagnoses exploded. During the first year of IDEA (1976), students with learning disabilities comprised less than 24 percent of all disabled children covered; by 1992, they constituted 52.4 percent. These 2,369,385 learning disabled students received over $1 billion in benefits. In recent years, the annual increases in the number of disabled students under IDEA is almost totally attributable to the growth in the number of learning disabled children. It will be interesting to see if the number of personality-disorder diagnoses similarly skyrockets as the ADA works its way into public consciousness.

A more serious question concerns the effects on the moral fabric of our society as character faults come to be viewed as no different from physical disabilities. What happens to a society that accommodates people who are excessively narcissistic, antisocial, histrionic, dependent, or compulsive rather than insisting that they accommodate themselves to society? How will workers react when they see chronically late, socially difficult, temperamental, or unlikable colleagues being given special privileges? What will workers think of sensitivity-training sessions that encourage them to tolerate, and even empathize with, a co-worker who is rude or lacks self-control? . . .

Clarify the Definitions of Disability

What is to be done? First, new regulations must clarify and further limit the definition of mental disability. Congress's handling of sexual disorders, drug addiction, and alcoholism can serve as a model. Although all three appear in the DSM, the ADA explicitly excludes sexual disorders from coverage, includes drug addiction only under very circumscribed conditions, and limits coverage of alcoholism. Similar qualifications are in order for other mental disorders. While it may make some sense to protect and accommodate people with schizophrenia who lack control over their illness, the same is not true for people with personality disorders. Their actions, attitudes, and qualities of character are commonly disapproved of in our society, and they should be held morally responsible for them. They should be encouraged to accommodate to society rather than the reverse. At the same time, we can recognize their suffering and perhaps help provide them with the appropriate psychotherapy.

While limiting the application of the ADA, we should not lose sight of some of its good intentions. Successful businesses have come to understand that good management means recognizing psychological differences among employees and creating working environments that maximize each individual's potential. Often this means tailoring jobs to fit an employee's weaknesses, as well as strengths, even if this entails some expense in providing the necessary supports. This is the sort of enlightened self-interest that employers have to some extent practiced even without the ADA. Thus there is reason to hope that a reformed and narrowed ADA, coupled with competitive market forces, will bring about a more humane, productive workplace.

Choosing to Read Critically Questions

1. Summarize the goals of the Americans with Disabilities Act (ADA).
2. In your own words, explain what Zuriff sees as the problem with the ADA.
3. In paragraph 2, Zuriff writes, "When most Americans think of the ADA, they imagine people in wheelchairs or with visual impairments working productively, attending college for the first time, or using accessible buses, all because the law now requires that their special needs be met." His next sentence begins with the word "However." Why does Zuriff establish what "most Americans think" of the ADA, and what does the word "however" signal? What is Zuriff's next point?
4. How does Zuriff end this piece? Explain whether or not you find his concluding remarks convincing.

Choosing to Respond Questions

1. Drawing on your own experiences and observations, respond to Zuriff's overarching argument.

2. Explain and respond to Zuriff's claim that, "What were in earlier times considered to be faults of mind and flaws of character are today regarded as 'psychological disorders.'"

Wide Awake to Connections Questions

1. Zuriff points to an increase in the number of students who qualify for entitlements under the Individuals with Disabilities Education Act (IDEA) (see paragraph 8). Conduct some research, and write an essay in which you evaluate the success or failure of IDEA. If you have personal experience with IDEA, you might choose to include your own observations and analysis in the essay.

2. In paragraph 2, Zuriff claims that Americans already have a "fragile sense of personal responsibility." First, establish what you think Zuriff means by this phrase. Then, review the articles in the next chapter, "What to Eat? Difficult Decisions About Food in America." Some of the authors in Chapter 10 (most notably Radley Balko and Kelly Brownell) use the concept of personal responsibility in their discussions of America's current "obesity crisis." In addition, some individuals view obesity as a type of disability. Sort out these multiple threads in an essay in which you take positions on whether or not obesity is a form of disability as well as to what extent individuals, corporations, and/or the government should be held responsible for the "obesity crisis."

Nancy Mairs, from "On Being a Cripple"

›› Prereading Check-In

1. How important are names and labels? Is there a name or label that you use that others find inappropriate? Are there names and labels that others use that you find offensive or inappropriate? Why and how?

2. A "euphemism" is an expression that is vague and perhaps less offensive than a more straightforward expression; people often use them to avoid upsetting others. (For example, one might say that someone "passed away" rather than "he died"). Come up with a list of two or three common euphemisms to discuss. Do you think these euphemisms are helpful in that they enable us to talk about difficult topics, or do you think they are dishonest in that they gloss over important issues? Use the list you've generated as fodder for your analysis.

Nancy Mairs *(b. 1943) is an award-winning poet and essayist. Mairs, who has multiple sclerosis, has published numerous books, including* Waist-High in the World: A Life Among the Nondisabled *(1997) and* Plaintext: Deciphering a Woman's Life *(1986), from which the following essay is excerpted.* Plaintext *is composed of personal essays. In the following selection, taken from the beginning of an essay in which she discusses the word "cripple," Mairs examines the importance of language and naming.*

From "On Being a Cripple"

The other day I was thinking of writing an essay on being a cripple. I was thinking hard in one of the stalls of the women's room in my office building, as I was shoving my shirt into my jeans and tugging up my zipper. Preoccupied, I flushed, picked up my book bag, took my cane down from the hook, and unlatched the door. So many movements unbalanced me, and as I pulled the door open I fell over backward, landing fully clothed on the toilet seat with my legs splayed in front of me: the old beetle-on-its-back routine. Saturday afternoon, the building deserted, I was free to laugh aloud as I wriggled back to my feet, my voice bouncing off the yellowish tiles from all directions. Had anyone been there with me, I'd have been still and faint and hot with chagrin. I decided that it was high time to write the essay.

First, the matter of semantics. I am a cripple. I choose this word to name me. I choose from among several possibilities, the most common of which are "handicapped" and "disabled." I made the choice a number of years ago, without thinking, unaware of my motives for doing so. Even now, I'm not sure what those motives are, but I recognize that they are complex and not entirely flattering. People—crippled or not—wince at the word "cripple," as they do not at "handicapped" or "disabled." Perhaps I want them to wince. I want them to see me as a tough customer, one to whom the fates/gods/viruses have not been kind, but who can face the brutal truth of her existence squarely. As a cripple, I swagger.

But, to be fair to myself, a certain amount of honesty underlies my choice. "Cripple" seems to me a clean word, straightforward and precise. It has an honorable history, having made its first appearance in the Lindisfarne Gospel in the tenth century. As a lover of words, I like the accuracy with which it describes my condition: I have lost the full use of my limbs. "Disabled," by contrast, suggests any incapacity, physical or mental. And I certainly don't like "handicapped," which implies that I have deliberately been put at a disadvantage, by whom I can't imagine (my God is not a Handicapper General), in order to equalize chances in the great race of life. These words seem to me to be moving away from my condition, to be widening the gap between word and reality. Most remote is the recently coined euphemism "differently abled," which partakes of the same semantic hopefulness that transformed countries from "undeveloped" to "underdeveloped," then to "less developed," and finally to "developing" nations. People have continued to starve during the shift. Some realities do not obey the dictates of language.

Mine is one of them. Whatever you call me, I remain crippled. But I don't care what you call me, so long as it isn't "differently abled," which strikes me as pure verbal garbage designed, by its ability to describe anyone, to describe no one. I subscribe to George Orwell's thesis that "the slovenliness of our language makes it easier for us to have foolish thoughts." And I refuse to participate in the degeneration of the language to the extent that I deny that I have lost anything in the course of this calamitous disease; I refuse to pretend that the only differences between you and me are the various ordinary ones that distinguish any one person from another. But call me "disabled" or "handicapped" if you like. I have long since grown accustomed to use them myself. Society is no readier to accept crippledness than to accept death, war, sex, sweat, or wrinkles. I would never refer to another person as a cripple. It is the word I use to name only myself.

Choosing to Read Critically Questions

1. What is Mairs' attitude toward the word "crippled"? What is her attitude toward the term "differently-abled"?

2. Explain the Orwell quotation that Mairs includes: "the slovenliness of our language makes it easier for us to have foolish thoughts."

3. Describe how Mairs opens her essay and what effect it had on you.

4. Why do you think Mairs decides to write this essay after her mishap in the bathroom?

Choosing to Respond Questions

1. Mairs writes, "Society is no readier to accept crippledness than to accept death, war, sex, sweat, or wrinkles." Using Mairs' quote as a starting point, agree or disagree with her contention, backing up your position with evidence and reasoning.

2. Mairs' essay seems to suggest that we should use language honestly. The names we assign things and people often reveal their status in society. What does the word "cripple," as well as most people's distaste for the word, reveal or suggest about the status of the disabled in our society?

Wide Awake to Connections Questions

1. Building on your answer to Choosing to Respond Question #2, agree or disagree with Orwell's statement, using examples to back up your position.

2. Read Eli Clare's "The Mountain" (in this chapter), and write an essay in which you discuss Mairs' embrace of the word "cripple" alongside of Clare's use of the word "supercrip." Alternately, write an essay in which you explain Mairs' dislike of the term "differently-abled" alongside of John Callahan's use of this term (in the cartoons included below in this chapter).

Eli Clare, from "The Mountain"

>> **Prereading Check-In**

1. Discuss an obstacle you've felt you've had to "overcome" in order to be successful.

2. When you think about images of disability, what comes to mind? Brainstorm a list of depictions of disability.

Eli Clare *(b. 1963) is a transgendered activist, speaker, and writer who has cerebral palsy. He has written a collection of essays,* Exile and Pride *(1999), from which the following excerpt is taken, and a collection of poetry,* The Marrow's Telling: Words in Motion *(2007). In this selection from "The Mountain," Clare investigates the stories we tell about disability, as well as the differences between "disability" and "impairment."*

From "The Mountain"

I: A Metaphor

The mountain as metaphor looms large in the lives of marginalized people, people whose bones get crushed in the grind of capitalism, patriarchy, white supremacy. How many of us have struggled up the mountain, measured ourselves against it, failed up there, lived its shadow? We've hit our heads on glass ceilings, tried to climb the class ladder, lost fights against assimilation, scrambled toward the phantom called normality.

We hear from the summit that the world is grand from up there, that we live down here at the bottom because we are lazy, stupid, weak, and ugly. We decide to climb that mountain, or make a pact that our children will climb it. The climbing turns out to be unimaginably difficult. We are afraid; every time we look ahead we can find nothing remotely familiar or comfortable. We lose the trail. Our wheelchairs get stuck. We speak the wrong languages with the wrong accents, wear the wrong clothes, carry our bodies the wrong ways, ask the wrong questions, love the wrong people. And it's goddamn lonely up there on the mountain. We decide to stop climbing and build a new house right where we are. Or we decide to climb back down to the people we love, where the food, the clothes, the dirt, the sidewalk, the steaming asphalt under our feet, our crutches, all feel right. Or we find the path again, decide to continue climbing only to have the very people who told us how wonderful life is at the summit booby-trap the trail. They burn the bridge over the impassable canyon. They redraw our topo maps so that we end up walking in circles. They send their goons—those working-class and poor people they employ as their official brutes—to push us over the edge. Maybe we get to the summit but probably not. And the price we pay is huge.

Up there on the mountain, we confront the external forces, the power brokers who benefit so much from the status quo and their privileged position at the very summit. But just as vividly, we come face-to-face with our own bodies, all that we cherish and despise, all that lies imbedded there. This I know because I have caught myself lurching up the mountain.

II: A Supercrip Story

I am a gimp, a crip, disabled with cerebral palsy. The story of me lurching up the mountain begins not on the mountain, but with one of the dominant images of disabled people, the supercrip. A boy without hands bats .486 on his Little League team. A blind man hikes the Appalachian Trail from end to end. An adolescent girl with Down syndrome learns to drive and has a boyfriend. A guy with one leg runs across Canada. The nondisabled world is saturated with these stories: stories about gimps who engage in activities as grand as walking 2,500 miles or as mundane as learning to drive. They focus on disabled people "overcoming" our disabilities. They reinforce the superiority of the nondisabled body and mind. They turn individual disabled people, who are simply leading their lives, into symbols of inspiration.

Supercrip stories never focus on the conditions that make it so difficult for people with Downs to have romantic partners, for blind people to have adventures. For disabled kids to play sports. I don't mean medical conditions. I mean material, social, legal conditions. I mean lack of access, lack of employment, lack of education, lack of personal attendant services. I mean stereotypes and attitudes. I mean oppression. The dominant story about disability should be about ableism, not the inspirational supercrip crap, the believe-it-or-not disability story.

I've been a supercrip in the mind's eye of nondisabled people more than once. Running cross-country and track in high school, I came in dead last in more races than I care to count. My tense, wiry body, right foot wandering out to the side as I grew tired, pushed against the miles, the stopwatch, the final back stretch, the last muddy hill. Sometimes I was lapped by the front runners in races as short as the mile, sometimes I trailed everyone on a cross-country course by two, three, four minutes. I ran because I loved to run, and yet after every race, strangers came to thank me, cry over me, tell me what an inspiration I was. To them, I was not just another hopelessly slow, tenacious high school athlete, but supercrip, tragic, brave kid with CP, courageous cripple. It sucked. The slogan on one of my favorite t-shirts, black cotton inked with big fluorescent pink letters, one word per line, reads PISS ON PITY.

Me lurching up the mountain is another kind of supercrip story, a story about internalizing supercripdom, about becoming supercrip in my own mind's eye, a story about climbing Mount Adams last summer with my friend Adrianne. We had been planning this trip for years. Adrianne spent her childhood roaming New Hampshire's White Mountains and wanted to take me to her favorite haunts. Six times in six years, we set the trip up, and every time something fell through at the last minute. Finally, last summer everything stayed in place.

. . . The night before our hike, it rained. In the morning we thought we might have to postpone. The weather reports from the summit still looked uncertain, but by 10 a.m. the clouds started to lift, later than we had planned to begin but still okay. The first mile of trail snaked through steep jumbles of rock, leaving me breathing hard, sweat drenching my cotton t-shirt, dripping into my eyes. I love this pull and stretch, quads and calves, lungs and heart, straining.

The trail divides and divides again, steeper and rockier now, moving not around but over piles of craggy granite, mossy and a bit slick from the night's rain. I start having to watch where I put my feet. Balance has always been somewhat of a problem for me, my right foot less steady than my left. On uncertain ground, each step becomes a studied move. Especially when my weight is balanced on my right foot. I take the trail slowly, bringing both feet together, solid on one stone, before leaning into my next step. This assures my balance, but I lose all the momentum gained from swinging into a step, touching ground, pushing off again in the same moment. There is no rhythm to my stop-and-go clamber. I know that going down will be worse, gravity underscoring my lack of balance. I watch Adrianne ahead of me hop from one rock to the next up this tumble trail of granite. I know that she's breathing hard, that this is no easy climb, but also that each step isn't a strategic game for her. I start getting scared as the trail steepens, then steepens again, the rocks not letting up. I can't think of how I will ever come down this mountain. Fear sets up a rumble right alongside the love in my bones. I keep climbing. Adrianne starts waiting every 50 yards or so. I finally tell her I'm scared.

She's never hiked this trail before so can't tell me if this is as steep as it gets. We study the topo map, do a time check. We have many hours of daylight ahead of us, but we're both thinking about how much time it might take me to climb down, using my hands and butt when I can't trust my feet. I want to continue up to treeline, the pines shorter and shorter, grown twisted and withered, giving way to scrub brush, then to lichen-covered granite, up to the sun-drenched cap where the mountains all tumble out toward the hazy blue horizon. I want to so badly, but fear rumbles next to love next to real lived physical limitations, and so we decide to turn around. I cry, maybe for the first time, over something I want to do, had many reasons to believe I could, but really can't. I cry hard, then get up and follow Adrianne back down the mountain. It's hard and slow, and I use my hands and butt often and wish I could use gravity as Adrianne does to bounce from one flat spot to another, down this jumbled pile of rocks.

I thought a lot coming down Mount Adams. Thought about bitterness. For as long as I can remember, I have avoided certain questions. Would I have been a good runner if I didn't have CP? Could I have been a surgeon or pianist, a dancer or gymnast? Tempting questions that have no answers. I refuse to enter the territory marked bitterness. I wondered about a friend who calls herself one of the last of the polio tribe, contracting the disease just before the vaccine's discovery. Does she ever ask what her life might look like if she had been born five years later? On a topo map, bitterness would be outlined in red.

I thought about the model of disability that separates impairments from disability. Disability theorist Michael Oliver defines impairment as "lacking part of or all of a limb, or having a defective limb, organism or mechanism of the body." I lack a fair amount of fine motor control. My hands shake. I can't play a piano, place my hands gently on a keyboard, or type even 15 words a minute. Whole paragraphs never cascade from my fingertips. My long hand is a slow scrawl. I have trouble picking up small objects, putting them down. Dicing onions with a sharp knife puts my hands at risk. A food processor is not a yuppie kitchen luxury in my house, but an adaptive device. My gross motor skills are better but not great. I can walk mile after mile, run and jump and skip and hop, but don't expect me to walk a balance beam. A tightrope would be murder; boulder hopping and rock climbing, not much better. I am not asking for pity. I am telling you about impairment.

Oliver defines disability as "the disadvantage or restriction of activity caused by a contemporary social organisation which takes no or little account of people who have physical [and/or cognitive/developmental/mental health impairments] and thus excludes them from the mainstream of society." I write slowly enough that cashiers get impatient as I sign my name to checks, stop talking to me, turn to my companions, hand them my receipts. I have failed timed tests, important tests, because teachers wouldn't allow me extra time to finish the sheer physical act of writing, wouldn't allow me to use a typewriter. I have been turned away from jobs because my potential employer believed my slow, slurred speech meant I was stupid. Everywhere I go people stare at me, in restaurants as I eat, in grocery stores as I fish coins out of my pocket to pay the cashier, in parks as I play with my dog. I am not asking for pity. I am telling you about disability.

In large part, disability oppression is about access. Simply being on Mount Adams, halfway up Air Line Trail, represents a whole lot of access. When access is measured by curb cuts, ramps, and whether they are kept clear of snow and ice in the winter; by the width of doors and height of counters; by the presence or absence of Braille, closed captions, ASL, and TDDs; my not being able to climb all the way to the very top of Mount Adams stops being about disability. I decided that turning around before reaching the summit was more about impairment than disability.

But even as I formed the thought, I could feel my resistance to it. To neatly divide disability from impairment doesn't feel right. My experience of living with CP has been so shaped by ableism—or to use Oliver's language, my experience of impairment has been so shaped by disability—that I have trouble separating the two. I understand the difference between failing a test because some stupid rule doesn't give me more time and failing to summit Mount Adams because it's too steep and slippery for my feet. The first failure centers on a socially constructed limitation, the second on a physical one.

At the same time, both center on my body. The faster I try to write, the more my pen slides out of control, muscles spasm, then contract trying to stop the tremors, my shoulder and upper arm growing painfully tight. Even though this socially constructed limitation has a simple solution—access to a typewriter, computer, tape recorder, or person to take dictation—I experience the problem on a very physical level. In the case of the bodily limitation, my experience is similarly physical. My feet simply don't know the necessary balance. I lurch along from one rock to the next, catching myself repeatedly as I start to fall, quads quickly sore from exertion, tension, lack of momentum. These physical experiences, one caused by a social construction, the other by a bodily limitation, translate directly into frustration, making me want to crumple the test I can't finish, hurl the rocks I can't climb. This frustration knows no neat theoretical divide between disability and impairment. Neither does disappointment nor embarrassment. On good days, I can separate the anger I turn inward at my body from the anger that needs to be turned outward, directed at the daily ableist shit, but there is nothing simple or neat about kindling the latter while transforming the former. I decided that Oliver's model of disability makes theoretical and political sense but misses important emotional realities.

I thought of my nondisabled friends who don't care for camping, hiking, or backpacking. They would never spend a vacation sweat-drenched and breathing hard halfway up a mountain. I started to list their names, told Adrianne what I was doing. She reminded me of other friends who enjoy easy day hikes on smooth, well-maintained trails. Many of them would never even attempt the tumbled trail of rock I climbed for an hour and a half before turning around. We added their names to my list. It turned into a long roster. I decided that if part of what happened up there was about impairment, another part was about desire, my desire to climb mountains.

I thought about supercrips. Some of us—the boy who bats .486, the man who through-hikes the A.T.—accomplish something truly extraordinary and become supercrips. Others of us—the teenager with Downs who has a boyfriend, the kid with CP who runs track and cross-country—lead entirely ordinary lives and still become supercrips. Nothing about having a boyfriend or running cross-country is particularly noteworthy. Bat .486 or have a boyfriend, it doesn't matter; either way we are astonishing. In the creation of supercrip stories, nondisabled people don't celebrate any particular achievement, however extraordinary or mundane. Rather, these stories rely upon the perception that disability and achievement contradict each other and that any disabled person who overcomes this contradiction is heroic.

To believe that achievement contradicts disability is to pair helplessness with disability, a pairing for which crips pay an awful price. The nondisabled world locks us away in nursing homes. It deprives us the resources to live independently. It physically and sexually abuses us in astoundingly high numbers. It refuses to give us jobs because even when a workplace is accessible, the speech impediment, the limp, the ventilator, the seeing-eye dog are read as signs of inability. The price is incredibly high.

Choosing to Read Critically Questions

1. In your own words, describe the distinction Oliver makes between a disability and an impairment.
2. What is the "supercrip" story, and why does Clare dislike it?
3. How does Part I: "A Metaphor" connect to Part II: "A Supercrip Story"? What is Clare suggesting by using the metaphor of the mountain, as well as his own experiences climbing a literal mountain?
4. Describe Clare's tone in this piece. Do you find it compelling and effective? Why or why not?

Choosing to Respond Questions

1. Does Clare's essay make you reconsider any of your own assumptions about disabled individuals? Why or why not and how?
2. What do you think of Clare's use of words like "crip" and "gimp"? Do you find them offensive? Why or why not?

Wide Awake to Connections Questions

1. Check out the blogs of some self-proclaimed "crips" and disability-rights activists. (You may want to start with http://uppity-crip.blogspot.com, http://thegimpparade.blogspot.com or http://cripconfessions.com.) Select one or two blogs to summarize and evaluate.
2. Drawing on the above essay as well as Winstone Zulu's "I Had Polio. I Also Have Sex" and John Callahan's cartoons (both in this chapter), write an essay in which you discuss common ideas and misconceptions about individuals who have disabilities. You may choose to include a discussion of how and why the above writers are combating some of these misconceptions.

John Callahan, *Cartoons*

>> **Prereading Check-In**

1. How, do you think, have attitudes toward disability and disabled people changed in recent decades?
2. Have you any experience with people with disabilities? If so, what have they been?

John Callahan *(1951–2010) became a quadriplegic in 1972 as a result of a car accident. With the partial use of one hand, Callahan became an acclaimed, controversial and politically incorrect cartoonist, often making light of his own disability. The cartoons that follow originally appeared in his autobiography,* Don't Worry, He Won't Get Far on Foot *(1990). In them, Callahan reminds us through humor that people with disabilities are really no different than "temporarily"-abled people.*

1. **In the past, handicapped people weren't an issue because they weren't seen around much. They were "shut-ins."**

John Callahan/Levin Represents

II. Today, handicapped people are more visible than ever. Yet people are often still uncomfortable around them. In an attempt to be appropriate, people tend to overcompensate.

John Callahan/Levin Represents

III. The first thing to realize is that the handicapped are just like you or me!

(SOME ARE HAPPY)

(SOME ARE DEPRESSED)

(SOME ARE COOL)

(SOME ARE FAT)

(SOME ARE GEEKS)

John Callahan/Levin Represents

IV. The correct way to approach a handicapped person.

John Callahan/Levin Represents

V. Don't be afraid to ask questions—children are spontaneous and uninhibited in their curiosity. Take a lesson from them. . . .

VIII. If you enjoy a handicapped person's company, what's next?

DON'T BE AFRAID
TO COMPLIMENT HIM:

"nice cane!"

HANDICAPPED PEOPLE
EAT THE SAME FOOD
YOU DO - INVITE THEM
TO DINNER

Sorry Bill!
We'll try to
get a ramp
for those
stairs before
our next
dinner party!
Need more
potatoes?

DON'T BE AFRAID OF
INTIMACY WITH A HAND-
ICAPPED PERSON IF THE
MOMENT ARISES...

John Callahan/Levin Represents

IX. Over the years many myths have arisen. Here are a few we've heard one too many times!

HANDICAPPED PEOPLE
DON'T HAVE SEX.

<u>FAT</u> MANIC-DEPRESSIVES
ARE JOLLY ½ THE TIME

DEAF PEOPLE ARE
GRATEFUL FOR PEACE
AND QUIET.

BLIND PEOPLE HANG
BY THEIR FEET IN A
CAVE WHEN THEY SLEEP.

DWARVES ARE
TO BE TOSSED
AND NOT
HEARD.

Choosing to Read Critically Questions

1. What, do you think, is the main point that Callahan is trying to make?
2. Explain Callahan's observation in IV: "Of course one of the problems of being in a wheelchair isn't the fact that you're in it, but that people react to you in the weirdest ways."
3. Not all of Callahan's advice should be taken seriously. Cite a few instances when he is being ironic.
4. Some people don't find Callahan's cartoons funny at all. In groups, discuss whether or not you find his cartoons funny. Why?

Choosing to Respond Questions

1. In II (above), Callahan illustrates the discomfort people feel when they encounter a person with a disability. The autobiography that the cartoons appeared in was published in 1990. Do the same or similar inappropriate reactions to people with disabilities still occur today?
2. In IX (above), Callahan displays the myths that persist about people with disabilities. Do these myths still exist today?

Wide Awake to Connections Questions

1. There are political underpinnings to the various cartoons. To understand the changes that Callahan tracks, take a look at the Disability History Timeline (http://www.disabilityhistory.org/timeline_new.html; you don't have to begin at the beginning) to get a sense of how attitudes toward and inclusion of people with disabilities occurred globally over time. Then concentrate on the timeline of the twentieth-century United States to see what kinds of serious criticisms Callahan makes about conditions for people with disabilities.
2. Find another text, either in this chapter or in another chapter in this book, in which an author uses humor to deal with a serious issue. Write an essay in which you compare and contrast that author's approach with Callahan's.

QUESTIONS AND SUGGESTIONS FOR FURTHER RESEARCH AND WRITING

1. Identify some of the recurring and important ideas addressed in this chapter. Then, drawing on two or three of these texts, construct an essay that provides an overview of contemporary attitudes toward

disability. You may note that most of the texts in this chapter are created by individuals who self-identify as disabled. Describe how they deal with disability in their work, what they identify as some of the issues that currently need addressing, and what solutions they propose. You may conclude the essay by presenting your own ideas on these topics.

2. Using the excerpt from Helen Keller's *The Story of My Life* as a springboard, construct an essay focused on the role and importance of education in an individual's development. You may also choose to draw on your own experience and/or one or two articles from Chapter 12: Choosing School.

3. Conducting independent research, investigate recent connections between disability and the environment. You may define "environment" in a number of different ways as you approach this assignment. Environment can mean the "built environment" or the role that public and private spaces play in creating, maintaining, or alleviating disability. Alternately, you may choose to examine disabilities like asthma and some kinds of cancer that may be caused or exacerbated by environmental conditions. Use your research to construct an argument about the relationships between individuals and their surroundings.

4. Disability studies scholars have pointed out that representations of disability appear everywhere in literature, film, and art. (See, for example, Helen Keller in either version of *The Miracle Worker*; Tiny Tim in *A Christmas Carol*; the short stories of authors Noria Jablonski, Anne Finger, Flannery O'Connor [see "Good Country People"], and Raymond Carver [see "Cathedral"], Hillary Swank's character in *Million Dollar Baby*; the character Lt. Dan in *Forest Gump*; the character David in *Vanilla Sky*; the hunchback in *The Hunchback of Notre Dame*; the figures in David Hevey and Diane Arbus's photography; Salvador Dalí's sketches and paintings.) Of course, many of these depictions are problematic in that authors and artists use a disability simplistically to symbolize villainy or inferiority. Select one or two depictions from film or literature that you think would lead to a fruitful analysis. First, decide whether or not this is a complex depiction of disability or if it is a stereotype. Then explain what you think this character represents and how.

5. Chances are that there is a center for students with disabilities on your campus. If so, check out its website to get a feel for what goes on in the center. Next, call or email a counselor or faculty member there and ask for an appointment to interview him or her concerning how the center operates, what kinds of students it serves, what accommodations it offers, and what

federal laws are in place that guide the center. (Before you meet with the counselor or faculty member, develop questions in writing so that you cover as many of the topics that interest you.) Synthesize your findings in an essay describing accessibility on your campus, what services it provides for its students, and what the school can do to further provide for students with disabilities.

10 Chapter Ten
What to Eat:
Difficult Decisions About Food in America

>> Prereading Check-In

1. How much time do you spend thinking about what you will eat? Do you care about where your food comes from, what's in it, and whether or not it is "good" for you? If these questions are important to you, explain why. If these aren't important considerations, explain your perspective on the purpose of food.

2. From your observations, what are some of the current controversies surrounding food production and consumption?

The most basic reason that we eat food is that we need to do so in order to survive. However, we also eat food because eating can be a pleasurable experience. Further, food plays an important role in our religious and cultural rituals, our social gatherings and celebrations. Thus, we often share meals or eat food in the company of others as part of a larger social act. For example, "first dates," or our first official romantic meetings, are often "dinner dates"; Thanksgiving is a national holiday structured around a meal; and the Catholic mass takes as its center Jesus' "last supper," itself a ritual meal that is part of the Jewish celebration of Passover.

The above list is just a sampling of traditions accompanying the deceptively simple act of eating and sharing food and begins to suggest that, although it might seem uncomplicated at first, eating is actually an extremely complex activity. Particularly at the dawn of the twenty-first century in America, producing and consuming food has become an act with political consequences. How we grow and make our food can have negative effects on our environments and also on our bodies. The United States is currently in the midst of an "obesity crisis" that has been linked to the low cost and convenience of much of our industrial food. Yet Americans have come to expect food to be cheap; further, our lifestyles make it difficult for many individuals to enjoy fresh or "home-cooked" foods on a daily basis. In addition, there are some who argue that alarm over the "obesity epidemic" is used as an excuse to persecute fat people. Thus, the topic of what we eat allows us to investigate the intersections of economic policies, environmental practices, health concerns, and social issues such as prejudice. We hope that this section encourages you to think critically about how food functions in your life, as well as what kinds of choices you make about the food you purchase and consume.

Wendell Berry, "The Pleasures of Eating"

›› Prereading Check-In

1. What are some of the pleasures of eating for you? Do they include shopping for, preparation of, and anticipation of a meal, as well as dining with companions? If so, discuss what goes into the process and why it's pleasurable for you.
2. Brainstorm on the concept of "eating responsibly." What ideas does that phrase conjure for you?

American "man of letters" **Wendell Berry** *(b. 1934) is a poet, essayist, and novelist. In addition, Berry became a farmer in the 1960s, and he continues to work his land without modern equipment. In the following essay from his book* What Are People For? *(1990), Berry discusses food consumption in America and calls for a return to the simple pleasures of eating by growing one's own food.*

"The Pleasures of Eating"

Many times, after I have finished a lecture on the decline of American farming and rural life, someone in the audience has asked, "What can city people do?"

"Eat responsibly," I have usually answered. Of course, I have tried to explain what I meant by that, but afterwards I have invariably felt that there was more to be said than I had been able to say. Now I would like to attempt a better explanation.

I begin with the proposition that eating is an agricultural act. Eating ends the annual drama of the food economy that begins with planting and birth. Most eaters, however, are no longer aware that this is true. They think of food as an agricultural product, perhaps, but they do not think of themselves as participants in agriculture. They think of themselves as "consumers." If they think beyond that, they recognize that they are passive consumers. They buy what they want—or what they have been persuaded to want. But one can be thus liberated only by entering a trap (unless one sees ignorance and helplessness as the signs of privilege, as many people apparently do). The trap is the ideal of industrialism: a walled city surrounded by valves that let merchandise in but no consciousness out. How does one escape this trap? Only voluntarily, the same way that one went in: by restoring one's consciousness of what is involved in eating; by reclaiming responsibility for one's own part in the food economy. Eaters, that is, must understand that eating takes place inescapably in the world, that it is inescapably an agricultural act, and that how we eat determines, to a considerable extent, how the world is used. This is a simple way of describing a relationship that is inexpressibly complex. To eat responsibly is to understand and enact, so far as one can, this complex relationship. What can one do? Here is a list, probably not definitive:

1. Participate in food production to the extent that you can. If you have a yard or even just a porch box or a pot in a sunny window, grow something to eat in it. Make a little compost of your kitchen scraps and use it for fertilizer. Only by growing some food for yourself can you become acquainted with the beautiful energy cycle that revolves from soil to seed to flower to fruit to food to offal to decay, and around again. You will be fully responsible for any food that you grow for yourself, and you will know all about it. You will appreciate it fully, having known it all its life.

2. Prepare your own food. This means reviving in your own mind and life the arts of kitchen and household. This should enable you to eat more cheaply, and it will give you a measure of "quality control": you will have some reliable knowledge of what has been added to the food you eat.

3. Learn the origins of the food you buy, and buy the food that is produced closest to your home. The idea that every locality should be, as much as possible, the source of its own food makes several kinds of sense. The locally produced food supply is the most secure, the freshest, and the easiest for local consumers to know about and to influence.

4. Whenever possible, deal directly with a local farmer, gardener, or orchardist. All the reasons listed for the previous suggestion apply here. In addition, by such dealings you eliminate the whole pack of merchants, transporters, processors, packagers, and advertisers who thrive at the expense of both producers and consumers.

5. Learn, in self-defense, as much as you can of the economy and technology of industrial food production. What is added to food that is not food, and what do you pay for these additions?

6. Learn what is involved in the best farming and gardening.

7. Learn as much as you can, by direct observation and experience if possible, of the life histories of the food species.

The last suggestion seems particularly important to me. Many people are now as much estranged from the lives of domestic plants and animals (except for flowers and dogs and cats) as they are from the lives of the wild ones. This is regrettable, for these domestic creatures are, in diverse ways, attractive; there is much pleasure in knowing them. And farming, animal husbandry, horticulture, and gardening, at their best, are complex and comely arts; there is much pleasure in knowing them, too.

It follows that there is great displeasure in knowing about a food economy that degrades and abuses those arts and those plants and animals and the soil from which they come. For anyone who does know something of the modern history of food, eating away from home can be a chore. My own inclination is to eat seafood instead of red meat or poultry when I am traveling. Though I am by no means a vegetarian, I dislike the thought that some animal has been made miserable in order to feed me. If I am going to eat meat, I want it to be from an animal that has lived a pleasant, uncrowded life outdoors, on bountiful pasture, with good water nearby and trees for shade. And I am getting almost as fussy about food plants. I like to eat vegetables and fruits that I know have lived happily and healthily in good soil, not the products of the huge, bechemicaled factory-fields that I have seen, for example, in the Central Valley of California. The industrial farm is said to have been patterned on the factory production line. In practice, it looks more like a concentration camp.

The pleasure of eating should be an extensive pleasure, not that of the mere gourmet. People who know the garden in which their vegetables have grown and know that the garden is healthy will remember the beauty of the growing plants, perhaps in the dewy first light of morning when gardens are at their best. Such a memory involves itself with the food and is one of the pleasures of eating. The knowledge of the good health of the garden relieves and frees and comforts the eater. The same goes for eating meat. The thought of the good pasture and of the calf contentedly grazing flavors the steak. Some, I know, will think it bloodthirsty or worse to eat a fellow creature you have known all its life. On the contrary, I think it means that you eat with understanding and with gratitude. A significant part of the pleasure of eating is in one's accurate consciousness of the lives and the world from which food comes. The pleasure of eating, then, may be the best available standard of our health. And this pleasure, I think, is pretty fully available to the urban consumer who will make the necessary effort.

I mentioned earlier the politics, esthetics, and ethics of food. But to speak of the pleasure of eating is to go beyond those categories. Eating with the fullest pleasure—pleasure, that is, that does not depend on ignorance—is perhaps the profoundest enactment of our connection with the world. In this pleasure we experience and celebrate our dependence and our gratitude, for we are living from mystery, from creatures we did not make and powers we cannot comprehend. When I think of the meaning of food, I always remember these lines by the poet William Carlos Williams, which seem to me merely honest:

> There is nothing to eat,
>   seek it where you will,
>   but the body of the Lord.
> The blessed plants
>   and the sea, yield it
>   to the imagination
> intact.

Choosing to Read Critically Questions

1. Explain what kinds of animals and plants Berry chooses to eat and why.
2. Explain Berry's statement in paragraph 3 that "how we eat determines, to a considerable extent, how the world is used."
3. Analyze the poem that Berry includes at the end of the essay. What, if anything, does this inclusion add to the main text?

4. This selection is an attempt to further explain Berry's advice to "eat responsibly." Do you find Berry's explanation effective and compelling? Does it make you think differently about food? Why or why not?

Choosing to Respond Questions

1. Berry writes that many people see "ignorance and helplessness as the signs of privilege" (paragraph 3). Explain what Berry means by this and whether or not you agree with him, providing examples to back up your ideas.

2. Given that most of the food production in this country involves vast feedlots, less-than-humane conditions for farm animals, pesticides, additives, artificial color and flavors, many of us choose not to think about where our food comes from. Yet, at the very end of the article, Berry seems to suggest that the pleasure of eating will only increase once eaters become familiar with how food is grown—including animals—and produced. Working together in groups, decide how you could reconcile these two positions.

Wide Awake to Connections Questions

1. Do a little research at your local supermarket. What kinds of foods are most available and most inexpensive? Can you find out where different products come from? Is there an "organic" section, or are "organic" products distributed throughout the store? You may also choose to comparison shop: Go to supermarkets in neighborhoods that are markedly different: rural and urban, poor and rich, racially/ethnically homogenous and diverse and see how their offerings might be different. Write an essay in which you present your findings, and draw some conclusions about the store or stores or about how food is marketed and sold more generally.

2. Read Bryan Walsh's "Getting Real About the High Price of Cheap Food," available online, which describes some of the startling realities of industrial food production. Write an essay in which you include references to both Berry and Walsh's work as you discuss whether or not individuals should educate themselves about where their food comes from.

Kelly Brownell and Katherine Battle Horgen, from *Food Fight: The Inside Story of the Food Industry, America's Obesity Crisis, and What We Can Do About It*

›› Prereading Check-In

1. How often do you eat fast food? Why do you or don't you choose to eat at fast-food restaurants?

2. To what extent do you see obesity as a public health issue?

Kelly Brownell *(b. 1951), director of the Rudd Center for Food Policy and Obesity at Yale, is a professor of epidemiology and public health and of psychology. He is the author of numerous books and articles, including* Food Fight: The Inside Story of the Food Industry, America's Obesity Crisis & What We Can Do About It *(2003) with* Katherine Battle Horgen, *from which the following excerpt is taken.* **Katherine Battle Horgen** *also works at the Yale Center for Eating and Weight Disorders and has published on the topic of obesity. The piece that follows is part of the Introduction to Brownell and Horgen's book and serves to establish obesity as a crisis that, according to the authors, must be addressed through both individual and institutional change.*

From *Food Fight*

Big Food, Big Money, Big People

It came quickly, with little fanfare, and was out of control before the nation noticed. Obesity, diabetes, and other diseases caused by poor diet and sedentary lifestyle now affect the health, happiness, and vitality of millions of men, women, and, most tragically, children and pose a major threat to the health care resources of the United States. Most alarming has been the national inaction in the face of crisis, the near-total surrender to a powerful food industry, and the lack of innovation in preventing further havoc.

The Centers for Disease Control and Prevention (CDC) labels the obesity problem an "epidemic." Within the United States, 64.5 percent of Americans are either overweight or obese, with the number growing. For many reasons, some obvious and some not, the increase in overweight children is twice that seen in adults.

Other nations are in hot pursuit. Country after country follows the American lead and grows heavier. Overconsumption has replaced malnutrition as the world's top food problem. From Banff to Buenos Aires . . . the world need only look to America to see its future. There are now clinics for obese children in Beijing.

Similar to a new virus without natural enemies, our lifestyle of abundant food and inactivity faces little opposition. Quite the contrary, powerful forces push it forward, spreading the problem to all segments of the population. These forces are woven so tightly into our social systems (economics, health care system, even education) that change seems almost beyond imagination. Despite talk of an obesity crisis, government reports, and presidents pushing exercise, obesity is increasing in all races, ages, income groups, and areas of the world.

The picture with children is sad. Projecting ahead to their adult years, today's children face a life of serious health problems and severely impaired quality of life. Children are targeted in relentless ways by the food companies. Institutions such as schools that would like to protect children instead must sell soft drinks and snack foods to function.

While writing this chapter, one of us (KB) visited his brother, wife, and three-year-old niece. This girl, the daughter of educated, successful, health-conscious parents, ran by, so a quick interview was conducted.

"What's your favorite breakfast?"

"I like Buzz Lightyear," was her reply.

"Where do you like to go out to eat?"

"I like to go everywhere," she said.

"What's your most favorite place of all?"

"McDonald's," she answered.

It is easy to blame parents, but they face off every day with an environment that grabs their children and won't let go. Children and the parents who raise them do not get what they deserve—conditions that support healthy eating and physical activity. The environment wins in most cases, and we have an epidemic to show for it.

By any definition, we face an emergency.

The reasons for this growing problem are simple and complex at the same time. People eat too much and exercise too little, but this easy truth masks a fascinating dance of genetics with modern lifestyle. Economics, breakthroughs in technology, how our nation thinks about food, and, of course, the powerful and sophisticated food industry, are all actors in this tragic play. Our environment is textured with risk. It intersects with genes in a way that makes an obese population a predictable consequence of modern life.

Some individuals have the biological fortune or the skills to resist this risk, leading to arguments that weight control is a matter of personal responsibility. Choices people make are important, but the nation has played the willpower and restraint cards for years and finds itself trumped again and again by an environment that overwhelms the resources of most people.

The cost of inaction will multiply human suffering, place our nation at a strategic disadvantage, and have a massive impact on health care costs.

The Toxic Environment

Biology comes undone when confronted by modern eating and exercise conditions, what we call the toxic environment. *Toxic* is a powerful word, but powerful language is needed to describe the situation. Names we give our food say it all: Double Whopper with Cheese, Super Supreme Pizza, Bacon Double Cheeseburger, Colossal Burger, Double Decker Taco Supreme, and Extreme Gulp. Chicken requires a "bucket." Food is

- available 24 hours a day
- accessible in restaurants, machines, and stores as never before
- sold in places previously unrelated to eating (gas station, drugstores)
- cheap
- promoted heavily and, in some cases, deceptively
- designed by food technologists to taste really good and keep people coming back for more

The second half of the energy equation, physical activity, has also been affected in disastrous ways. Few children walk or bike to school; there is little physical education; computers, video games, and television keep children inside and inactive; and parents are reluctant to let children roam free to play.

The American landscape has been altered in profound ways. Cheeseburgers and French fries, drive-in windows and supersizes, soft drinks and candy, potato chips and cheese curls, once unusual, are as much our background as trees, grass, and clouds. We now take notice when food isn't there. Gas stations *without* a mini-market look old-fashioned and unappealing . . . .

Food, not just fast food, is everywhere. . . . Accessibility of bad food is coupled with a key economic reality: unhealthy food is cheap. It is also convenient, fast, packaged attractively, and tasty. Healthy foods are more difficult to get, less convenient, and more expensive. If you came from Mars and knew nothing but this about a country, an epidemic of obesity is exactly what you'd predict.

This confluence of declining physical activity and an altered eating environment, both in toxic proportions, has created a human crisis.

Is a Braver New World Possible?

The nation's reticence to tackle the obesity problem has allowed an epidemic to flourish, our children to be victimized, and business to prevail over health . . . .

Individuals can act, as can parents, families, schools, communities, states, businesses, the nation, and the world. But there must be a stimulus. That stimulus is now beginning to take shape. It is concern, even outrage, over the human suffering caused by this environment, especially in children. Suffering is least defensible when children are affected, and children are the most startling victims of the toxic environment.

Mobilizing both individuals and the nation requires as its centerpiece bold and decisive changes in public policy. Progress is possible, but only if the nation, from its individual citizens to the largest corporations, from the local school board to the president, takes several steps:

1. Acknowledge the massive nature of problems caused by poor diet, inactivity, and obesity, appreciate the resulting human suffering, and recognize the costs to the nation.
2. Resist the seductive argument that people are doing this to themselves, thus justifying inaction.
3. Appreciate that there are victims—our children deserve more from us.
4. Understand that prevention must take priority and that children are the logical initial focus.
5. Stand up to the food companies to prevent undue influence on nutrition policy and obesity initiatives.
6. Hold the food industry accountable for targeting children.
7. Provide parents and children skills to deal with the toxic environment.
8. Develop creative ways for institutions such as schools to help solve the national problem.
9. Do everything possible to allow and encourage the population to be more physically active.
10. Change the basic economics of food so that it is easier and less expensive to eat a healthy diet.

The environment should produce healthy and happy citizens. It must help parents raise healthy children, provide schools with alert and vigorous pupils, offer businesses healthy employees, and create conditions in which the nation's people can thrive. Profound change is necessary.

Choosing to Read Critically Questions

1. What is the central argument or point of this excerpt?
2. In your own words, explain what Brownell and Horgen mean when they use the term "toxic environment."

3. Does this Introduction spark your interest and make you want to read the rest of the book *Food Fight?* Why or why not?

4. Brownell and Horgen often include lists in order to organize their ideas and get their points across. How effective do you find this format? Explain why you do or do not like it.

Choosing to Respond Questions

1. Although the article does not explicitly address this issue, obesity is, in part, a problem because of the high health insurance costs that are passed on to taxpayers. Write a paragraph or two in which you examine the relationship between the obesity epidemic and the health care industry.

2. In the section titled "Toxic Environment," Brownell and Horgen state that "Names we give our food say it all: Double Whopper with Cheese, Super Supreme Pizza, Bacon Double Cheeseburger, Colossal Burger, Double Decker Taco Supreme, and Extreme Gulp." Rather than allowing them to "say it all," select a few fast-food names and analyze them. What kinds of adjectives do these companies use? What are those adjectives usually associated with, and what are they meant to suggest to the consumer?

Wide Awake to Connections Questions

1. Near the end of the article, Brownell and Horgen present a list of steps that the nation and individuals should take to resist what the authors term a "toxic environment." Choose one item on this list to further research and discuss. For example, you might write an essay on the topic of #6, holding "the food industry responsible for targeting children."

2. Using the articles written by Brownell, Horgen, and/or Winter (below), construct an argument about the urgency of the "obesity epidemic." In this essay, you should use summaries, paraphrases, and quotations from the articles you select.

Radley Balko, "Health Care Should Be a Personal Responsibility"

>> Prereading Check-In

1. Do you think that you make good food and exercise choices? Why or why not?

2. Do you think the government should play a role in fighting increasing rates of obesity? Explain your reasons why or why not and, if appropriate, how you think the government should intervene.

Formerly a policy analyst with the Cato Institute and a senior editor at Reason *and* Reason.com, **Radley Balko** *(b. 1975) has written articles for numerous publications, including* FoxNews. com, *the* Wall Street Journal, *and the* Washington Post. *He is now an investigative reporter with the* Huffington Post *and maintains a blog,* The Agitator. *In the following selection, originally published on* Techcentralstation.com *in 2004, Balko contends that obesity is a private, not a public, matter.*

"Health Care Should Be a Personal Responsibility"

This June [2004], *Time* magazine and ABC News will host a three-day summit on obesity. ABC News anchor Peter Jennings, who last December anchored the prime time special "How to Get Fat Without Really Trying" will host. Judging by the scheduled program, the summit promises to be a pep rally for media, nutrition activists, and policy makers—all agitating for a panoply of government antiobesity initiatives, including prohibiting junk food in school vending machines, federal funding for new bike trails and sidewalks, more demanding labels on foodstuffs, restrictive food marketing to children, and prodding the food industry into more "responsible" behavior. In other words, bringing government between you and your waistline.

Politicians have already climbed aboard. President Bush earmarked $200 million in his budget for antiobesity measures. State legislatures and school boards across the country have begun banning snacks and soda from school campuses and vending machines. Sen. Joe Lieberman and Oakland Mayor Jerry Brown, among others, have called for a "fat tax" on high-calorie foods. Congress is now considering menu-labeling legislation, which would force restaurants to send every menu item to the laboratory for nutritional testing.

This is the wrong way to fight obesity. Instead of manipulating or intervening in the array of food options available to American consumers, our government ought to be working to foster a sense of responsibility in and ownership of our own health and well-being. But we're doing just the opposite.

For decades now, America's health care system has been migrating toward socialism. Your well-being, shape, and condition have increasingly been deemed matters of "public health," instead of matters of personal responsibility. Our lawmakers just enacted a huge entitlement that requires some people to pay for other people's medicine. Sen. Hillary Clinton just penned a lengthy article in *the New York Times Magazine* calling for yet more federal control of health care. All of the Democrat candidates for president boasted plans to push health care further into the public sector. More and more, states are preventing private health insurers from charging overweight and obese clients higher premiums, which effectively removes any financial incentive for maintaining a healthy lifestyle.

We're becoming less responsible for our own health, and more responsible for everyone else's. Your heart attack drives up the cost of my premiums and office visits. And if the government is paying for my anticholesterol medication, what incentive is there for me to put down the cheeseburger?

This collective ownership of private health then paves the way for even more federal restrictions on consumer choice and civil liberties. A society where everyone is responsible for everyone else's well-being is a society more apt to accept government restrictions, for example—on what McDonald's can put on its menu, what Safeway or Kroger can put on grocery shelves, or holding food companies responsible for the bad habits of unhealthy consumers.

A growing army of nutritionist activists and food industry foes are egging the process on. Margo Wootan of the Center for Science in the Public Interest has said, "we've got to move beyond 'personal responsibility.'" The largest organization of trial lawyers now encourages its members to weed jury pools of candidates who show "personal responsibility bias." The title of Jennings' special from last December—"How to Get Fat Without Really Trying"—reveals his intent, which is to relieve viewers of responsibility for their own condition. Indeed, Jennings ended the program with an impassioned plea for government intervention to fight obesity.

The best way to alleviate the obesity "public health" crisis is to remove obesity from the realm of public health. It doesn't belong there. It's difficult to think of anything more private and of less public concern than what we choose to put into our bodies. It only becomes a public matter when we force the public to pay for the consequences of those choices. If policymakers want to fight obesity, they'll halt the creeping socialization of medicine, and move to return individual Americans' ownership of their own health and well-being back to individual Americans.

That means freeing insurance companies to reward healthy life-styles, and penalize poor ones. It means halting plans to further social-ize medicine and health care. Congress should also increase access to medical and health savings accounts, which give consumers the option of rolling money reserved for health care into a retirement account. These accounts introduce accountability into the health care system, and encourage caution with one's health care dollar. When money we spend on health care doesn't belong to our employer or the government, but is money we could devote to our own retirement, we're less likely to run to the doctor at the first sign of a cold.

We'll all make better choices about diet, exercise, and personal health when someone else isn't paying for the consequences of those choices.

Choosing to Read Critically Questions

1. What is Balko's thesis? Where is it located?

2. In paragraph 1, Balko lists some possible government antiobesity initia-tives and then writes, "In other words, bringing government between you and your waistline." What is Balko saying about these initiatives? Do you agree with his characterization?

3. In your own words, summarize the argument that you think Balko is re-sponding to in this article.

4. Balko references the title of Peter Jennings' program "How to Get Fat Without Really Trying" twice. Why? What does Balko see this title suggesting?

Choosing to Respond Questions

1. Have you eaten at a restaurant that posted calories for food items on the menu? How did you feel about this practice?

2. Working in a group, try to come to a consensus: Do you agree, disagree, or partly agree with what Balko is arguing here? Write up your group's response. If you cannot agree, outline the points your group finds particu-larly contentious.

Wide Awake to Connections Questions

1. Balko is critical of what he calls the "socialization of medicine." As he suggests, obesity may be a matter of public concern if the "crisis" forces up health insurance costs for all taxpayers. This article appeared in 2004; research recent developments in the health care debate and changes in American health care policy. Then, write an essay in which you evaluate Balko's recommendations for his approach to health care policies that appear in the second-to-last paragraph. Then, write an essay in which you evaluate Balko's recommendations for changes in health care policies. (These appear in the second-to-last paragraph.)

2. Write an essay in which you contrast the ideas presented in this article with those presented in the article by Kelly Brownell that is included in this chapter. Is obesity a matter of personal responsibility? Your answer to that question may be your thesis statement.

Michelle Obama, "Remarks by the First Lady to the NAACP National Convention in Kansas City, Missouri"

>> **Prereading Check-In**

1. How do you think your race, class, gender, or background affects your eating habits and choices? Even if you feel that these factors have no effect, describe the eating habits you developed as a child.

2. What have you heard or read about childhood obesity? Why do you think that some people are alarmed by rising rates of childhood obesity?

First Lady of the United States, **Michelle Obama** *(b. 1964) is a lawyer and has held positions in government and nonprofit organizations. As First Lady, Obama initiated the "Let's Move" campaign to combat childhood obesity. In the following speech, delivered on July 12, 2010 to the National Association for the Advancement of Colored People (NAACP) Convention in Kansas City, Missouri, Obama urges members to take seriously the threat of obesity, particularly in the African American community.*

"Remarks by the First Lady to the NAACP National Convention in Kansas City, Missouri"

One hundred and one years ago, the NAACP was established in pursuit of a simple goal and that was to spur this nation to live up to the founding ideals, to secure those blessings of liberty, to fulfill that promise of equality.

And since then, the work of this organization has been guided by a simple belief: that while we might not fully live out that promise or those blessings for ourselves, if we worked hard enough, and fought long enough, and believed strongly enough, that we could secure them for our children and for our grandchildren, and give them opportunities that we never dreamed of for ourselves.

So, for more than a century, the men and women of the NAACP have marched and protested. You have lobbied presidents and fought unjust laws. You've stood up and sat in and risked life and limb so that African Americans could take their rightful places, not just at lunch counters and on buses, but at universities and on battlefields—and in hospitals and boardrooms; in Congress, the Supreme Court; and, yes, even the White House. Think about it—even the White House . . .

. . . [But] when so many of our children still attend crumbling schools, and a black child is still far more likely to go to prison than a white child, I think the founders of this organization would agree that our work is not yet done.

When African American communities are still hit harder than just about anywhere by this economic downturn, and so many families are just barely scraping by, I think the founders would tell us that now is not the time to rest on our laurels.

When stubborn inequalities still persist—in education and health, in income and wealth—I think those founders would urge us to increase our intensity and to increase our discipline and our focus and keep fighting for a better future for our children and our grandchildren.

And that's why I really wanted to come here today—because I wanted to talk with you about an issue that I believe cries out for our attention— one that is of particular concern to me, not just as First Lady, but as a mother who believes that we owe it to our kids to prepare them for the challenges that we know lie ahead. And that issue is the epidemic of childhood obesity in America today.

Now, right now in America, one in three children is overweight or obese, putting them at greater risk of obesity-related conditions like diabetes and cancer, heart disease, asthma.

And we're already spending billions of dollars in this country a year to treat these conditions, and that number is only going to go up when these unhealthy children reach adulthood.

But it's important to be clear that this issue isn't about how our kids look. It's not about that. It's about how our kids feel. It's about their health and the health of our nation and the health of our economy.

And there's no doubt that this is a serious problem. It's one that is affecting every community across this country. But just like with so many other challenges that we face as a nation, the African American community is being hit even harder by this issue.

We are living today in a time where we're decades beyond slavery, we are decades beyond Jim Crow; when one of the greatest risks to our children's future is their own health.

African American children are significantly more likely to be obese than are white children. Nearly half of African American children will develop diabetes at some point in their lives. People, that's half of our children.

And if we don't do something to reverse this trend right now, our kids won't be in any shape to continue the work begun by the founders of this great organization. They won't be in any condition to confront all those challenges that we know still remain.

So we need to take this issue seriously, as seriously as improving under-achieving schools, as seriously as eliminating youth violence or stopping the spread of HIV/AIDS or any of the other issues that we know are devastating our communities.

But in order to address this challenge, we also need to be honest with ourselves about how we got here, because we know that it wasn't always like this for our kids and our communities.

The way we live today is very different from even when I was growing up. And I like to tell my kids I'm not that old. They don't agree.

Many of you probably grew up like I did—in a community that wasn't rich, not even middle class, but where people knew their neighbors, and they looked out for each other's kids.

In these kind of strong African American communities, we went to neighborhood schools around the corner. So many of us had to walk to and from school every day, rain or shine. I know you've told that story. And in Chicago, where I was raised, we did it in the dead of winter. No shoes on our feet—it was hard, but we walked!

And in school, we had recess twice a day and gym class twice a week, like it or not. And then when we got home in the afternoon, after school or in the summer, there was no way we'd be allowed to lie around the house watching TV. First of all, there wasn't that many channels.

Our parents made us get up and play outside. Had to get up, get out, didn't have to—just couldn't be inside. And we would spend hours riding bikes, playing softball, freeze tag, jumping double-dutch. Kids nowadays don't even know how to jump double-dutch!

. . . And eating was a totally different experience back then. In my house, we rarely ate out—rarely. Even when both parents worked outside of the home, most families in my neighborhood sat down at the table together as a family for a meal. And in my house, Marian Robinson's house, we ate what we were served. My mother never cared whether me or my brother liked what was on our plates. We either ate what was there or we didn't eat. It was as simple as that.

We never ate anything fancy, but the portion sizes were reasonable and there were rarely seconds—maybe for your father, but not for you. And there was always a vegetable on the plate.

And many of our grandparents tended their own gardens or they relied on, as my father told me, "The Vegetable Man" who brought fresh produce. That was how people got by back then—they had fresh fruits and vegetables in their own backyards, and in jars in their cellar during the winter. And that wasn't just being thrifty—that was healthy too, little did we know.

And unless it was Sunday, or somebody's birthday, there was no expectation of dessert after our meals. And we didn't dream of asking for soda or pop. That was for special occasions . . .

Back then, without any expert advice and without spending too much money, we managed to lead pretty healthy lives. But things are a little different today, and many kids these days aren't so fortunate.

So many kids can't attend neighborhood schools or don't, so instead of walking to school, they ride in a car or they're in a bus. And in too many schools, recess and gym class have been slashed because of budget cuts.

Fears about safety mean that those afternoons outside have been replaced by afternoons inside with TV, video games, the Internet.

In fact, studies have found that African American children spend an average of nearly six hours a day watching TV—and that every extra hour of TV they watch is associated with the consumption of an additional 167 calories.

. . . Most folks don't grow their own food the way many of our parents and grandparents did. A lot of folks also just don't have the time to cook at home on a regular basis. So instead, they wind up grabbing fast food or something from the corner store or the mini-mart—places that have few, if any, healthy options.

And we've seen how kids in our communities regularly stop by these stores on their way to school—buying themselves sodas and pop and chips for breakfast. And we've seen how they come right back to those same stores after school to buy their afternoon snack of candy and sugary drinks.

According to one study, on average, a trip to the corner store, a child will walk out of that store with more than 350 calories worth of food and beverage—this is on average. So if they're going two and three times a day, that can really add up.

And taken together, all of these things have made for a perfect storm of bad habits and unhealthy choices—a lifestyle that's dooming too many of our children to a lifetime of poor health and undermining our best efforts to build them a better future.

See, we can build our kids the best schools on earth, but if they don't have the basic nutrition they need to concentrate, they're still going to have a challenge learning. And we can create the best jobs in the world—we must—but that won't mean that folks will have the energy and the stamina to actually do those jobs.

. . . And surely the men and women of the NAACP haven't spent a century organizing and advocating and working day and night only to raise the first generation in history that might be on track to live shorter lives than their parents.

And that's why I've made improving the quality of our children's health one of my top priorities . . . [My] "Let's Move," the campaign, has four components.

The first, we're working to give parents the information they need to make healthy decisions for their families.

For example, we're working with the FDA and the food industry to provide better labeling, something simple, so folks don't have to spend hours squinting at labels, trying to figure out whether the food they're buying is healthy or not . . .

But we also know that giving better information to parents is not enough, because with 31 million American children participating in federal school meal programs, many of our kids are consuming as many as half their daily calories at school.

That's why the second part of "Let's Move" is to get healthier food into our schools.

And we're working to reauthorize our child nutrition legislation that will make significant new investments to revamp our school meals and improve the food that we offer in those school vending machines, so that we're serving our kids less sugar, salt and fat, and more vegetables, fruits and whole grains . . .

But we also know that healthy eating is only half the battle. Experts recommend at least 60 minutes a day of activity. That's at least the bare minimum, and many of our kids aren't even close.

So the third part of "Let's Move" is to help our kids get moving, to find new ways for them to get and stay active and fit. And we're working to get more kids participating in daily physical education classes and to get more schools offering recess for their students . . .

But we know that even if we offer the most nutritious school meals, and we give kids every opportunity to be fit, and we give parents the information they need to prepare healthy food for their families, all that won't mean much if our families still live in communities where that healthy food simply isn't available in the first place.

And that brings me to the fourth and final component of the campaign, and that is to ensure that all families have access to fresh, affordable food in their communities where they live.

And one of the most shocking statistics for me in all of this is that right now, 23.5 million Americans, including 6.5 million children, live in what we call "food deserts"—areas without a single supermarket.

This is particularly serious in African American communities where folks wind up buying their groceries at places like gas stations and bodegas and corner stores where they often pay higher prices for lower-quality food.

But the good news is that we know that this trend is reversible, because when healthier options are available in our community, we know that folks will actually take advantage of those options.

One study found that African Americans ate 32 percent more fruits and vegetables for each additional supermarket in their community. So we know the kind of difference that we can make with some changes. We know that when we provide the right incentives—things like grants and tax credits, and help securing permits and zoning—businesses are willing to invest and lay down roots in our communities . . .

So, I know these goals are ambitious, and there are many, many more. And as First Lady, I am going to do everything that I can to ensure that we meet them.

But I also know that at the end of the day, government can only do so much.

I have spoken to so many experts about this issue, and not a single one of them said that the solution is to have government tell people what to do. It's not going to work. Instead, this is about families taking responsibility and making manageable changes that fit with their budgets and their needs and their tastes. That's the only way it's going to work.

It's about making those little changes that can really add up—simple things like taking the stairs instead of the elevator, walking instead of riding in a car or bus, even something as simple as turning on the radio and dancing with your children in the middle of your living room for hours. That will work up a sweat.

How about replacing all of that soda and those sugary drinks with water? Kids won't like it at first, trust me. But they'll grow to like it. Or deciding that they don't get dessert with every meal. As I tell my kids, dessert is not a right . . .

Or just being more thoughtful about how we prepare our food—baking instead of frying. I know. Don't shoot me. And cutting back on those portion sizes.

Look, no one wants to give up Sunday meal. No one wants to say goodbye to mac and cheese and fried chicken and mashed potatoes—oh, I'm getting hungry—forever. No one wants to do that. Not even the Obamas, trust me.

. . . But let's be clear, this isn't just about changing what our kids are eating and the lifestyles they're leading—it's also about changing our own habits as well. Because believe it or not, if you're obese, there's a 40 percent chance that your kids will be obese as well. And if both you and the child's other parent are obese, that number jumps to 80 percent.

And this is more than just genetics at work. The fact is, we all know we are our children's first and best teachers and role models. We teach them healthy habits not just by what we say but by how we live. Shoot, I can't tell Malia and Sasha to eat their vegetables if I'm sitting around eating French fries—trust me, they will not let that happen. And I can't tell them to go run around outside if I'm spending all my free time on the couch watching TV . . .

So if there's anybody here, after all this talking I've done, who feels a little overwhelmed by this challenge—because it can be overwhelming— if there is anyone here who might even already be losing hope thinking about how hard it will be to get going, or giving up, I just want you to take a look around at all the things that are already being accomplished, because I want folks to learn from each other and to be inspired by each other, because that's what we've always done.

That is exactly what happened here in this city half a century ago. See, because back in 1958, folks right here in Kansas City saw what folks down in Montgomery had achieved with their bus boycott. So they were inspired by all those men and women who walked miles—walked miles home each day on aching feet because they knew there was a principle at stake.

So folks here organized their own boycott of department stores that refused to serve African Americans. Handbills publicizing their meetings stated, and this is a quote: "They stopped riding in Montgomery, so let's stop buying in Kansas City."

A local music teacher even composed a song that became the anthem for their efforts. It was entitled "Let's take the walk that counts."

And then, as you know, a few years later, in April of 1964, folks turned out in droves to pass a public accommodations law mandating that all residents, regardless of their skin color, be served in restaurants, hotels and other public places. Even folks who were too sick to walk showed up to vote.

One organizer recalled that they used wheelchairs to get people to the polls and even brought one man in on a stretcher. So think about that—being carried to the ballot box on a stretcher. Those folks didn't do all that just for themselves. They did it because they wanted something better for their children and for their grandchildren. That's why they did it.

And in the end, that's what has driven this organization since its founding.

It is why Daisy Bates endured hate mail and death threats to guide those nine young men and women who would walk through those schoolhouse doors in Little Rock.

It is why Thurgood Marshall fought so hard to ensure that children like Linda Brown, and children like my daughters and your sons and daughters, would never again know the cruel inequality of separate but equal.

It is why so many men and women—legends and icons and ordinary folks—have faced down their doubts, their cynicism and their fears, and they've taken that walk that counts.

So we owe it to all those who've come before us to ensure that all those who come after us—our children and our grandchildren—that they have the strength and the energy and the enduring good health that they need to continue and complete that journey.

So I'm asking you, NAACP, will you move with me? Let's move! I'm going to need you, NAACP. This is not an endeavor that I can do by myself. We cannot change the health of our community alone. I'm going to need each and every single one of you to work together for this campaign for our children's future. If we do this together, we can change the way our children think about their health forever.

Choosing to Read Critically Questions

1. Why, according to Obama, is childhood obesity of particular concern to African Americans? In your own words, summarize some of the causes of obesity that Obama highlights here.

2. How does Obama contextualize her comments about combating obesity? That is, how and why does she comment on the NAACP's legacy at the beginning and ending of the speech?

3. Obama often uses humor to get her point across. Identify one or two places where you think Obama might be making a joke. What kind of joke is she making, and why do you think she includes it?

4. In paragraph 7, Obama makes reference to herself as a mother. Why does she do this? Find another part of the essay in which Obama speaks specifically about her own family. Do you think it was effective for Obama to draw on her own experiences? What did you like or not like about it?

Choosing to Respond Questions

1. Imagine you are an advisor to Mrs. Obama and she gave you a draft of this speech to comment on. In a brief essay, give her some feedback. Tell her what you particularly liked and what you thought could have been stronger; you may also provide suggestions for improvement.

2. As of this printing, you can watch Obama's speech on YouTube or on the NAACP website. (Google "Obama NAACP speech obesity" to find sites.) After reading the speech, watch it. How was the experience of watching different from reading? Which did you find more compelling? Explain your reaction.

Wide Awake to Connections Questions

1. Research the "Let's Move" campaign. Has it been successful? Why or why not?

2. In this speech, Obama emphasizes that she doesn't feel the government should "tell people what to do." If you read carefully, however, you'll see that Obama both recommends changes that individuals can make as well as describes government initiatives to support those choices. Drawing on one or two articles from this or another chapter, discuss the role of government in promoting "positive" or healthy behaviors.

Julie Gunlock, "Federalizing Fat"

>> **Prereading Check-In**

1. Brainstorm reasons for an increase in childhood obesity in the United States. What are some of the different factors you see affecting this rise?

2. What, if anything, do you think should be done to combat childhood obesity?

Columnist and commentator **Julie Gunlock** *is a senior fellow with the Independent Women's Forum, an organization dedicated, in part, to limited government. Gunlock's articles on food and obesity have appeared in publications including the* Washington Post *and the* Washington Examiner. *In the following essay, which originally appeared in the* National Review Online, *Gunlock critiques the ideas underpinning Michelle Obama's "Let's Move" initiative.*

"Federalizing Fat"

Michelle Obama has recently taken up childhood obesity as one of her major policy priorities. Interviewed about this "epidemic," the first lady discussed in some detail her own children's supposed weight problems as an illustration of her personal experience with her new signature issue.

Mrs. Obama revealed that her daughters' pediatrician had "warned that he was concerned that something was getting off balance." She then decided that she needed to take a greater role in her children's nutrition: "Even though I wasn't exactly sure at that time what I was supposed to do with this information about my children's BMI [body mass index], I knew that I had to do something."

After first getting over my complete mortification on behalf of the tween Obama girls, ages eight and eleven, at seeing their weight issues discussed in a national forum, I started to think about their home situation. They are obviously loved, indeed doted on, by their parents and grandmother. The family employs a personal chef, who is himself a leader in the healthy-food and locavore movements, and who often brags about preparing healthy meals for the first family. A look at the weekly lunch menu served at the girls' school reveals such items as grilled veggie wraps, local squash gratin, natural local rosemary chicken, and local vegetable risotto. And, of course, the Obamas have within the White House a gym, a bowling alley, a basketball court, and an outdoor pool.

Despite all this, the Obama girls' weight went "off balance." The first lady took action immediately, making small but significant changes to her daughters' diets and habits: less television, more colorful vegetables at dinner, more water and low-fat milk. In other words, Mrs. Obama promptly took a greater role in her children's food decisions. Now, according to her, the girls' weight is back "on track."

Good for Mrs. Obama for taking responsibility for her children's health. Her personal attention to the matter clearly made a difference.

Her decision to embarrass her children by talking about the rather delicate issue of their weight in a national interview was presumably intended to inspire other parents to take a more active role in their children's food choices. She had presumably learned from her own family's experience that responsible parenting is the best way to combat childhood obesity.

But apparently the first family's own success has had no impact on Mrs. Obama's policy prescriptions. Her solution for the rest of America is more government intervention.

Speaking about the issue during a meeting with cabinet members and congressional leaders, the first lady said: "It's going to require us working together—not just the administration, but Congress, governors, mayors, parents, teachers. Anyone who has access to children in their lives is going to have to work together. And one of the things that's also very clear is that this problem won't be solved by any single federal solution. This is going to require national action."

Mrs. Obama is certainly correct about one thing: The problem won't be solved by a federal solution—not even the one she went on to propose.

. . . [T]he first lady's new plan involves four basic initiatives. She wants to increase the number of "healthy" schools, and she also wants to increase the number of physical-activity programs made available by them. She hopes to improve the "accessibility and affordability" of food for all Americans. (Apparently, Mrs. Obama is unaware that Americans pay far less for their food than citizens of other nations do, spending only 7 percent of annual income on it, according to a 2009 Department of Labor study.) Lastly, she wants to "empower" consumers to make better food choices—whatever that means.

The first lady made no mention of how much this new initiative will cost, but, according to a 2009 Congressional Research Report, federally funded child-nutrition programs, along with the WIC (Women, Infants, and Children) program, cost American taxpayers $19 billion in 2007. How much more will Mrs. Obama propose we spend to overhaul these programs, especially at a time when her husband is calling for a government-wide spending freeze?

Most children are smart enough to make good decisions for themselves when given guidance and attention from their parents. Considering the vast number of resources available to the Obama girls even before their move to the White House, it's clear that nothing had a greater impact on these young ladies' health than their mother's involvement. When Michelle Obama was advised by the doctor to pay attention to her children's food decisions, her reaction was that of a concerned parent ready to take responsibility, not a parent looking for a government program to step in.

By all means, let the first lady urge American parents to follow her example and take the lead in making better food choices for their children. Just as parents need to ensure that their children get enough sleep, do their homework, and avoid dangerous activities, they need to teach their children proper eating habits. Parental involvement, not the federal government, is the only long-term cure for childhood obesity—as Mrs. Obama has shown by her example, if not by her policy proposals.

Choosing to Read Critically Questions

1. Compose a formal summary of Gunlock's article.
2. Prepare a paraphrase of the final two paragraphs of Gunlock's article.
3. Explain how and why Gunlock includes a summary of Michelle Obama's anecdote about taking her daughter to the doctor.
4. Gunlock's skepticism of Obama's agenda appears as early as the first paragraph. Work through the article and underline words and phrases that suggest that Gunlock disagrees with or disapproves of ideas that she is presenting.

Choosing to Respond Questions

1. Compose an essay in which you use your own background and experiences to respond to Gunlock's article. How has your family influenced the food choices that you make?
2. Gunlock writes that she experienced "complete mortification on behalf of the tween Obama girls" when Mrs. Obama discussed their weight issues publicly. What does Gunlock mean and why do you think she had this reaction? Do you agree with Gunlock's reaction? Why or why not?

Wide Awake to Connections Questions

1. In paragraph 10, Gunlock asserts that Americans spend less money on food than individuals in other countries do. After conducting some research, compose an essay in which you compare Americans' spending with that of other nations and provide some reasons for why Americans might be spending less. You may also begin to address how and why the amount of money a nation's citizens spends on food may be related to issues such as obesity.

2. In this article, Gunlock argues that parents should be the primary source for information about what their children should or shouldn't eat and she takes issue with Michelle Obama's "Let's Move" campaign, which includes an initiative to get healthier foods into schools. Where do you land on this issue? Drawing on this article, Obama's speech, the article "Students Behave Better With Healthy Lunches" (available online from *ABC News*), and/or one or two articles from Chapter 12's "American Education," compose an essay in which you explore what we are learning (or not learning) about food and nutrition in our homes and in our schools. You may ask whether or not schools are the appropriate places to be learning about food and nutrition.

Amy Winter, "The Biggest Losers & the Lies They Feed Us"

>> **Prereading Check-In**

1. What is your attitude toward overweight people? Should losing weight be their goal? Why or why not?
2. If you are or have ever been overweight (or if you have a family member or friend who is overweight), have you ever experienced or observed teasing or ridicule? Describe the situation and your feelings about it.

A self-identified "radical lesbian feminist blogger," **Amy Winter** *writes on issues that affect women. In this article, which originally appeared in a news journal dedicated to women's issues,* Off Our Backs, *Winter argues that the supposed health risks of obesity are overstated.*

"The Biggest Losers & the Lies They Feed Us"

I have a love-hate relationship with television; as a radical fat feminist, the mainstream values paraded across the screen make steam come out of my ears, but often a state of horrified fascination prevents me from tearing my eyes away. This happened most recently with NBC's "The Biggest Loser," the latest in the series of mainstream mind candy like "Extreme Makeover," "I Want a Famous Face," and "The Swan." Unlike the latter shows, where participants go under the knife, the transformations on "The Biggest Loser"—a show where fat people compete to lose the most weight, while being coached by "celebrity trainers" and tempted by "disallowed" foods—are left to willpower and self-denial.

Misinformation About Weight and Dieting

"The Biggest Loser" is completely dependent on the assumptions and misinformation about weight and dieting that saturate mainstream media, reinforced by the increasing hysteria about the "obesity epidemic." The argument goes something like this: Fat people are fat because they eat too much and lay around all day, and fat is ugly, plus unhealthy! If fat people just worked out and didn't eat so much, they could become thin and beautiful like the rest of us, and all their problems would be solved. A *People* magazine article speculating on the motivation behind the makeover-show trend states, "As obesity becomes an epidemic and fully two-thirds of all Americans are overweight, authentically slim, good-looking people are becoming rarer and rarer. In other words, we are in the throes of a beauty shortage. And we have applied our typically optimistic, boot-strap attitude to the situation: If we can't grow pretty people, we'll make them. What used to be solely a function of luck can now actually be an accomplishment, something earned through hard work and persistence."

Enter "The Biggest Loser." Despite the supposed ugliness of fat people, the participants on this show seem to have been chosen for their good looks, and their curves in the form-fitting tank tops and shorts they wear throughout the program are very appealing. As I watch the show, I realize how unusual it is to see really fat bodies on television. However, neither participant nor viewer can be allowed to appreciate their appearance as it is. The contestants are filmed deriding themselves and their bodies for being weak, ugly, and unhealthy. As part of the first episode, the two teams are made to compete at pulling cars around a track; a camera inside the car focuses on their t-shirts tightening across their bellies and thighs as they squeeze through the car window to take their required turn at the wheel. Rather than demonstrating the strength of fat people—able to pull a car!—the contest fosters fat hatred by displaying the bodies this culture disparages in vulnerable, uncomfortable positions.

. . . Underlying all the interactions between the participants is the assumption that body weight is completely subject to manipulation of food intake and exercise; I want to cry as I experience viscerally the expectation that these fat people can control their own body size. As the show ends, the contestants line up to be weighed; their hope that they will be judged worthy is practically visible as we learn that on this extreme, punishing, self-denying, ultimately unsustainable regimen, some participants have lost over 20 pounds in one week—all in the quest for "health," of course.

Some Simple Common Sense

But let's apply some simple common sense to the conventional attitude toward weight that "The Biggest Loser" promotes. Given the vast array of weight-loss diets that have made the rounds since the 1950s, you'd think fat would be a thing of the past, wouldn't you? Surprise, surprise—diets don't work. And in a stroke of capitalist genius, the diet industry has not only made billions of dollars selling us products that don't work, they've convinced us that it's our fault! If we only had more willpower, we'd be thin—we have no one to blame but ourselves. But just in case we were thinking of resisting wasting money on diets, with stultifying regularity the media obediently produce some new scare tactic about the "health risks of obesity" to maintain the public frenzy over weight and dieting. So, once more, with feeling, a summary of the current state of medical knowledge about fat:

There's no clear explanation for why fat people are fat. The *New England Journal of Medicine* calls fat people "ordinary people who happen to be heavier than average, probably from some mixture of nature, nurture, and choice."

There's no known method for fat people to permanently lose weight. The few studies that follow dieters long-term demonstrate failure rates between 85% and 95% for all diets studied; often participants gain back more weight than was lost.

There's no evidence that fat people are unhealthy. There are no diseases that only fat people get, and there are many diseases that fat people get at lower rates than thin people. Furthermore, people with diabetes, hypertension, and other so-called "obesity-related" diseases often have better blood sugar and blood pressure readings with lifestyle changes that cause little to no weight loss, suggesting that fat itself is not the cause of these problems. In fact, the world's largest study to date found the highest life expectancy in the group of people 60 to 75 pounds overweight by current U.S. government standards . . .

Health at Every Size

This information is not new. Feminists have been critiquing the diet industry, the medical system, and mainstream ideas about body size and weight loss for decades. In an article written in the 1970s, Vivian Mayer exposed the biases and conflicts of interest inherent in research on body size, and suggested the need for a paradigm shift.

Fortunately, some researchers and health practitioners have begun to heed the call. Dietitian Karin Kratina developed four principles that have been adopted as the Health At Every Size (HAES) movement. HAES advocates leaving behind the focus on weight; instead, we're encouraged to abandon attempts at weight loss and accept that healthy bodies come in different sizes. HAES encourages us to eat simple, unprocessed foods as much as we can rather than processed diet foods, to eat when we're hungry and stop when we're full, and to engage in physical movement that we enjoy for its own sake, rather than forcing ourselves into strenuous, regimented workouts with weight loss as a goal. And, unlike diet plans, pills, shakes, and weight loss surgery, these suggestions do not stigmatize or penalize fat people; they constitute a lifestyle that encourages all of us to be as healthy as we can be. The HAES movement has great potential to break the assumed connection between thinness and good health; it's simple, gentle and encourages all people to make healthy food and exercise choices while loving ourselves and our bodies, rather than punishing ourselves with diets and workouts under the mistaken assumption that we can control our body size.

Choosing to Read Critically Questions

1. How and why does Winter include a discussion of the television show, "The Biggest Loser"?

2. In your own words, summarize the recommendations of the HAES movement.

3. Winter has a very distinct voice, and she employs more than one tone here; at some points, she even uses sarcasm to make her point. Identify one area in which you find Winter's tone particularly effective or ineffective; explain what you think she is doing and why you think she is doing it.

4. Explain and evaluate Winter's condemnation of the diet industry (paragraph 5).

Choosing to Respond Questions

1. Do you agree with Winter that shows such as "The Biggest Loser" foster fear and hatred of fat people?

2. Do you think that people are more critical of their own and others' bodies in American culture than in other cultures or other times in history? Back up your answer with specific examples and details.

Wide Awake to Connections Questions

1. Watch and analyze an episode of a show like "The Biggest Loser" that features overweight and obese individuals. How does fat feature on the show, and what attitudes toward fat are presented? Overall, do you think the program presents positive or negative messages?

2. In this article, Winter suggests that misinformation about weight leads to stereotypes about fat people (for example, that fat people are lazy). Using this selection, as well as one or two articles from Chapter 9, "Disability Studies," construct an essay discussing the persistence of discrimination based on physical appearance.

QUESTIONS AND SUGGESTIONS FOR FURTHER RESEARCH AND WRITING

1. This chapter introduces a number of different topics within the larger topic of "Food Politics," including the obesity epidemic, the effects of industrial food and farming, the role of government, and prejudice against fat people. Select at least two articles from this chapter in order to examine how at least two of these topics are related to each other. Your essay, then, will explore the connections between, for example, topics such as obesity and industrial food or government regulation and cheap food.

2. The selection from Plato's "Allegory of the Cave" in Chapter 12, "American Education," describes how the journey from ignorance to enlightenment might be a painful one. Drawing on one or two articles from this section (Berry's piece might work well), construct an essay about what, if anything, you have learned about contemporary food production and consumption. Do you think that more people should

think about where their food comes from, even if that knowledge upsets them? Why or why not?

3. Some of the authors of selections in this chapter have a clear political perspective. For example, Radley Balko is a "libertarian" and Amy Winter is a "feminist." Explain how what we eat is a political issue. Should it be? You might choose to put one or two authors in dialogue with each other, to research different authors' politics and positions, and/or to read other articles an author has written as you develop your position on how and why what we eat has become a part of our national conversation.

4. There are currently a number of excellent documentaries about the food industry. Select one or two items from the list below to view or read. Compose an essay in which you identify and evaluate the texts' arguments.

> *Soul Food Junkies,* 2011 Dir. Byron Hurt
>
> *Food, Inc.,* 2008 Dir. Robert Kenner
>
> *Fast Food Nation,* 2006 Dir. Richard Linklater
>
> *Our Daily Bread,* 2005 Dir. Nikolaus Geyrhalter
>
> *Supersize Me: A Film of Epic Portions,* 2004 Dir. Morgan Spurlock
>
> *The Future of Food,* 2004 Dir. Deborah Koons
>
> *Vegucated,* 2010 Dir. Marisa Miller Wolfson

5. In an article titled "Rules to Eat By," which originally appeared in *the New York Times Magazine,* Michael Pollan urges readers to listen to their common sense and cultures when making decisions about what to eat. After locating and reading Pollan's article, as well as one or two other articles from this chapter, discuss the role of culture in one's approaches to food and to health. In this essay, you are invited to include reflections on your own background and experiences. What are some of your culture's ideas about food? What role does food play in your culture, community, or family's traditions? How has your culture influenced your food choices?

11 Chapter Eleven

Ecological Consciousness:
A Challenge for the 21st Century

>> **Prereading Check-In**

1. Write about a time when you felt you were present in "nature." This memory might be fond, or vivid, or unpleasant. Tell the story, including as many details as possible.

2. Write down what you know about current environmental concerns. Are there any issues that you feel are particularly important to you or that affect you personally?

Currently, an island of trash bigger than the state of Texas, known as the "Great Pacific Garbage Patch" is floating in the Pacific Ocean, increasing in size every day and endangering marine life. Meanwhile, in the Arctic, polar bears are dying because their habitats—the polar ice caps—are disappearing at alarming rates. Among humans, cancer rates, although they've plateaued in recent years, have increased 50 percent in the 50 years between 1950 and 2000. Rising rates of asthma have been linked to air pollution. Some experts suggest that we should anticipate and prepare for increasingly severe storms and weather events as a result of climate change.

Human activities have always had an impact on the world. However, it seems as though human behaviors are damaging the Earth and are endangering human life and health as well. As we all know, activists have been calling for changes in our habits, and individuals and institutions across the political and social spectrum are taking action. Many consumers are opting for energy-efficient lightbulbs and cars and are buying more foods that claim to be "organic" and "sustainably" produced. Many colleges and universities, including the State University of New York system, have announced their decisions to "go green." Further, cities and suburbs are providing incentives to encourage businesses and citizens to embrace green technology in order to decrease their "carbon footprints."

Many individuals make these efforts because they want to preserve the Earth for future generations, while others are concerned about preventing or remediating damage in their immediate and local communities; still others are indifferent to environmental concerns. The readings in this chapter will cover questions about the importance of place, the role of "nature" in our lives and our children's lives, and current controversies within discussions of the environmental crisis.

Henry David Thoreau, from *Walden; Or, Life in the Woods,* "Where I Lived and What I Lived For"

>> **Prereading Check-In**
1. Brainstorm on the concept of "simplicity."
2. Describe your favorite outdoor spot. This might be a vacation area, a park, a backyard, or any other outdoor place that you enjoy.

Henry David Thoreau *(1817–1862) was an American author associated with the transcendentalist movement. His work,* Walden *(1854), which is excerpted below, described his experiences living in a cabin in the woods. In "Where I Lived and What I Lived For," Thoreau describes his situation and the benefits of living simply in the natural world.*

"Where I Lived and What I Lived For"

When first I took up my abode in the woods, that is, began to spend my nights as well as days there, which, by accident, was on Independence Day, or the Fourth of July, 1845, my house was not finished for winter, but was merely a defense against the rain, without plastering or chimney, the walls being of rough, weather-stained boards, with wide chinks, which made it cool at night. The upright white hewn studs and freshly planed door and window casings gave it a clean and airy look, especially in the morning, when its timbers were saturated with dew, so that I fancied that by noon some sweet gum would exude from them. To my imagination it retained throughout the day more or less of this auroral character, reminding me of a certain house on a mountain which I had visited a year

before. This was an airy and unplastered cabin, fit to entertain a traveling god, and where a goddess might trail her garments. The winds which
passed over my dwelling were such as sweep over the ridges of mountains, bearing the broken strains, or celestial parts only, of terrestrial
music. The morning wind forever blows, the poem of creation is uninter-
rupted; but few are the ears that hear it. Olympus is but the outside of the
earth everywhere.

The only house I had been the owner of before, if I except a boat, was
a tent, which I used occasionally when making excursions in the summer,
and this is still rolled up in my garret; but the boat, after passing from hand
to hand, has gone down the stream of time. With this more substantial
shelter about me, I had made some progress toward settling in the world.
This frame, so slightly clad, was a sort of crystallization around me and
reacted on the builder. It was suggestive somewhat as a picture in outlines.
I did not need to go outdoors to take the air, for the atmosphere within had
lost none of its freshness. It was not so much within doors as behind a door
where I sat, even in the rainiest weather. The Harivansa says, "An abode
without birds is like a meat without seasoning." Such was not my abode,
for I found myself suddenly neighbor to the birds; not by having imprisoned one, but having caged myself near them. I was not only nearer to
some of those which commonly frequent the garden and the orchard, but
to those smaller and more thrilling songsters of the forest which never, or
rarely, serenade a villager—the wood thrush, the veery, the scarlet tanager,
the field sparrow, the whip-poor-will, and many others.

I was seated by the shore of a small pond, about a mile and a half
south of the village of Concord and somewhat higher than it, in the midst
of an extensive wood between that town and Lincoln, and about two
miles south of that our only field known to fame, Concord Battle Ground;
but I was so low in the woods that the opposite shore, half a mile off, like
the rest, covered with wood, was my most distant horizon. For the first
week, whenever I looked out on the pond it impressed me like a tarn high
up on the side of a mountain, its bottom far above the surface of other
lakes, and, as the sun arose, I saw it throwing off its nightly clothing of
mist, and here and there, by degrees, its soft ripples or its smooth reflecting surface was revealed, while the mists, like ghosts, were stealthily
withdrawing in every direction into the woods, as at the breaking up of

some nocturnal conventicle. The very dew seemed to hang upon the trees later into the day than usual, as on the sides of mountains.

This small lake was of most value as a neighbor in the intervals of a gentle rainstorm in August, when, both air and water being perfectly still, but the sky overcast, mid-afternoon had all the serenity of evening, and the wood thrush sang around and was heard from shore to shore. A lake like this is never smoother than at such a time; and the clear portion of the air above it being, shallow and darkened by clouds, the water, full of light and reflections, becomes a lower heaven itself so much the more important. From a hilltop near by, where the wood had been recently cut off, there was a pleasing vista southward across the pond, through a wide indentation in the hills which form the shore there, where their opposite sides sloping toward each other suggested a stream flowing out in that direction through a wooded valley, but stream there was none. That way I looked between and over the near green hills to some distant and higher ones in the horizon, tinged with blue. Indeed, by standing on tiptoe I could catch a glimpse of some of the peaks of the still bluer and more distant mountain ranges in the northwest, those true-blue coins from heaven's own mint and also of some portion of the village. But in other directions, even from this point, I could not see over or beyond the woods which surrounded me. It is well to have some water in your neighborhood, to give buoyancy to and float the earth. One value even of the smallest well is, that when you look into it you see that earth is not continent but insular. This is as important as that it keeps butter cool. When I looked across the pond from this peak toward the Sudbury meadows, which in time of flood I distinguished elevated perhaps by a mirage in their seething valley, like a coin in a basin, all the earth beyond the pond appeared like a thin crust insulated and floated even by this small sheet of interverting water, and I was reminded that this on which I dwelt was but *dry land*.

Though the view from my door was still more contracted, I did not feel crowded or confined in the least. There was pasture enough for my imagination. The low shrub oak plateau to which the opposite shore arose stretched away toward the prairies of the West and the steppes of Tartary, affording ample room for all the roving families of men. "There are none happy in the world but beings who enjoy freely a vast horizon"—said Damodara, when his herds required new and larger pastures . . . .

Every morning was a cheerful invitation to make my life of equal simplicity, and I may say innocence, with Nature herself. I have been as sincere a worshipper of Aurora as the Greeks. I got up early and bathed in the pond; that was a religious exercise and one of the best things which I did. They say that characters were engraven on the bathing tub of King Tchingthang to this effect: "Renew thyself completely each day; do it again, and again, and forever again." I can understand that. Morning brings back the heroic ages. I was as much affected by the faint hum of a mosquito making its invisible and unimaginable tour through my apartment at earliest dawn, when I was sitting with door and windows open, as I could be by any trumpet that ever sang of fame. It was Homer's requiem; itself an Iliad and Odyssey in the air, singing its own wrath and wanderings. There was something cosmical about it; a standing advertisement, till forbidden, of the everlasting vigor and fertility of the world. The morning, which is the most memorable season of the day, is the awakening hour. Then there is least somnolence in us; and for an hour, at least, some part of us awakes which slumbers all the rest of the day and night. Little is to be expected of that day, if it can be called a day, to which we are not awakened by our Genius, but by the mechanical nudgings of some servitor, are not awakened by our own newly acquired force and aspirations from within, accompanied by the undulations of celestial music, instead of factory bells, and a fragrance filling the air—to a higher life than we fell asleep from; and thus the darkness bear its fruit, and prove itself to be good, no less than the light. That man who does not believe that each day contains an earlier, more sacred, and auroral hour than he has yet profaned, has despaired of life and is pursuing a descending and darkening way. After a partial cessation of his sensuous life, the soul of man, or its organs rather, are reinvigorated each day, and his Genius tries again what noble life it can make. All memorable events, I should say, transpire in morning time and in a morning atmosphere. The Vedas say, "All intelligences awake with the morning." Poetry and art, and the fairest and most memorable of the actions of men, date from such an hour. All poets and heroes, like Memnon, are the children of Aurora and emit their music at sunrise. To him whose elastic and vigorous thought keeps pace with the sun, the day is a perpetual morning. It matters not what the clocks say or the attitudes and labors of men. Morning is when

I am awake and there is a dawn in me. Moral reform is the effort to throw off sleep. Why is it that men give so poor an account of their day if they have not been slumbering? They are not such poor calculators. If they had not been overcome with drowsiness, they would have performed something. The millions are awake enough for physical labor; but only one in a million is awake enough for effective intellectual exertion, only one in a hundred millions to a poetic or divine life. To be awake is to be alive. I have never yet met a man who was quite awake. How could I have looked him in the face?

We must learn to reawaken and keep ourselves awake, not by mechanical aids, but by an infinite expectation of the dawn, which does not forsake us in our soundest sleep. I know of no more encouraging fact than the unquestionable ability of man to elevate his life by a conscious endeavor. It is something to be able to paint a particular picture, or to carve a statue, and so to make a few objects beautiful; but it is far more glorious to carve and paint the very atmosphere and medium through which we look, which morally we can do. To affect the quality of the day, that is the highest of arts. Every man is tasked to make his life, even in its details, worthy of the contemplation of his most elevated and critical hour. If we refused, or rather used up, such paltry information as we get, the oracles would distinctly inform us how this might be done.

I went to the woods because I wished to live deliberately, to front only the essential facts of life, and see if I could not learn what it had to teach, and not, when I came to die, discover that I had not lived. I did not wish to live what was not life, living is so dear; nor did I wish to practice resignation, unless it was quite necessary. I wanted to live deep and suck out all the marrow of life, to live so sturdily and Spartan-like as to put to rout all that was not life, to cut a broad swath and shave close, to drive life into a corner, and reduce it to its lowest terms, and, if it proved to be mean, why then to get the whole and genuine meanness of it, and publish its meanness to the world; or if it were sublime, to know it by experience and be able to give a true account of it in my next excursion. For most men, it appears to me, are in a strange uncertainty about it, whether it is of the devil or of God, and have *somewhat hastily* concluded that it is the chief end of man here to "glorify God and enjoy him forever."

Still we live meanly, like ants; though the fable tells us that we were long ago changed into men; like pygmies we fight with cranes; it is error upon error, and clout upon clout, and our best virtue has for its occasion a superfluous and evitable wretchedness. Our life is frittered away by detail. An honest man has hardly need to count more than his ten fingers, or in extreme cases he may add his ten toes, and lump the rest. Simplicity, simplicity, simplicity! I say, let your affairs be as two or three, and not a hundred or a thousand; instead of a million count half a dozen, and keep your accounts on your thumbnail. In the midst of this chopping sea of civilized life, such are the clouds and storms and quicksand and thousand-and-one items to be allowed for, that a man has to live, if he would not founder and go to the bottom and not make his port at all, by dead reckoning, and he must be a great calculator indeed who succeeds. Simplify, simplify.

Choosing to Respond Questions

1. Paraphrase the second-to-last paragraph (it begins "I went to the woods").
2. Explain and respond to Thoreau's charge: "Simplicity, simplicity, simplicity!"
3. Explain and respond to Thoreau's contention that "The millions are awake enough for physical labor; but only one in a million is awake enough for effective intellectual exertion, only one in a hundred millions to a poetic or divine life. To be awake is to be alive. I have never yet met a man who was quite awake."
4. Although he says it was an "accident," Thoreau begins living in his house in the woods on July 4th—Independence Day. How might this date be symbolically significant?

Choosing to Read Critically

1. Select a quotation or short passage from the above excerpt and discuss its implications for contemporary life.
2. Field trip: Go outside and find an artifact from the "natural world": a pinecone, a leaf, a blade of grass. Write an essay in which you describe the object and then discuss the object as a symbol of another aspect of life. (For example, the veins of the leaf might represent the branches of a human family or the surface of the rock is an analogy for the hardness of life.)

Wide Awake to Connections Questions

1. Research transcendental philosophy and the transcendentalists and write an essay in which you describe transcendentalism and explain how

Thoreau's ideas in the above excerpt dramatize some transcendentalist ideas. Then, discuss whether or not transcendentalism is relevant in contemporary life. If transcendentalist ideas can still be helpful, explain how.

2. Drawing on at least one other selection from Part II of this book as well as the above excerpt from *Walden*, explain and respond to Thoreau's statement that "I know of no more encouraging fact than the unquestionable ability of man to elevate his life by a conscious endeavor." Do you agree with this contention? Provide examples or counterexamples to back up your position.

Jeff Jacoby, "The Waste of Recycling"

>> **Prereading Check-In**

1. Brainstorm on the concept of "recycling." You may choose to focus on what the word literally means, what it means to you personally, or what it means culturally or nationally.

2. Do you choose to recycle? What? And why or why not?

Jeff Jacoby *(b. 1959), formerly chief editorial writer with the* Boston Herald, *has since provided a conservative perspective for the* Boston Globe, *in which he writes an op-ed column. The following, which originally appeared in the* Boston Globe, *questions some popular beliefs about the virtues of recycling and its challenges.*

"The Waste of Recycling"

I generally see her after dark: an old woman in a conical Vietnamese hat, making the rounds in my neighborhood the night before our weekly trash pickup. She is out in all kinds of weather, checking the bins that residents have set out on the curb, helping herself to the aluminum cans. I've smiled and nodded hello once or twice, but she looks right past me and moves on. I figure she's too busy working to lose any time on pleasantries.

That elderly woman engages in one of mankind's oldest means of employment: picking through rubbish, looking for things of value in other people's discards. Winslow Homer portrayed such scavengers—recyclers, we'd call them today—in *Scene on the Back Bay Lands, Boston*, an 1859 engraving of trash-pickers sorting through the landfill that eventually became one of Boston's most elegant neighborhoods.

Such "private sector recycling is as old as trash itself," notes Clemson University economist Daniel K. Benjamin, who reproduces the Homer image in *Recycling Myths Revisited*, a new monograph for PERC, the Montana-based Property & Environment Research Center. Like the "scow-trimmers" who once competed for the right to rummage through New York City's garbage barges, or like Cairo's modern-day "Zabbaleen," who collect much of that city's waste and support themselves by recycling what they find, Homer's Back Bay foragers were poor people who sifted through rubbish not because it was politically correct or required by law, but because it was a productive use of their time. It left them better off.

Similarly, the woman I see in my neighborhood pulls beverage cans out of trash bins not because she believes recycling is virtuous, but because there is a natural market demand for aluminum cans (bolstered by a 5-cent deposit) and she increases her wealth by supplying them.

By contrast, she doesn't take the old toothpaste tubes or Styrofoam cups that people have thrown out, because there is no natural market for them. That doesn't mean those items *couldn't* be recycled. It means that they're not *worth* recycling. To put it in environmental terms, recycling such rubbish would be a waste of resources.

Most of the stuff we throw out—aluminum cans are an exception—is cheaper to replace from scratch than to recycle. "Cheaper" is another way of saying "requires fewer resources." Green evangelists believe that recycling our trash is "good for the planet"—that it conserves resources and is more environmentally friendly. But recycling household waste consumes resources, too.

Extra trucks are required to pick up recyclables, and extra gas to fuel those trucks, and extra drivers to operate them. Collected recyclables have to be sorted, cleaned, and stored in facilities that consume still more fuel and manpower; then they have to be transported somewhere for post-consumer processing and manufacturing. Add up all the energy, time, emissions, supplies, water, space, and mental and physical labor involved, and mandatory recycling turns out to be largely unsustainable—an environmental burden, not a boon.

"Far from saving resources," Benjamin writes, "curbside recycling typically wastes resources—resources that could be used productively elsewhere in society."

Popular impressions to the contrary notwithstanding, we are not running out of places to dispose of garbage. Not only is US landfill capacity at an all-time high, but all of the country's rubbish for the next 100 years could comfortably fit into a landfill measuring 10 miles square. Benjamin puts that in perspective: "Ted Turner's Flying D ranch outside Bozeman, Mont., could handle all of America's trash for the next century—with 50,000 acres left over for his bison."

Nor do modern landfills—which are regulated by the Environmental Protection Agency—pose a threat to human health or the environment. They must be sited far from wetlands and groundwater, thickly lined with clay and plastic, covered daily with fresh layers of soil, and equipped for drawing off the methane gas created by decomposition (the gas, in turn, is collected and purified for sale). Eventually they are capped, landscaped, and turned into public parks or other open space.

Recycling makes many people feel good, but feelings are not the best test of environmental soundness. When it makes more sense to recycle than to throw something away; government compulsion isn't needed. And when recycling is a profligate use of natural and human resources, government mandates can't change the fact. Big Brother can force you to recycle your garbage, but that doesn't make garbage-recycling green.

Choosing to Read Critically Questions

1. What is Jacoby's central argument?
2. Explain how, according to Jacoby, recycling might be "unsustainable."
3. Articulate the position that Jacoby is arguing against. That is, write up the attitude that Jacoby is responding to.
4. In paragraph 3, Jacoby invokes the "scow trimmers" and "Zabbaleen" of Cairo. Why do you think he includes these examples? Do you think they are effective?

Choosing to Respond Questions

1. Over the course of a week, keep track of every single item that you throw out or recycle. Using this as your data, write an essay discussing your personal consumption and waste habits. Do you think you are an average, above-average, or below-average consumer? Did you learn anything about yourself or your priorities by doing this exercise?

2. Find a copy of the Winslow Homer painting that Jacoby describes and, in a group, analyze the image. What kind of people are represented? What are they doing? What is the overall tone or feel of the painting? Does viewing the painting supplement your understanding and/or opinion of the Jacoby article?

Wide Awake to Connections Questions

1. Check out the website www.thestoryofstuff.com, where you can view the animated video "The Story of Stuff" about where all the "stuff" we use comes from and where it all goes when we're done with it. (The site also provides some other relevant information about what's happening to our resources globally.) You may choose to critique the site or draw on the information it provides in order to compose an essay in which you comment on and discuss the above article and, in particular, the question: Why don't we often think about what happens to our trash? Should we? Why or why not?

2. In this article, Jacoby attempts to debunk or challenge a widespread belief (i.e., recycling is inherently virtuous and good for the environment). Find another article in any chapter of this book in which an author makes a similar move—that is, he or she attempts to challenge what he or she perceives as the status quo or a commonly held assumption. Write an essay in which you discuss and evaluate each author's work.

Nel Noddings, from "Place and Nature"

>> **Prereading Check-In**

1. Describe a place that you love. Explain what you love about it.
2. Do you think it is important for people to spend time in "natural" settings such as the woods, the shore, or the mountains? If you think this is important, explain how and why. If you don't, explain why you don't think this kind of experience is valuable.

Philosopher, educator, and feminist **Nel Noddings** *(b. 1929) has worked in a variety of capacities in the field of education. She has also published several books, including* Happiness and Education *(2003), from which the below excerpt is taken. In the following, Noddings argues that "happiness" should be one end of education. She goes further to suggest that children should be taught a "love of place."*

From "Place and Nature"

There is some evidence that a connection between people and nature, beyond the need for food, is inherently necessary. The biophilia hypothesis holds that human beings have a genetically based need to affiliate with nature. For those of us who feel a strong affiliation with other life forms, water, rocks, and geophysical phenomena such as tides and sunrises, the biophilia hypothesis sounds right. We have to acknowledge, however, that there are people—increasingly many—who seem to feel no need to connect with nature and prefer to live as far from it as possible. That so many people *do* feel the need and that others might if given the appropriate educational exposure is reason enough for us to explore how education should approach the human-nature relationship . . . .

We must educate for love of place, and then we must gather and disseminate the knowledge required to preserve the places we love. Love alone is not enough because, through ignorance, we can unintentionally destroy what we love. With happiness as a primary aim of education, we have another strong incentive to teach for both love and knowledge of place.

One of the most interesting and useful things we could teach in suburban schools is, in the words of Sara Stein, "restoring the ecology of our own back yards." Huge and useless lawns that require gas-guzzling machines to mow them and poisons to keep them free of weeds could be, at least partially, replaced by trees, shrubs, thickets, vegetable gardens, and wild flowers, and these plantings would provide homes for birds and other wild life. They would also provide the wild places so loved by children and now largely missing in the suburban landscape.

When children live in contact with nature, they gradually come to know that the relations among living things and their environments are enormously complex. The gentle, much-loved cat becomes a killer when mice appear. Some seedlings fail to thrive even though we have not neglected them. Some plants will not do well in the presence of certain others. Killing one set of marauders may deprive a beneficial insect or spider of food. An ugly, scraggly plant may be the main food for the larvae of the beautiful butterfly. Problems are seldom simple, and we have to work observantly and thoughtfully in the environment we wish to preserve.

Understanding the complexity, observing the mixture of beauty and horror, and accepting the feelings of happiness and sadness engendered by their connections to nature, young people should be less prone to either carelessness or fanaticism. To cultivate our happiness, we must enjoy situations and relationships that are less than perfect but, as we are open to them, yield moments of great joy. Our commitments should not turn us into grouches, violent protestors, or single-minded proselytizers. For example, a young woman committed to conserving water may insist on taking short showers, but she may make everyone else miserable by harping on her virtue and the vice of others. A hot shower is a sensuous luxury to be enjoyed. One can avoid excessive use but still take delight in what she *is* using. Similarly, one can be dedicated to recycling without going into fits of guilt over occasional lapses . . . .

Young people today face environmental problems that were rarely discussed years ago. (One could argue, of course, that if they had been discussed and treated effectively, the problems of today would not be so acute.) Some of today's more tender attitudes would have worked against survival years ago . . . .

If the problems of today are in part products of prosperity and leisure, they are not entirely so. We have the time now to recognize and ponder the lives of animals, for example, but their suffering has always been part of the natural condition. Our relationship to non-human animals is a topic that education can no longer avoid, but it should be guided by the quest for balance.

Choosing to Read Critically Questions

1. In your own words, define "biophilia."
2. Explain what Noddings means in paragraph 5 when she writes, "Understanding the complexity, observing the mixture of beauty and horror, and accepting the feelings of happiness and sadness engendered by their connections to nature, young people should be less prone to either carelessness or fanaticism."
3. Who do you think Noddings' audience is? Who do you think would most benefit from considering the ideas presented in this essay?
4. In paragraph 4, Noddings provides some examples of the complex relationships between living things and their environments. Using her work as a guide, write your own descriptions of elements in nature that are revealed as complex when closely examined.

Choosing to Respond Questions

1. What do you think Noddings means when she suggests that many of today's environmental problems are "in part products of prosperity and leisure"? Do you agree or disagree with Noddings' claim?

2. Using the ideas presented in Noddings' essay, construct a lesson plan that you would use in order to teach elementary school students about the natural world.

Wide Awake to Connections Questions

1. Richard Louv has written about "nature deficit disorder," or what he describes as children's behavioral and emotional problems resulting from a lack of exposure to the outdoors. Read Louv's book *The Last Child in the Woods: Saving Our Children From Nature Deficit Disorder* (2005), or do some research on "nature deficit disorder." Do you think Louv has identified an urgent problem or do you feel he is misattributing or misunderstanding the issues? You may draw on your personal experiences as well as Noddings' article for your response.

2. Do you agree that happiness is or should be a goal of education? You may choose to check out Noddings' book *Happiness and Education,* from which the above excerpt is taken, as well as some of the articles in the "American Education" and "Happiness" chapters of this textbook, to include in your essay.

Ward M. Clark, "Why Hunt?"

>> **Prereading Check-In**

1. Do you hunt? Describe your experiences. If you don't hunt, explain why not—even if those reasons are purely "practical."

2. Do you think hunting is ethical? That is, do you approve or disapprove of hunting? Are there kinds of hunting that you think are "better" than others? Explain your perspective.

Writer and hunter **Ward M. Clark** *has written several fiction and nonfiction books, including* Misplaced Compassion: The Animal Rights Movement Exposed. *In the following article, which originally appeared in* Wildfowling Magazine, *Clark argues that hunting is an important human activity that brings us a better appreciation of the natural world.*

"Why Hunt?"

Modern hunters seem to find they are answering that question [why hunt?] frequently. Sometimes the question is put by the genuinely curious; sometimes it is a hostile demand for justification. In the first case, the answer is complex and thought provoking. In the second, the answer is simple—"because it suits me to do so." Hunting in and of itself requires no justification. The hunt is not only natural and healthful; it's an inextricable part of our heritage as human beings.

Man is and has long been a terminal predator, as marvelously equipped for hunting by our intellect as a lion is by his claws and fangs, as a wolf by his swift legs and pack instinct. No matter whether humans today hunt directly, or employ middlemen to prepare their prey for them on farms and meat packing plants, the fact of our status as predator is in our very DNA. We owe the very fact of our world-conquering intellect on the hunt, on the stimulus that drove us to overcome the handicap of our clawless, blunt-toothed bodies, to develop weapons to match the feats of the greatest of animal predators; we owe our great brains to the access to high-quality diets of meat, marrow, and fat that predatory behavior allowed.

But, the question remains nonetheless. Why, now, do we hunt?

Some hunt for the meat. A good reason in itself; game meat is lean, healthy, and free from additives; the process of obtaining it provides exercise and time in the outdoors, away from work pressures and the temptations of couches and televisions. The fruits of the hunt, properly cared for, are welcomed on the most discriminating of tables. Some hunt for the camaraderie, another fine reason; for many of these, the actual hunt is secondary to the outing with friends, sharing the campfire with others of like mind and feeling. Another good reason; it is in the enjoyment of fine companions that we grow as social animals. The annual ritual of the mountain elk camp is a vital part of the year for many.

But, there is frequently another reason. A reason that's more compelling, and at the same time harder to explain.

Henry David Thoreau, in the great classic *Walden*, wrote "Go fish and hunt far and wide day by day—farther and wider—and rest thee by many brooks and hearth-sides without misgiving. Remember thy Creator in the days of thy youth. Rise free from care before the dawn, and seek adventures. Let the noon find thee by other lakes, and the night overtake thee everywhere at home. There are no larger fields than these, no worthier games than may here be played." Thoreau spoke for many hunters in those words, hunters who hunt not solely for the meat, or for the company, but for the ageless, timeless experience of the hunt itself.

For it's true that for some of us the hunt is an answer in itself. It's enough to awake hours before the dawn, and to know the utter silence of a late autumn morning. To hear the crunch of snow under your boots as you begin the hike into the distant, silent mountains. To smell the pines along the trail, and see the silent sentinel spruces on the ridges, barely glimpsed in the pre-dawn dark. It's enough to sit, shivering, at that best spot on the top rim of a remote basin, watching the east grow bright, waiting for the first rays of warm sunshine to break through the trees and drive away the bitter cold of night.

But those moments, treasured as they are, pale before the ultimate goal of the hunt. It's a part of the hunter's soul, to carry the knowledge that somewhere, out among the pines, in the dark timber or the frost-covered meadows, a bull awaits, and the chance of the day may bring him within your awareness. The snap of a branch, the ghosting shape of antlers through the aspens, the sudden ringing bugle of a bull elk, as he appears, suddenly, where no bull was a moment before. His breath plumes out in the cold as he screams his challenge, and your hands and will freeze momentarily in awe of his magnificence. It's enough to know that the day may bring the chance of a stalk, through the darkness under the trees, along the edges of the golden grasses of a meadow, creeping, creeping, under the streamside willows, silently, slowly, ever closer, testing the wind, watching underfoot for twigs, whispering a silent prayer to the forests and fields to allow you to close the gap, to make the shot.

With luck, you'll raise your rifle or draw your bow, and make your shot. More often than not, though, the bull escapes, to play the game of predator and prey another day, in another valley.

You can't buy moments like that; you can't find them on the Internet, or at the movie theater. . . .

For hunting requires a level of participation unknown in any other human venture—hunting requires a communion with the very primal forces of Nature, taking life so that life may be. Hunting requires a contact that the non-hunter can never know, a contact with life itself. The hunter eschews supporting his or her life through a middleman; knowing the cost of one's diet, engenders respect for the lives that must be taken to sustain one's own life.

. . . Perhaps the answer lies in the very understanding of our role in Nature. Nature has but one law; Life feeds on Life, and Life gives Life to Life. People who obtain their steaks, chicken, and burgers from supermarkets and butcher's shops can lose sight of this fundamental truth, and perhaps they would prefer to have that process sanitized in just such a manner. In our modern, urbanized society, many like to imagine their own existence is bloodless, clean, and sanitary. But such an outlook is self-deluding.

The hunter knows very well the cost for the steaks that grace his plate. . . . Most of all, the hunter has seen the sudden transition from a living animal to an inanimate food source, from animate life to meat for the table. The non-hunting urbanite likely has never seen this take place, and would not care to do so; but the hunter knows, with bittersweet regularity, the price that must be paid for continued existence.

It is for this very reason that the hunter reveres his prey. . . . Reverence for the game, reverence for the wellspring of life, reverence for the great, largely unknowable cycles of the Earth, all come from the intimacy with Nature found in the hunt. . . .

It's unfortunate that the non-hunter often cannot see past the fact that the hunt results in the death of an animal. The death of an animal, it's true, is the goal of the hunt; but a greater goal is to be found in the overall experience, of which the actual kill is only the climactic moment. . . . And, indeed, in the final moment of success, when the hunter approaches, cautiously, the downed bull, lying still now against the bed of needles; the heart-pounding thrill of success, weighted against the bittersweet regret of the necessity of taking the life, facing the final truth that for life to be, another life must give way.

Life feeds on Life, and Life gives Life to Life. The hunter in success understands this great truth as no other human possibly can.

We hunt to pay homage to Nature, to Life, to the Earth. To make our annual pilgrimage to our beginnings, to lay hands on our heritage as members of the biotic community. To affirm once more that Life feeds on Life, and Life gives Life to Life. We hunt for the gift of an elk to a family, the gift of life from the Earth. In the hunt lies an affirmation, a recognition that we too will one day return to the Earth that has fed and nurtured us, and the elk will then feed on the minerals and nutrients returned to the soil from our bodies.

That affirmation alone is enough for many of us who hunt, to send us once more out of our tents, trailers, and ranch houses, out into the freezing darkness under the glittering stars, to climb an unseen mountain for the chance at an elk.

Hunting has a fundamental truth that few non-hunters understand. It's not about death. It's about life.

That's why.

Choosing to Read Critically Questions

1. In your own words, what is the answer to the question, "Why hunt"?
2. Why, according to Clark, does the hunter have respect for his or her prey?
3. Throughout the article, Clark uses the word "man." Do you think Clark means "humankind," or is he specifically referring to males? Explain your answer and explain why you think Clark makes this semantic choice.
4. Evaluate the stylistic choices, tone, and rhythm of this article. Did you find it compelling? Why or why not?

Choosing to Respond Questions

1. Clark quotes Henry David Thoreau's advice to let "the night overtake thee everywhere at home." Reread the entire quotation and explain what Thoreau means. Do you think this is good advice? Do you have any experience of ever feeling "everywhere at home"?
2. Elsewhere, pro-hunting authors have argued that some of the most vehement nature conservationists are hunters. See, for example, Randall L. Eaton's article "Modern Hunters are Stewards of Wildlife and the Environment" (originally in *Outdoor Edge Magazine*). Drawing on Clark's article, write an essay in which you discuss why hunters and fishers might feel passionately about animals and nature.

Wide Awake to Connections Questions

1. Locate and read *Walden; Or Life in the Woods* (1854), an important book by Henry David Thoreau, a transcendentalist philosopher who wrote about his experiences living in a cabin on Walden pond. After reading

Walden, write an essay in which you first summarize Thoreau's arguments and then discuss whether or not his perspectives are relevant to life in 21st-century America.

2. Clark writes that "People who obtain their steaks, chicken, and burgers from supermarkets and butcher's shops can lose sight of this fundamental truth" that "Life feeds on Life, and Life gives Life to Life." Drawing on one or two articles from Chapter 10, construct an essay in which you discuss the relationship between how one obtains food and one's attitude toward one's food.

Al Gore, from Nobel Peace Prize Acceptance Speech

>> **Prereading Check-In**

1. Do you consider climate change an urgent problem? Why or why not?
2. Write down anything you already know about former Vice President Al Gore.

Albert "Al" Gore Jr. *(b. 1948), Vice President of the United States from 1993–2001, won the Nobel Peace Prize with the Intergovernmental Panel on Climate Change for his work publicizing the global climate crisis, including the production of the documentary* An Inconvenient Truth *(2006). Gore has held several political offices and has long worked to raise awareness of environmental issues. The text below is excerpted from Gore's speech at the Nobel Prize acceptance ceremony in Oslo, Norway, on December 10, 2007. In it, Gore insists that we must act swiftly and decisively to confront climate change.*

From Nobel Peace Prize Acceptance Speech

Sometimes, without warning, the future knocks on our door with a precious and painful vision of what might be. One hundred and nineteen years ago, a wealthy inventor read his own obituary, mistakenly published years before his death. Wrongly believing the inventor had just died, a newspaper printed a harsh judgment of his life's work, unfairly labeling him "The Merchant of Death" because of his invention—dynamite.

Shaken by this condemnation, the inventor made a fateful choice to serve the cause of peace.

Seven years later, Alfred Nobel created this prize and the others that bear his name.

Seven years ago tomorrow, I read my own political obituary in a judgment that seemed to me harsh and mistaken—if not premature. But that unwelcome verdict also brought a precious if painful gift: an opportunity to search for fresh new ways to serve my purpose.

Unexpectedly, that quest has brought me here. Even though I fear my words cannot match this moment, I pray what I am feeling in my heart will be communicated clearly enough that those who hear me will say, "We must act."

. . . We, the human species, are confronting a planetary emergency— a threat to the survival of our civilization that is gathering ominous and destructive potential even as we gather here. But there is hopeful news as well: we have the ability to solve this crisis and avoid the worst—though not all—of its consequences, if we act boldly, decisively and quickly.

However, despite a growing number of honorable exceptions, too many of the world's leaders are still best described in the words Winston Churchill applied to those who ignored Adolf Hitler's threat: "They go on in strange paradox, decided only to be undecided, resolved to be irresolute, adamant for drift, solid for fluidity, all powerful to be impotent."

So today, we dumped another 70 million tons of global-warming pollution into the thin shell of atmosphere surrounding our planet, as if it were an open sewer. And tomorrow, we will dump a slightly larger amount, with the cumulative concentrations now trapping more and more heat from the sun.

As a result, the earth has a fever. And the fever is rising. The experts have told us it is not a passing affliction that will heal by itself. We asked for a second opinion. And a third. And a fourth. And the consistent conclusion, restated with increasing alarm, is that something basic is wrong.

We are what is wrong, and we must make it right.

. . . In the last few months, it has been harder and harder to misinterpret the signs that our world is spinning out of kilter. Major cities in North and South America, Asia and Australia are nearly out of water due to massive droughts and melting glaciers. Desperate farmers are losing their livelihoods. Peoples in the frozen Arctic and on low-lying Pacific islands are planning evacuations of places they have long called home. Unprecedented wildfires have forced a half million people from their homes in one country and caused a national emergency that almost brought down the government in another. Climate refugees have migrated into areas already inhabited by people with different cultures, religions, and traditions, increasing the potential for conflict. Stronger storms in the Pacific and Atlantic have threatened whole cities. Millions have been displaced by massive flooding in South Asia, Mexico, and 18 countries in Africa. As temperature extremes have increased, tens of thousands have lost their lives. We are recklessly burning and clearing our forests and driving more and more species into extinction. The very web of life on which we depend is being ripped and frayed.

We never intended to cause all this destruction, just as Alfred Nobel never intended that dynamite be used for waging war. He had hoped his invention would promote human progress. We shared that same worthy goal when we began burning massive quantities of coal, then oil and methane.

. . . In the years since this prize was first awarded, the entire relationship between humankind and the earth has been radically transformed. And still, we have remained largely oblivious to the impact of our cumulative actions.

Indeed, without realizing it, we have begun to wage war on the earth itself. Now, we and the earth's climate are locked in a relationship familiar to war planners: "Mutually assured destruction."

. . . It is time to make peace with the planet.

We must quickly mobilize our civilization with the urgency and resolve that has previously been seen only when nations mobilized for war. These prior struggles for survival were won when leaders found words at the 11th hour that released a mighty surge of courage, hope and readiness to sacrifice for a protracted and mortal challenge.

These were not comforting and misleading assurances that the threat was not real or imminent; that it would affect others but not ourselves; that ordinary life might be lived even in the presence of extraordinary threat; that Providence could be trusted to do for us what we would not do for ourselves.

No, these were calls to come to the defense of the common future. They were calls upon the courage, generosity and strength of entire peoples, citizens of every class and condition who were ready to stand against the threat once asked to do so. Our enemies in those times calculated that free people would not rise to the challenge; they were, of course, catastrophically wrong.

Now comes the threat of climate crisis—a threat that is real, rising, imminent, and universal. Once again, it is the 11th hour. The penalties for ignoring this challenge are immense and growing, and at some near point would be unsustainable and unrecoverable. For now we still have the power to choose our fate, and the remaining question is only this: Have we the will to act vigorously and in time, or will we remain imprisoned by a dangerous illusion?

. . . We must abandon the conceit that individual, isolated, private actions are the answer. They can and do help. But they will not take us far enough without collective action. At the same time, we must ensure that in mobilizing globally, we do not invite the establishment of ideological conformity and a new lock-step "ism."

That means adopting principles, values, laws, and treaties that release creativity and initiative at every level of society in multifold responses originating concurrently and spontaneously.

. . . In the Kanji characters used in both Chinese and Japanese, "crisis" is written with two symbols, the first meaning "danger," the second "opportunity." By facing and removing the danger of the climate crisis, we have the opportunity to gain the moral authority and vision to vastly increase our own capacity to solve other crises that have been too long ignored.

We must understand the connections between the climate crisis and the afflictions of poverty, hunger, HIV-AIDS and other pandemics. As these problems are linked, so too must be their solutions. We must begin by making the common rescue of the global environment the central organizing principle of the world community.

. . . No one should believe a solution will be found without effort, without cost, without change. Let us acknowledge that if we wish to redeem squandered time and speak again with moral authority, then these are the hard truths:

The way ahead is difficult. The outer boundary of what we currently believe is feasible is still far short of what we actually must do. Moreover, between here and there, across the unknown, falls the shadow.

That is just another way of saying that we have to expand the boundaries of what is possible. In the words of the Spanish poet, Antonio Machado, "Pathwalker, there is no path. You must make the path as you walk."

We are standing at the most fateful fork in that path. So I want to end as I began, with a vision of two futures—each a palpable possibility—and with a prayer that we will see with vivid clarity the necessity of choosing between those two futures, and the urgency of making the right choice now.

The great Norwegian playwright, Henrik Ibsen, wrote, "One of these days, the younger generation will come knocking at my door."

The future is knocking at our door right now. Make no mistake, the next generation will ask us one of two questions. Either they will ask: "What were you thinking; why didn't you act?"

Or they will ask instead: "How did you find the moral courage to rise and successfully resolve a crisis that so many said was impossible to solve?"

We have everything we need to get started, save perhaps political will, but political will is a renewable resource.

So let us renew it, and say together: "We have a purpose. We are many. For this purpose we will rise, and we will act."

Choosing to Read Critically Questions

1. The speech has two purposes. One is to say thanks and accept the award. What is the second? Quoting from the text, summarize the argument Gore makes in this speech.

2. What are some of the recent events that Gore points to in order to demonstrate that we are in a "planetary emergency"?

3. Explain why Gore invokes Alfred Nobel at the beginning and ending of the speech.

4. Gore quotes many sources in his speech. What did you think of his use of quotations? Do they strengthen his argument? Choose one or two to further discuss.

Choosing to Respond Questions

1. Gore uses several metaphors, including that the "earth has a fever" and that we are at "war" with our own planet, in order to describe the current crisis as well as how we should respond. Choose one metaphor and

unpack it. What are the implications of this metaphor? Does the metaphor make the situation clearer for you? Do you agree with what Gore is saying with the metaphor?

2. Gore provides a general idea of what he thinks the world's response to climate change should be. Building on Gore's recommendations, develop *specific* plans that governments around the world—including our own—should institute in order to combat climate change.

Wide Awake to Connections Questions

1. In paragraph 3, Gore refers to his "own political obituary." Do some research to figure out what Gore is referring to here. Write an essay in which you outline Gore's political history.

2. Read the next article, Wray and Flanagan's "An Inconvenient Truth About Youth," and then write an essay responding to Gore's claim that "We are what is wrong, and we must make it right."

Laura Wray and Constance Flanagan, "An Inconvenient Truth About Youth"

> **》》 Prereading Check-In**
>
> 1. Have you altered your behaviors in any way in order to lessen your "carbon footprint?" Describe any differences you've noted in your own life as a result of widespread increased environmental awareness.
> 2. Drawing on your own observations, describe young people's attitudes about the environment. Do young people today seem to care?

Laura Wray *and* **Constance Flanagan** *have collaborated on a number of publications, in addition to working together on the MacArthur Research Network on Transitions to Adulthood that documents and analyzes trends among young people and is referenced in the article below. The following opinion-editorial piece originally appeared in the* Washington Post *in 2006. In it, Wray and Flanagan suggest that young people are distressingly complacent when it comes to environmental issues.*

An Inconvenient Truth About Youth

"An Inconvenient Truth," Al Gore's movie on global warming, is now the fourth-largest-grossing documentary of all time. But apparently it isn't young adults who are paying the price of the ticket—or, more important, taking the truth about the environment to heart. In fact, the inconvenient truth today is that youths' willingness to conserve gas, heat and energy has taken a precipitous plunge since the 1980s.

According to data from Monitoring the Future, a federally funded national survey on trends in the attitudes, values and behavior of high school seniors since 1976, there has been a clear decline in conservation behavior among 18-year-olds over the past 27 years—although we are not yet sure whether these attitudes follow youths into adulthood. This decline, interestingly, is coupled with a rise in materialistic values.

In fact, trends in materialism and conservation are highly related: At times when youths place higher value on material goods, they are also much less likely to say they would conserve resources. And when youths are more materially driven, they are also less likely to believe that natural resources will become scarce in the future.

Since the 1990s, the trends in materialism seem to have topped out at a steady high level, while willingness to conserve keeps declining. These opposing values should raise a red flag about the consumer culture and its influence on youth.

Youths also consistently believe that government is more responsible for the environment than they are personally. Importantly, when they perceive that the government's role in solving environmental problems is declining, so does their belief that they, personally, must do their part to save the environment.

Conservation is a collective responsibility. Likewise, in the minds of youth, their own actions to preserve the environment are inextricably linked to their perception of the government's role in environmental conservation.

Indeed, environmental attitudes of youth seem to mirror the opinions of those in the White House at the time. The highest levels of conservation occurred in the mid- to late 1970s, at the same time President Jimmy Carter was publicly petitioning citizens to take individual responsibility for conserving resources. The steepest decline in conservation occurred during the Reagan administration, which has been widely criticized for its environmental policies. Willingness to conserve enjoyed a slight surge around 1992–93, when Bill Clinton first took office, but this increase was short-lived. (Al Gore must not have been speaking up too loudly about the environment back then.)

The good news in these trends is that when government responds, so do youth. If our country's leaders follow the example of Al Gore and start to genuinely explore sustainable solutions, it's likely that young people will follow suit.

Policymakers and elected officials might also want to note that when youths embrace conservation and pro-environmental attitudes, they are more likely to engage in conventional politics, from writing to officials to giving money to a political campaign, or working on a campaign.

Gore argues that in America, "political will is a renewable resource." Perhaps one way to renew this resource is to start focusing more on young people and their understanding of, as well as contribution to, environmental problems.

Choosing to Read Critically Questions

1. What connections do Wray and Flanagan make between materialism and conservationism?

2. Compose a one-paragraph formal summary in which you present Wray and Flanagan's thesis statement, as well as all of their important points.

3. This article appeared as an opinion-editorial, or op-ed, piece. What do you think its purpose is? Who, do you think, is Wray and Flanagan's audience?

4. Does this piece convince you that action should be taken? What action? Why or why not?

Choosing to Respond Questions

1. What do you see as the government's role regarding environmentalism and conservation? What is your role? Do you feel that your attitude toward the environment is influenced by government policies?

2. Propose some steps that local governments could take in order to get youth more interested in making positive contributions to their communities. (These contributions may or may not be related to environmental and conservationist causes.)

Wide Awake to Connections Questions

1. Conduct a survey of a peer or friend group in order to gauge your peers' opinions about and interest in conservation. Of course, your survey is "unscientific," but you will nevertheless analyze your data in order to compose an article modeled on Wray and Flanagan's in which you argue that your peer group (whether they be young adults, middle-aged adults, teens, seniors, etc.) either does or does not care about the environment.

2. Drawing on this article as well as one or two articles from Chapter 13, "Social Networking," write an essay in which you evaluate the ways in which young people are characterized in academic and popular media and whether or not you find these characterizations to be true. For example, you might choose to discuss the excerpt from Mark Bauerlein's *The Dumbest Generation* in order to argue that young people are apathetic and uninformed or, rather, to argue that writers such as Wray, Flanagan, and Bauerlein misunderstand and misrepresent the attitudes of today's young people.

The Christian Science Monitor's Editorial Board, "Why Earth Day Needs a Regreening"

›› Prereading Check-In

1. Have you ever seen or experienced something that caused you to be concerned about the environment? (This environment could be your home community or the world more broadly.) Describe the situation. If you haven't, you might choose to answer the next Prereading question.

2. In a paragraph or two, describe one of the most important issues that you feel is now facing your local neighborhood or community. (Examples of issues might include crime, pollution, noise, or the economy.)

According to its website, the goal of the Christian Science Monitor *is to shed "light and understanding with the conviction that truth is the beginning of solutions." Begun by Mary Baker Eddy in 1908, the* Monitor *uses multiple platforms, including a website and a weekly magazine, to deliver national and international news and commentary.*

"Why Earth Day Needs a Regreening"

This year's Earth Day comes with a faded shade of green.

The portion of Americans concerned about the planet has dropped significantly in three years (from 43 percent to 34 percent). People are wasting more water and buying fewer all-natural products, according to a Harris poll. Only a quarter now describe themselves as "environmentally conscious."

At the same time, the percentage of Americans who feel "green guilt"—defined as knowing they could do more for the environment—has risen from 12 percent to 29 percent during the same period, another survey finds.

And, as one might expect after a recession, Americans have flipped their views and now see economic growth as more important than environmental protection, by a 49 percent to 41 percent margin, per yet another survey.

The most surprising report on public opinion, published in the *Journal of Personality and Social Psychology*, reveals that young adults, known as Millennials, have less concern for the environment than any generation of the past four decades. This shaky commitment to the environment may have two causes:

One is that the issues, such as climate change, have become just too big and complex to comprehend. It was easy to stop littering. But give up oil and that SUV?

And two, after four decades of government action to protect nature and cut pollution, everyday folk simply take less responsibility for doing much on their own unless pushed.

What can be done to bolster this sagging support for this little blue ball called Earth?

One of Britain's most famous philosophers, Roger Scruton, offers some hope in a new book, "Green Philosophy: How to Think Seriously About the Planet," due out in the United States next month. He argues for a return to a love of home and one's local community and surroundings, or what he calls "settlement"—and less focus on global schemes, coercive law, and alarmist rhetoric.

Environmental problems must be seen by "all of us in our everyday circumstances, and should not be confiscated by the state," he writes. Once these big issues seem like our problems, then we can start to solve them with "our given moral equipment."

"When problems pass to governments, they pass out of our hands."

He sees small-scale civic actions tied to friendships and local connections as the best way to deal with the most fundamental issue: How to
convince people—and companies—not to pass the costs of their consumption and pollution to future generations.

Or, as President Obama once described the problem, "We are borrow-
ing this planet from our children and our grandchildren."

Only when people are settled in a community and feel a spirit of coop-
eration, duty, and obligation will they start to respect the environment—
and to sustain it for those to come.

Stronger communities based on a sense of place provide a moral con-
straint on individual ambition to pollute. Without it, Mr. Scruton says, the
state rushes in to fill a vacuum, with rules, fines, and bureaucracy. Then
individuals take less responsibility in conserving their habitat.

His idea of bottom-up solutions based on loyalty to place is bearing out.

Much of the action on climate change, for example, is happening
locally, in states and cities, rather than at the federal or global level. Just
look at the explosion of public bike-rentals in cities and state initiatives
on energy conservation—despite the fact that four in ten Americans say
there is no proof of global warming.

Scruton's book merely gives us the big picture, pointing out the trends
already under way, such as the "local food," "slow food," and "local
economy" movements.

When people stop treating each other as objects and form bonds of
community, he proposes, then they will stop treating the planet as an
object, suitable only to be used up for personal benefit.

Choosing to Read Critically Questions

1. What is "environmental guilt?"
2. Explain Roger Scruton's contention that "environmental problems . . .
   should not be confiscated by the state." What does Scruton propose as
   an alternative?
3. Discuss the polling data provided. What do the authors conclude from the
   data? Can you draw other, perhaps contradictory, conclusions?
4. Explain and respond to the idea presented in the final paragraph.

Choosing to Respond Questions

1. Drawing on your own experiences and observations, test Scruton's argument that fostering a sense of community is fundamental to encouraging individuals to care about the environment. Provide specific examples to back up your response.

2. Research the "slow food," "local food," or "local economy" movements described in the above article. After summarizing the central concept, provide examples. Finally, evaluate the movement and/or the examples. Is this an effective project? Has it been successful? Should it be more successful? Why or why not and how?

Wide Awake to Connections Questions

1. According to the United Church of Christ's study "Toxic Waste and Race at Twenty," people of color disproportionately live near toxic waste sites. (See www.ucc.org/environmental-ministries/environment/toxic-waste-20.) How does this happen? What should be done to remedy what some people call "environmental racism"?

2. Drawing on this excerpt and another selection from this chapter, write an essay in which you describe what kinds of actions individuals can and should take when they are confronted with an environmental crisis. Articles such as Laura Wray and Constance Flanagan's "An Inconvenient Truth about Youth" and Vice President Al Gore's Nobel Prize acceptance speech might prove to be useful for this assignment.

Selection of Cartoons: Dean Young, Mike Peters, and Bob Englehart

›› Prereading Check-In

1. How important do you think your personal choices and actions are when it comes to the environment? Explain.

2. Do you know anybody who calls themself an "environmentalist"? Describe that person. If you don't, describe your perceptions of those who are committed to environmental issues. Where do your perceptions come from?

"Blondie," which first appeared in 1930, was originally created by "Chic" Young *and was passed on to his son,* **Dean Young**. *"Blondie"*

has appeared in more than 2,000 newspapers worldwide. The cartoon below appeared during celebrations of Earth Day.

Mike Peters *began his career as a cartoonist in 1969 with the* Dayton Daily News, *and in 1981, he won a Pulitzer Prize for Journalism. His political cartoons have appeared in over 400 newspapers. His strip, "Mother Goose and Grimm," from which the below was taken, has appeared in over 800 newspapers. In it, Peters responds to the popularity of Al Gore's* An Inconvenient Truth.

Bob Englehart's *first cartoons appeared in 1966 in* Chicago Today. *His work has since been featured in numerous publications, including* USA Today, Time, *the* New York Times, *and the* Hartford Courant. *The cartoon below mocks a number of attitudes, including self-righteousness and hypocrisy.*

Blondie, by Dean Young

Blondie copyright © 2008 King Features Syndicate

Mother Goose and Grimm, by Mike Peters

Mother Goose & Grimm copyright © 2008 Grimmy, Inc. King Features Syndicate

Bob Englehart/PoliticalCartoons.com

"NO PLASTIC BAGS, PLEASE. I DON'T WANT TO CONTRIBUTE TO GLOBAL WARMING!"

Choosing to Read Critically Questions

1. What is the punch line of the "Blondie" cartoon? Why is it supposed to be funny?

2. What is the punch line of the "Mother Goose" cartoon? Why is it supposed to be funny?

3. What is the punch line of Englehart's cartoon? Why is it supposed to be funny?

4. Did you find these cartoons effective in conveying a point? Did you find them funny? Explain.

Choosing to Respond Questions

1. What kinds of stereotypes does the "Blondie" cartoon draw on? Discuss whether or not you find this cartoon accurate or not, funny or not.

2. All three cartoons focus on individual behaviors that will have little to no impact on larger environmental issues. Using these cartoons as evidence you will analyze, make some suggestions about contemporary attitudes about the environmental crisis.

Wide Awake to Connections Questions

1. Draw your own cartoon strip that dramatizes some element of the environmental crisis and our response to it. In a two-to-three-paragraph essay accompanying the cartoon, explain what attitudes or behaviors you were trying to capture in your work.

2. Look at John Callahan's cartoons in Chapter 9 as well as the "Peanuts" cartoon in Chapter 14. Using Callahan and/or Shulz's work, as well as the above comics, write an essay in which you discuss the use of humor to deal with serious issues. Do you feel these cartoons reach people or do you feel they oversimplify the subjects? (You may also want to suggest that each piece is different and does something different than the others and may be more or less effective.)

QUESTIONS AND SUGGESTIONS FOR FURTHER RESEARCH AND WRITING

1. Imagine you are a developer who has just purchased a large tract of land outside a metropolitan area. As part of the deal to buy the land, you agreed to make many "green" innovations in your development. After conducting research into green initiatives in building and development and finding out what works and what doesn't work, write up a description of the development you plan to create for the local government, explaining all the environmentally friendly aspects of the community you will construct, as well as those you won't include and why. (In addition, you might choose to include plans for making your community accessible to all people. If you choose to do so, you may draw on Graham Pullin's article, "An Introduction to Universal Design," in Chapter 9 of this text.)

2. Drawing on articles from Chapter 10, "What to Eat: Difficult Decisions About Food in America," compose an essay exploring the relationships between environmental degradation and the food we produce and consume. You may choose to focus on how certain kinds of farming, food, or consumption affect the environment or the foods that are produced and/or how these foods affect our bodies and health. Some articles you might include are Clark's "Why Hunt?" and Berry's "The Pleasures of Eating," as well as articles available online, such as Bryan Walsh's "Getting Real About the High Price of Cheap Food."

3. Mark Schapiro's excellent book *Exposed: The Toxic Chemistry of Everyday Products and What's at Stake for American Power* (2009) describes the ways in which the United States has fallen behind the European Union in the regulation of toxic substances in the products we use in daily life. In addition to conducting your own research, make use of Schapiro's bibliography as you write a research paper

further exploring one of the areas, for instance the cosmetics or electronics industries, that is included in Schapiro's discussion.

4. A number of wonderful films tell the "true" stories of individuals who discover illegal pollution and who work tirelessly to protect affected communities and neighborhoods. There are also films that call attention to pollution and toxicity that affect our everyday lives. Watch one or two of the following films, and write an essay analyzing their depictions of toxicity. How, according to these films, is progress made? How are the protagonists depicted? What do these films suggest about contemporary society?

Films Depicting the Discovery of Illegal Pollution:

A Civil Action (1998)

Erin Brockovich (2000)

Michael Clayton (2007) (This film is not based on a true story.)

Silkwood (1983)

Films Depicting the Effects of Toxicity and Pollution on Everyday People:

Gasland (2010) (This film is a documentary.)

Blue Vinyl (2002) (This film is a documentary.)

The Incredible Shrinking Woman (1981)

Safe (1995)

No Impact Man (2009) (This documentary deals with attempts not to "impact" the environment.)

5. An important aspect of discussions of the environment right now is the tension between what individuals can and should do and what larger organizations, such as institutions and governments, can and should do. Research the events surrounding the discovery of toxicity and government intervention at the Love Canal neighborhood in Niagara Falls, New York. You might start by consulting Lois Gibbs' memoir about the experience, *Love Canal: My Story.* What lessons can be learned from Love Canal? Is the story still relevant? A second step might be to research citizen-activist groups in your community and to attend some meetings. Describe your experiences and suggest what role citizen-activists are playing or will play in your community.

12 Chapter Twelve

Choosing School:
American Education in the 21st Century

>> **Prereading Check-In**

1. Describe a situation in which you learned something really important. (This situation, of course, could have taken place in an educational setting, but may also have occurred elsewhere.) Describe what you learned and how you learned it.

2. What is the purpose of education?

If you sometimes feel that school is irrelevant to your nonacademic life or that it is unnecessarily boring or otherwise unpleasant, it might be helpful to remember that the opportunity to study, to learn, to pursue an education is a luxury unknown to many citizens of the world. There are places right now in which girls and young women literally risk their lives to go to school. And remember that before the American Civil War, it was *illegal* to teach an African American slave to read. Remember, too, that until recently, many members of minority groups, including blacks, women, and Jews, were specifically barred from certain educational institutions. Finally, scholars suggest that, both globally and nationally on the individual and community levels, pursuing an education is the most effective strategy for combating poverty. Education can be a path to personal and social power.

At the same time, it is quite possible that your educational experiences to date have been less than fulfilling. There are plenty of stories of students who claim to have "never read a book" in high school or who boast about the amount of time they spent cutting class. What's saddest about these stories is that often students don't realize that they have lost out on something valuable and rewarding. They have been denied—and have participated in denying themselves—an opportunity to develop their intellects at a time in their lives that has been specifically set aside for just that purpose.

Unfortunately, one of the realities of the universal education system we have in place in the United States, or the commitment to provide an education for every student from kindergarten through high school, is that, while this is an ambitious and noble cause, it is also an extremely difficult goal to achieve. (The title of former President George W. Bush's No Child Left Behind plan, for example, suggests that, previously, children were, in fact, being left behind.) Students who graduate from high school never having read a book, for example, have "fallen through the cracks"; that is, no one seems to have noticed or cared that these students were not motivated or inspired to learn. Many of the articles in this section focus on problems within our current system of education. This is not to suggest that America's educational system is not, in many respects, a success that we should be proud of. Instead, the focus on problems and possible solutions suggests that we must stay alert and not take education for granted; nor should we simply accept that the system is screwed up and there's nothing we can do about it. These readings highlight the complications involved in educating: School can function as a holding pen for young people, as a place of enlightenment, as a place of confusion and bafflement. This chapter invites you to look critically at your own past, present, and future learning, as well as the current state of schooling in the United States, and to choose to be an active participant rather than a passive recipient of your education.

Plato, "The Allegory of the Cave"

>> **Prereading Check-In**

1. Describe a time in your life when you discovered that something you believed to be true was, in fact, false or only partially true. How did you feel when you made this discovery?

2. Describe, in whatever language you see fit (i.e., technical, metaphorical, conversational), the process of learning as you understand it.

Greek philosopher **Plato** *(born around 427 B.C.), a crucial figure in the development of philosophy, was the founder of the Academy of Athens, the first academy for higher learning. The following, which is excerpted from Benjamin Jowett's translation, is presented as a dialogue between two speakers, Socrates (the "I" of the dialogue) and Glaucon (the "he" of the dialogue). In it, Socrates explores the questions of how we know what we know about the world and how our senses might deceive us.*

"The Allegory of the Cave"

And now, I said, let me show in a figure how far our nature is enlightened or unenlightened:—Behold! human beings living in an underground den, which has a mouth open towards the light and reaching all along the den; here they have been from their childhood, and have their legs and necks chained so that they cannot move, and can only see before them, being prevented by the chains from turning round their heads. Above and behind them a fire is blazing at a distance, and between the fire and the prisoners there is a raised way; and you will see, if you look, a low wall built along the way, like the screen which marionette players have in front of them, over which they show the puppets.

I see.

And do you see, I said, men passing along the wall carrying all sorts of vessels, and statues and figures of animals made of wood and stone and various materials, which appear over the wall? Some of them are talking, others silent.

You have shown me a strange image, and they are strange prisoners.

Like ourselves, I replied; and they see only their own shadows, or the shadows of one another, which the fire throws on the opposite wall of the cave?

True, he said; how could they see anything but the shadows if they were never allowed to move their heads?

And of the objects which are being carried in like manner, they would only see the shadows?

Yes, he said.

And if they were able to converse with one another, would they not suppose that they were naming what was actually before them?

Very true.

And suppose further that the prison had an echo which came from the other side, would they not be sure to fancy when one of the passers-by spoke that the voice which they heard came from the passing shadow?

No question, he replied.

To them, I said, the truth would be literally nothing but the shadows of the images.

That is certain.

And now look again, and see what will naturally follow if the prisoners are released and disabused of their error. At first, when any of them is liberated and compelled suddenly to stand up and turn his neck round and walk and look towards the light, he will suffer sharp pains; the glare will distress him, and he will be unable to see the realities of which in his former state he had seen the shadows; and then conceive some one saying to him, that what he saw before was an illusion, but that now, when he is approaching nearer to being and his eye is turned towards more real existence, he has a clearer vision,—what will be his reply? And you may further imagine that his instructor is pointing to the objects as they pass and requiring him to name them,—will he not be perplexed? Will he not fancy that the shadows which he formerly saw are truer than the objects which are now shown to him?

Far truer.

And if he is compelled to look straight at the light, will he not have a pain in his eyes which will make him turn away to take refuge in the objects of vision which he can see, and which he will conceive to be in reality clearer than the things which are now being shown to him?

True, he said.

And suppose once more, that he is reluctantly dragged up a steep and rugged ascent, and held fast until he is forced into the presence of the sun himself, is he not likely to be pained and irritated? When he approaches the light his eyes will be dazzled, and he will not be able to see anything at all of what are now called realities.

Not all in a moment, he said.

He will require to grow accustomed to the sight of the upper world. And first he will see the shadows best, next the reflections of men and other objects in the water, and then the objects themselves; then he will gaze upon the light of the moon and the stars and the spangled heaven; and he will see the sky and the stars by night better than the sun or the light of the sun by day?

Certainly.

Last of all he will be able to see the sun, and not mere reflections of him in the water, but he will see him in his own proper place, and not in another; and he will contemplate him as he is.

Certainly.

He will then proceed to argue that this is he who gives the season and the years, and is the guardian of all that is in the visible world, and in a certain way the cause of all things which he and his fellows have been accustomed to behold?

Clearly, he said, he would first see the sun and then reason about him.

And when he remembered his old habitation, and the wisdom of the den and his fellow-prisoners, do you not suppose that he would felicitate himself on the change, and pity them?

Certainly, he would.

And if they were in the habit of conferring honors among themselves on those who were quickest to observe the passing shadows and to remark which of them went before, and which followed after, and which were together; and who were therefore best able to draw conclusions as to the future, do you think that he would care for such honors and glories, or envy the possessors of them? Would he not say with Homer,

'Better to be the poor servant of a poor master,' and to endure anything, rather than think as they do and live after their manner?

Yes, he said, I think that he would rather suffer anything than entertain these false notions and live in this miserable manner.

Imagine once more, I said, such a one coming suddenly out of the sun to be replaced in his old situation; would he not be certain to have his eyes full of darkness?

To be sure, he said.

And if there were a contest, and he had to compete in measuring the shadows with the prisoners who had never moved out of the den, while his sight was still weak, and before his eyes had become steady (and the time which would be needed to acquire this new habit of sight might be very considerable), would he not be ridiculous? Men would say of him that up he went and down he came without his eyes; and that it was better not even to think of ascending; and if any one tried to loose another and lead him up to the light, let them only catch the offender, and they would put him to death.

No question, he said.

This entire allegory, I said, you may now append, dear Glaucon, to the previous argument; the prison-house is the world of sight, the light of the fire is the sun, and you will not misapprehend me if you interpret the journey upwards to be the ascent of the soul into the intellectual world according to my poor belief, which, at your desire, I have expressed— whether rightly or wrongly God knows. But, whether true or false, my opinion is that in the world of knowledge the idea of good appears last of all, and is seen only with an effort; and, when seen, is also inferred to be the universal author of all things beautiful and right, parent of light and of the lord of light in this visible world, and the immediate source of reason and truth in the intellectual; and that this is the power upon which he who would act rationally either in public or private life must have his eye fixed.

I agree, he said, as far as I am able to understand you.

Moreover, I said, you must not wonder that those who attain to this beatific vision are unwilling to descend to human affairs; for their souls are ever hastening into the upper world where they desire to dwell; which desire of theirs is very natural, if our allegory may be trusted.

Yes, very natural.

And is there anything surprising in one who passes from divine contemplations to the evil state of man, misbehaving himself in a ridiculous manner; if, while his eyes are blinking and before he has become accustomed to the surrounding darkness, he is compelled to fight in courts of law, or in other places, about the images or the shadows of images of justice, and is endeavoring to meet the conceptions of those who have never yet seen absolute justice?

Anything but surprising, he replied.

Any one who has common sense will remember that the bewilderments of the eyes are of two kinds, and arise from two causes, either from coming out of the light or from going into the light, which is true of the mind's eye, quite as much as of the bodily eye; and he who remembers this when he sees any one whose vision is perplexed and weak, will not be too ready to laugh; he will first ask whether that soul of man has come out of the brighter life, and is unable to see because unaccustomed to the dark, or having turned from darkness to the day is dazzled by excess of light. And he will count the one happy in his condition and state of being, and he will pity the other; or, if he have a mind to laugh at the soul which comes from below into the light, there will be more reason in this than in the laugh which greets him who returns from above out of the light into the den.

That, he said, is a very just distinction.

But then, if I am right, certain professors of education must be wrong when they say that they can put a knowledge into the soul which was not there before, like sight into blind eyes.

They undoubtedly say this, he replied.

Whereas, our argument shows that the power and capacity of learning exists in the soul already; and that just as the eye was unable to turn from darkness to light without the whole body, so too the instrument of knowledge can only by the movement of the whole soul be turned from the world of becoming into that of being, and learn by degrees to endure the sight of being, and of the brightest and best of being, or in other words, of the good.

Very true.

Choosing to Read Critically Questions

1. Draw the cave and write a paragraph or two explaining your drawing.

2. In your own words, summarize the allegory itself (what happens in the cave) as well as what the allegory means.

3. Plato describes how, after an individual has left the cave, he might return and share his knowledge with those still in the cave. However, when he returned, those still in the cave might say, "better not even to think of ascending." Explain why those in the cave might feel this way.

4. If you've had difficulty with this selection, check out one of the many YouTube videos dramatizing the allegory. (The claymation version, available at http://www.youtube.com/watch?v=69F7GhASOdM is quite good.) After watching the video, read the selection again, and then write a few paragraphs explaining if and how the video helped your comprehension. What didn't you get before and what do you understand now?

Choosing to Respond Questions

1. Building on your answer to Choosing to Read Critically Question #3, find an application from your own life or observations for the attitude, "better not even to think of ascending." Have you ever thought this way or been confronted with this attitude?

2. Is learning painful? Does it have to be? Using the above selection, develop an essay in which you evaluate the relevance of Plato's ideas today.

Wide Awake to Connections Questions

1. "The Allegory of the Cave" has had many applications; most recently, some readers have identified correspondences between the allegory and

the 1999 film, *The Matrix.* If you're familiar with *The Matrix,* or any other film in which characters think they are living in reality when really they are not, write a short essay in which you discuss parallels. Don't consult the Internet on this one; rely on your own readings and ideas.

2. Read Mike Rose's "Finding Our Way" in this chapter. Building on Rose and Plato's ideas, compose an essay in which you discuss the ideal purposes of education. You may also choose to draw on your own experiences and observations.

John Taylor Gatto, "The Seven-Lesson Schoolteacher"

›› Prereading Check-In

1. Would you say that you have had different attitudes toward school at different stages of your life? Describe those attitudes and the situations they arose from.
2. As you probably know, there has been severe and sustained criticism of the American public school system. Do you agree that our public school system needs reforming?

New York City's Teacher of the Year in 1989, 1990, and 1991, and New York State's Teacher of the Year in 1991, **John Taylor Gatto** *(b. 1935) is the author of* Dumbing Us Down: The Hidden Curriculum of Compulsory Schooling *(1992),* The Exhausted School *(1993),* A Different Kind of Teacher: Solving the Crisis of American Schooling *(2002), and* Weapons of Mass Instruction: A Schoolteacher's Journey through the Dark World of Compulsory Schooling *(2008). Gatto is also working on a documentary about the public school system. The excerpt here, in which Gatto critiques contemporary education, is taken from* Dumbing Us Down: The Hidden Curriculum of Compulsory Schooling.

"The Seven-Lesson Schoolteacher"

Call me Mr. Gatto, please. Twenty-six years ago, having nothing better to do at the time, I tried my hand at schoolteaching. The license I hold certifies that I am an instructor of English language and English literature, but that isn't what I do at all. I don't teach English, I teach school—and I win awards doing it.

Teaching means different things in different places, but seven lessons are universally taught Harlem to Hollywood Hills. They constitute a national curriculum you pay more for in more ways than you can imagine, so you might as well know what it is. You are at liberty, of course, to regard these lessons any way you like, but believe me when I say I intend no irony in this presentation. These are the things I teach, these are the things you pay me to teach. Make of them what you will:

I.

1. Confusion

A lady named Kathy wrote this to me from Dubois, Indiana the other day:

"What big ideas are important to little kids? Well, the biggest idea I think they need is that what they are learning isn't idiosyncratic—that there is some system to it all and it's not just raining down on them as they helplessly absorb. That's the task, to understand, to make coherent."

Kathy has it wrong. **The first lesson I teach is confusion.** Everything I teach is out of context. . . . I teach the unrelating of everything. I teach disconnections. I teach too much: the orbiting of planets, the law of large numbers, slavery, adjectives, architectural drawing, dance, gymnasium, choral singing, assemblies, surprise guests, fire drills, computer languages, parent's nights, staff-development days, pull-out programs, guidance with strangers you may never see again, standardized tests, age-segregation unlike anything seen in the outside world . . . what do any of these things have to do with each other?

Even in the best schools a close examination of curriculum and its sequences turns up a lack of coherence, full of internal contradictions. Fortunately the children have no words to define the panic and anger they feel at constant violations of natural order and sequence fobbed off on them as quality in education. The logic of the school-mind is that it is better to leave school with a tool kit of superficial jargon derived from economics, sociology, natural science and so on than to leave with one genuine enthusiasm. But quality in education entails learning about something in depth. Confusion is thrust upon kids by too many strange adults, each working alone with only the thinnest relationship with each other, pretending for the most part, to an expertise they do not possess. Meaning, not disconnected facts, is what sane human beings seek, and education is a set of codes for processing raw facts into meaning. Behind the patchwork quilt of school sequences and the school obsession with facts and theories the age-old human search lies well concealed. This is harder to see in elementary school where the hierarchy of school experience seems to make better sense because the good-natured simple relationship of "let's do this" and "let's do that now" is just assumed to mean something and the clientele has not yet consciously discerned how little substance is behind the play and pretense.

Think of all the great natural sequences like learning to walk and learning to talk; following the progression of light from sunrise to sunset; witnessing the ancient procedures of a farm, a smithy, or a shoemaker; watching your mother prepare a Thanksgiving feast—all of the parts are in perfect harmony with each other, each action justifies itself and illuminates the past and future. School sequences aren't like that, not inside a single class and not among the total menu of daily classes. School sequences are crazy. There is no particular reason for any of them, nothing that bears close scrutiny. Few teachers would dare to teach the tools whereby dogmas of a school or a teacher could be criticized since everything must be accepted. School subjects are learned, if they can be learned, like children learn the catechism or memorize the 39 articles of Anglicanism. I teach the un-relating of everything, an infinite fragmentation the opposite of cohesion; what I do is more related to television programming than to making a scheme of order. In a world where home is only a ghost because both parents work or because too many moves or too many job changes or too much ambition or something else has left everybody too confused to stay in a family relation, I teach you how to accept confusion as your destiny. That's the first lesson I teach.

2. Class Position

The second lesson I teach is your class position. I teach that you must stay in class where you belong. I don't know who decides that my kids belong there but that's not my business. The children are numbered so that if any get away they can be returned to the right class. Over the years the variety of ways children are numbered has increased dramatically, until it is hard to see the human being plainly under the burden of numbers he carries. Numbering children is a big and very profitable business, though what the strategy is designed to accomplish is elusive. I don't even know why parents would allow it to be done to their kid without a fight.

In any case, again, that's not my business. My job is to make them like it, being locked in together with children who bear numbers like their own. Or at the least endure it like good sports. If I do my job well, the kids can't even imagine themselves somewhere else because I've shown how to envy and fear the better classes and how to have contempt for the dumb classes. Under this efficient discipline the class mostly polices itself into good marching order. That's the real lesson of any rigged competition like school. You come to know your place.

In spite of the overall class blueprint, which assumes that 99 percent of the kids are in their class to stay, I nevertheless make a public effort to exhort children to higher levels of test success, hinting at eventual transfer from the lower class as a reward. I frequently insinuate that the day will come when an employer will hire them on the basis of test scores and grades, even though my own experience is that employers are rightly indifferent to such things. I never lie outright, but I've come to see that truth and schoolteaching are, at bottom, incompatible just as Socrates said they were thousands of years ago. The lesson of numbered classes is that everyone has a proper place in the pyramid and that there is no way out of your class except by number magic. Failing that, you must stay where you are put.

3. Indifference

The third lesson I teach kids is indifference. I teach children not to care about anything too much, even though they want to make it appear that they do. How I do this is very subtle. I do it by demanding that they become totally involved in my lessons, jumping up and down in their seats with anticipation, competing vigorously with each other for my favor. It's heartwarming when they do that, it impresses everyone, even me. When I'm at my best I plan lessons very carefully in order to produce this show of enthusiasm. But when the bell rings I insist that they stop whatever it is that we've been working on and proceed quickly to the next work station. They must turn on and off like a light switch. Nothing important is ever finished in my class, nor in any other class I know of. Students never have a complete experience except on the installment plan.

Indeed, the lesson of the bells is that no work is worth finishing, so why care too deeply about anything? Years of bells will condition all but the strongest to a world that can no longer offer important work to do. Bells are the secret logic of schooltime; their argument is inexorable. Bells destroy the past and future, converting every interval into a sameness, as an abstract map makes every living mountain and river the same even though they are not. Bells inoculate each undertaking with indifference.

4. Emotional Dependency

The fourth lesson I teach is emotional dependency. By stars and red checks, smiles and frowns, prizes, honors and disgraces I teach you to surrender your will to the predestined chain of command. Rights may be granted or withheld by any authority, without appeal because rights do not exist inside a school—not even the right of free speech, the Supreme Court has ruled—unless school authorities say they do. As a schoolteacher I intervene in many personal decisions, issuing a pass for those I deem legitimate, or initiating a disciplinary confrontation for behavior that threatens my control. Individuality is constantly trying to assert itself among children and teenagers so my judgments come thick and fast. Individuality is a contradiction of class theory, a curse to all systems of classification. Here are some common ways it shows up: children sneak away for a private moment in the toilet on the pretext of moving their bowels; they trick me out of a private instant in the hallway on the grounds that they need water. I know they don't but I allow them to deceive me because this conditions them to depend on my favors. Sometimes free will appears right in front of me in children angry, depressed or happy by things outside my ken; rights in such things cannot be recognized by schoolteachers, only privileges that can be withdrawn, hostages to good behavior.

5. Intellectual Dependency

The fifth lesson I teach is intellectual dependency. Good people wait for a teacher to tell them what to do. It is the most important lesson, that we must wait for other people, better trained than ourselves, to make the meanings of our lives. The expert makes all the important choices; only I can determine what you must study, or rather, only the people who pay me can make those decisions which I enforce. If I'm told that evolution is fact instead of a theory I transmit that as ordered, punishing deviants who resist what I have been told to tell them to think.

This power to control what children will think lets me separate successful students from failures very easily. Successful children do the thinking I appoint them with a minimum of resistance and decent show of enthusiasm. Of the millions of things of value to study, I decide what few we have time for, or it is decided by my faceless employer. The choices are his, why should I argue? Curiosity has no important place in my work, only conformity.

Bad kids fight this, of course, even though they lack the concepts to know what they are fighting, struggling to make decisions for themselves about what they will learn and when they will learn it. How can we allow that and survive as schoolteachers? Fortunately there are procedures to break the will of those who resist; it is more difficult, naturally, if the kid has respectable parents who come to his aid, but that happens less and less in spite of the bad reputation of schools. Nobody in the middle class I ever met actually believes that their kid's school is one of the bad ones. Not a single parent in 26 years of teaching. That's amazing and probably the best testimony to what happens to families when mother and father have been well-schooled themselves, learning the seven lessons.

Good people wait for an expert to tell them what to do. It is hardly an exaggeration to say that our entire economy depends upon this lesson being learned. Think of what would fall apart if kids weren't trained to be dependent: The social-service businesses could hardly survive, they would vanish I think, into the recent historical limbo out of which they arose. Counselors and therapists would look on in horror as the supply of psychic invalids vanished. Commercial entertainment of all sorts, including television, would wither as people learned again how to make their own fun. Restaurants, prepared-food and a whole host of other assorted food services would be drastically down-sized if people returned to making their own meals rather than depending on strangers to plant, pick, chop and cook for them. Much of modern law, medicine, and engineering would go, too, the clothing business and schoolteaching as well, unless a guaranteed supply of helpless people poured out of our schools each year.

6. Provisional Self-Esteem

The sixth lesson I teach is provisional self-esteem. If you've ever tried to wrestle a kid into line whose parents have convinced him to believe they'll love him in spite of anything, you know how impossible it is to make self-confident spirits conform. Our world wouldn't survive a flood of confident people very long so I teach that your self-respect should depend on expert opinion. My kids are constantly evaluated and judged. A monthly report, impressive in its precision, is sent into students' homes to signal approval or to mark exactly down to a single percentage point how dissatisfied with their children parents should be. The ecology of good schooling depends upon perpetuating dissatisfaction just as much as commercial economy depends on the same fertilizer. Although some people might be surprised how little time or reflection goes into making up these mathematical records, the cumulative weight of the objective-seeming documents establishes a profile of defect which compels a child to arrive at certain decisions about himself and his future based on the casual judgment of strangers. Self-evaluation, the staple of every major philosophical system that ever appeared on the planet, is never a factor in these things. The lesson of report cards, grades, and tests is that children should not trust themselves or their parents, but need to rely on the evaluation of certified officials. People need to be told what they are worth.

7. One Can't Hide

The seventh lesson I teach is that you can't hide. I teach children they are always watched by keeping each student under constant surveillance as do my colleagues. There are no private spaces for children, there is no private time. Class change lasts three hundred seconds to keep promiscuous fraternization at low levels. Students are encouraged to tattle on each other, even to tattle on their parents. Of course I encourage parents to file their own child's waywardness, too. A family trained to snitch on each other isn't likely to be able to conceal any dangerous secrets. I assign a type of extended schooling called "homework", too, so that the surveillance travels into private households, where students might otherwise use free time to learn something unauthorized from a father or mother, or by apprenticing to some wise person in the neighborhood. Disloyalty to the idea of schooling is a Devil always ready to find work for idle hands. The meaning of constant surveillance and denial of privacy is that no one can be trusted, that privacy is not legitimate. Surveillance is an ancient urgency among certain influential thinkers, a central prescription set down in *The Republic, The City of God, The Institutes of the Christian Religion, New Atlantis, Leviathan* and a host of other places.

All these childless men who wrote these books discovered the same thing: children must be closely watched if you want to keep a society under tight central control. Children will follow a private drummer if you can't get them into a uniformed marching band.

II.

It is the great triumph of compulsory government monopoly mass-schooling that among even the best of my fellow teachers, and among the best of my student's parents, only a small number can imagine a different way to do things. "The kids have to know how to read and write, don't they?" "They have to know how to add and subtract, don't they?" "They have to learn to follow orders if they ever expect to keep a job."

Only a few lifetimes ago things were very different in the United States; originality and variety were common currency; our freedom from regimentation made us the miracle of the world, social class boundaries were relatively easy to cross, our citizenry was marvelously confident, inventive, and able to do many things independently, to think for themselves. We were something, we Americans, all by ourselves, without government sticking its nose into our lives, without institutions and social agencies telling us how to think and feel; no, all by ourselves we were something, as individuals.

We've had a society increasingly under central control in the United States since just before the Civil War and such a society requires compulsory schooling, government monopoly schooling to maintain itself. Before the society changed, schooling wasn't very important anywhere. We had it, but not too much of it and only as much as an individual wanted. People learned to read, write, and do arithmetic just fine anyway, there are some studies which show literacy at the time of the American Revolution, at least on the Eastern seaboard, as close to total.

The continuing cry for "basic skills" practice is a smoke screen behind which schools preempt the time of children for 12 years and teach them the seven lessons I've just taught you. School takes our children away from any possibility of an active role in community life—in fact it destroys communities by reserving the training of children to the hands of certified experts—and by doing so it ensures that they cannot grow up fully human. Aristotle taught that without a fully active role in community life you could not hope to become a healthy human being. Surely he was right. Look around you the next time you are near a school or an old people's reservation, that will be the demonstration. The current debate about whether we should have a national curriculum is phony—we already have one, locked up in the seven lessons I just taught you and a few more I decided to spare you. Such a curriculum produces physical, moral, and intellectual paralysis and no curriculum of content will be sufficient to reverse its hideous effects. What is currently under discussion in our national school hysteria about failing academic performance is a great irrelevancy that misses the point. Schools teach exactly what they are intended to teach and they do it well—How to be good and where your place is.

Choosing to Read Critically Questions

1. In your own words, provide an overview of Gatto's "seven lessons."
2. Explain how, according to Gatto, homework is a surveillance tool. What do you think of this claim?
3. As part of the fifth lesson, Gatto writes "Nobody in the middle class I ever met actually believes that their kid's school is one of the bad ones." What does Gatto mean by this? What do you think of this claim?
4. What is Gatto's tone in section I? Is it effective? What purpose does his tone serve?

Choosing to Respond Questions

1. If any of your experiences with education dovetail with any of Gatto's observations, pinpoint which one(s) of his observations has/have resonated with you and build a response around them. Be sure to include details in your descriptions.

2. As a group, evaluate and respond to Gatto's claim that, without schools teaching children "dependency," "The social-service businesses could hardly survive. . . .Counselors and therapists would look on in horror as the supply of psychic invalids vanished. Commercial entertainment of all sorts, including television, would wither as people learned again how to make their own fun. Restaurants, prepared-food and a whole host of other assorted food services would be drastically down-sized if people returned to making their own meals rather than depending on strangers to plant, pick, chop and cook for them. Much of modern law, medicine, and engineering would go, too, the clothing business and schoolteaching as well, unless a guaranteed supply of helpless people poured out of our schools each year." What is Gatto saying? Does your group agree or disagree? (It's also all right for there to be dissent within the group.) Prepare your ideas for presentation to the class.

Wide Awake to Connections Questions

1. Conduct some research on the notion of a "hidden curriculum" in schools. Select one or two definitions of the "hidden curriculum" and compose an essay in which you define and respond to these identifications of the implicit lessons that students learn in school settings.

2. In another part of this selection that is not included here, Gatto writes, "schoolchildren who face the 21st century cannot concentrate on anything for very long, they have a poor sense of time past and to come, they are mistrustful of intimacy like the children of divorce they really are (for we have divorced them from significant parental attention); they hate solitude, are cruel, materialistic, dependent, passive, violent, timid in the face of the unexpected, addicted to distraction."

   What's remarkable is that Gatto wrote this observation in 1992, before the age of the Internet, texting, Facebook, Twitter, Wii. Drawing on the above quote, as well as the selection from Mark Bauerlein's *The Dumbest Generation*, excerpted in Chapter 13 of this book, write an essay in which you respond to the negative characterizations of the current and previous generations of schoolchildren. In your experience, are these characterizations accurate? Why or why not?

George W. Bush, "President Bush Discusses No Child Left Behind"

>> Prereading Check-In

1. Describe your pre-college educational experiences. You might write about your time in elementary, middle, or high schools. Did you go to a "good" school? Explain.

2. Write down anything you already know or think about the No Child Left Behind Act.

George W. Bush *(b. 1946) served as the 43rd president from 2001 to 2009. Bush, who has written the book* Decision Points *(2010) about his presidency, signed the "No Child Left Behind Act" into law in 2002. In the following speech, which Bush delivered near the end of his presidency in 2009, Bush explains, celebrates, and defends the act.*

"President Bush Discusses No Child Left Behind"

THE PRESIDENT: Thank you for the warm welcome. And Laura and I are thrilled to be here at Kearny School. We have come because this is one of the really fine schools in the city of Philadelphia. We bring greetings from the Nation's Capital, but more importantly, we bring appreciation for those who are working so hard to make sure that every child can learn.

You know, seven years ago today, I had the honor of signing a bill that forever changed America's school systems. It was called the No Child Left Behind Act. I firmly believe that thanks to this law, more students are learning, an achievement gap is closing. And on this anniversary, I have come to talk about why we need to keep the law strong. If you find a piece of legislation that is working, it is important to make sure the underpinnings of that law remain strong.

. . . At the end of the presidency, you get to do a lot of "lasts." I don't know if you saw on TV, but I pardoned my last Thanksgiving turkey. This is my last policy speech. As President of the United States, this is the last policy address I will give. What makes it interesting is that it's the same subject of my first policy address as President of the United States, which is education and education reform.

I hope you can tell that education is dear to my heart. I care a lot about whether or not our children can learn to read, write, and add and subtract. When I was a governor of Texas, I didn't like it one bit when I'd go to schools in my state and realize that children were not learning so they could realize their God-given potential. I didn't like it because I knew the future of our society depended upon a good, sound education.

I was sharing this story with people that Laura and I just met with, and at the time I went to a high school in my state, one of our big city high schools. And I said, thanks for teaching—I met this teacher. I think his name is Brown, if I'm not mistaken. . . . Nelson Brown. And he taught geography and history, if I'm not mistaken. I said, "How is it going, Mr. Brown?" He said, "It's going lousy." I said, "Why?" He said, "Because my kids cannot read and they're in high school." You see, the system was just satisfied with just shuffling kids through—if you're 14 you're supposed to be here, if you're 16 you're supposed to be there. Rarely was the question asked: Can you read? Or can you write? Or can you add and can you subtract?

And so we decided to do something about it. We said such a system is unacceptable to the future of our state. And that's the spirit we brought to Washington, D.C. It's unacceptable to our country that vulnerable children slip through the cracks. And by the way, guess who generally those children are? They happen to be inner-city kids, or children whose parents don't speak English as a first language. They're the easiest children to forget about.

We saw a culture of low expectations. You know what happens when you have low expectations? You get lousy results. And when you get lousy results, you have people who say, there's no future for me in this country.

And so we decided to do something about it. We accepted the responsibility of the office to which I had been elected. It starts with this concept: Every child can learn. We believe that it is important to have a high quality education if one is going to succeed in the 21st century. It's no longer acceptable to be cranking people out of the school system and saying, okay, just go—you know, you can make a living just through manual labor alone. That's going to happen for some, but it's not the future of America, if we want to be a competitive nation as we head into the 21st century.

We believe that every child has dignity and worth. But it wasn't just me who believed that. Fortunately, when we got to Washington, a lot of other people believed it—Democrats and Republicans. I know there's a lot of talk about how Washington is divided, and it has been at times—at times. And it can get awfully ugly in Washington. But, nevertheless, if you look at the history over the past eight years, there have been moments where we have come together. And the No Child Left Behind Act is one such moment.

. . . The philosophy behind the law is pretty straightforward: Local schools remain under local control. In exchange for federal dollars, however, we expect results. We're spending money on schools, and shouldn't we determine whether or not the money we're spending is yielding the results society expects?

So states set standards. . . . And we hold schools accountable for meeting the standards. There—we set an historic goal, and that is to—every child should learn to read and do math at grade level by 2014.

The key to measuring is to test. And by the way, I've heard every excuse in the book why we should not test—oh, there's too many tests; you teach the test; testing is intrusive; testing is not the role of government. How can you possibly determine whether a child can read at grade level if you don't test? And for those who claim we're teaching the test, uh-uh. We're teaching a child to read so he or she can pass the test.

Testing is important to solve problems. You can't solve them unless you diagnose the problem in the first place. Testing is important to make sure children don't slip too far behind. The facts are, if you get too far behind in reading, for example, it's nearly impossible to catch up. That's why it's important to test early.

Measuring results allows us to focus resources on children who need extra help. And measuring gives parents something to compare other schools with. You oftentimes hear, oh, gosh, I wish parents were more involved. Well, one way to get parental involvement is to post results. Nothing will get a parent's attention more than if he or she sees that the school her child goes to isn't performing as well as the school around the corner.

Measurement is essential to success. When schools fall short of standards year after year, something has to happen. In other words, there has to be a consequence in order for there to be effective reforms. And one such thing that can happen is parents can enroll their children in another school. It's—to me, measurement is the gateway to true reform, and measurement is the best way to ensure parental involvement.

By the way, school choice was only open to rich people up until No Child Left Behind. It's hard for a lot of parents to be able to afford to go to any other kind of school but their neighborhood school. Now, under this system, if your public school is failing, you'll have the option of transferring to another public school or charter school. And it's—I view that as liberation. I view that as empowerment.

. . . Instead of looking the other way when students are falling behind, policymakers at all levels are now beginning to be focused on how to close the achievement gap. Achievement gap is—it means this: White students are reading here, and African American students are reading here, and Latino students are reading down here. And that is unacceptable for the United States of America.

In the classroom, students are learning from highly qualified teachers. In other words, that's part of the reforms of encouraged—the focus on highly qualified teachers. Schools have adopted research-proven strategies for reading instruction. There's a lot of debate, if you follow the public education debates closely, there's a lot of debate about what's the best kind of reading program as to how to best teach a child to read. Well, when you measure, it helps you determine which system works the best. . . .

There's a new Teacher Incentive Fund in place, as a result of No Child Left Behind reforms, and a city like Philadelphia are rewarding educators for taking jobs in this city's toughest classrooms, and those who are achieving results. In other words, there's an incentive to make sure good teachers get in the classrooms all throughout the city. And by the way, this is happening all across our country.

You know, I mentioned disclosure. More and more districts are producing annual report cards, and that's really important. And I did mention to you what they call supplemental services. Under the No Child Left Behind Act, when you find a disadvantaged child falling behind where he or she should be, there's extra money for tutoring. And across the country there's now about a half a million students benefiting from the tutoring that comes from No Child Left Behind. It makes sense, doesn't it? It says we're going to measure, and if we determine you need extra help, here's some money to help you—so that you don't fall behind, so that you catch up.

... The most important result of the No Child Left Behind is this: Fewer students are falling behind; more students are achieving high standards. We have what's called the Nation's Report Card. For those who wonder whether or not we should strengthen No Child Left Behind, I want you to hear this: 4th graders earned the highest reading and math scores in the history of the test. Minority and disadvantaged students made some of the largest gains, with African Americans and Hispanics posting all-time highs in several categories.

No Child Left Behind is working for all kinds of students in all kinds of schools in every part of the country. That is a fact. There's still a long way to go, however.... And one of the problems we've had, of course, is getting enough information out in a timely fashion to empower parents to be able to make wise decisions about the future of their children. And [Secretary Spellings] has worked steadily to make sure that information gets to parents in a timely fashion.

Obviously, a piece of legislation like this takes compromise. But there is no compromise to the basic premise of No Child Left Behind, and that is we need to measure on a clear set of goals. We need a few goals that have got maximum impact. And we need to know whether or not those goals are being met. People say, can you possibly meet the goal you set? And the answer is absolutely we can meet the goals that we've set. And not only is it absolutely—confident we can meet it, I know it is necessary that we do meet those goals.

Laura and I have been privileged to travel to schools over the past eight years such as this. And you'd be amazed at what we get to see. We get to see hardworking, decent citizens who dedicate their lives to making sure no child is left behind. And we have seen innovators who are willing to try different approaches to achieve the same result. So we went to Harlem to see a school district there. They attend school for 10 hours a day. So the educators, taking advantage of local control, said, what is required to make sure that we meet high standards? In this case, the educators said, well, we need to have school 10 hours a day. The teachers give parents their cell phone numbers, so that they can be called any time. And as the teachers told us, they do get called any time—to help solve problems. I was just thankful that there weren't cell phones when I was going to elementary school.

I have seen the resolve for reform and the belief in high standards in Chicago, where reading and math scores are soaring, and where every child still has time to study a foreign language and the fine arts. . . .

Laura and I will never forget the resolve that we saw in New Orleans after Katrina, and the determination by principals and teachers to get their schools up and running—and they did. And by the way, they have placed innovation at the center of a rebuilding school system. They believe in high standards and accountability to make sure that out of the rubble of Katrina comes a world-class education system.

And we've seen the resolve here at Kearny. That's why we're here. Every year—we met a mom, who told us her twins now come to this school. You know, it's interesting what happens when you post scores. Nobody cares more about a child's education, obviously, than the first teacher a child has, which is a parent. And this notion about how parents really don't seem to care—they care, believe me. And when there's transparency in the system it helps them make informed choices. And so the mom was saying her twins come here. She also said, by the way, they weren't really reading up to snuff initially, and yet they got extra help. And now, guess what. They're reading up to snuff. Kearny School works.

They commute for miles. Some of the families commute for miles because they understand it's a place of excellence. This is a school where a lot of community and faith-based groups come to help. And that is really, really great of you to do that. And by the way, it happens in other schools, too. And if you're interested in how you can serve America, why don't you volunteer in your local school? If you want to be a member of the army of compassion in America, help your schools. Help your schools help each child realize their God-given potential.

. . . There is a growing consensus across the country that now is not the time to water down standards or to roll back account-ability. There is a growing consensus that includes leaders of the business communities across America who see an increas-ingly global economy and, therefore, believe in standards and accountability. There's a growing consensus amongst leaders of civil rights organizations—like La Raza, and the Urban League, and the Education Equality Project. These leaders refuse to accept what I have called the soft bigotry of low expectations. There's a growing consensus—includes a lot of parents, and superintendents, and mayors, and governors who insist that we put our children first.

And so I've come to herald the success of a good piece of legis-lation. I have come to talk to our citizens about the results that this reform has yielded. And I call upon those who can determine the fate of No Child Left Behind in the future to stay strong in the face of criticism, to not weaken the law—because in weak-ening the law, you weaken the chance for a child to succeed in America—but to strengthen the law for the sake of every child.

Thank you for letting us come by for the last policy address that we have been honored to make. God bless you.

Choosing to Read Critically Questions

1. In your own words, describe the overarching point or points of Bush's speech.

2. What, according to Bush, is the "achievement gap"?

3. How would you characterize Bush's tone in this speech? Provide examples from the text to back up your claims. Do you find Bush's tone effective? Why or why not?

4. If you had the opportunity to work with Bush on this speech, what would you tell him that you liked about it? What would you encourage him to revise?

Choosing to Respond Questions

1. How important were tests when you were in school (before college)? Do you personally find testing effective?

2. Explain and respond to Bush's contention that testing and measurement are keys to diagnosing and improving the problems in the educational system.

Wide Awake to Connections Questions

1. Conduct some research on No Child Left Behind and write an essay in which you argue that the act has been a success or a failure.

2. Drawing on Bush's speech as well as one other selection in this chapter, compose an essay in which you discuss the more ideal goals of education and the difficulties in reaching those goals. Some selections to consider include Rose's "Finding Our Way" or Perez's "A Forgotten Child Remembers."

Laura Perez, "A Forgotten Child Remembers: Reflections on Education"

›› Prereading Check-In

1. Did you feel that your elementary school teachers knew you and cared about you? What about your college professors? Describe your relationships with your teachers.

2. What, do you think, are some of the biggest challenges facing teachers today?

Laura Perez *(b. 1985) grew up in Port Washington, New York. Although she did not have the opportunity to go through high school, Perez earned a G.E.D. and began her college career at a community college in Long Island, New York. She plans to pursue her degree in English Literature, to continue writing, and to someday practice medicine.*

"A Forgotten Child Remembers: Reflections on Education"

In 5th grade, I was able to recite all of the presidents. I sat at a corner desk by the door, and in front of me, above the chalkboard, a poster of the presidents' faces lined the wall in chronological order. Each morning

I would come in and read their names once, close my eyes, and recite them without peeking. However, in the middle of that year, my life at home became increasingly stressful. I wasn't able to pay attention in class, because all I could think about was my life outside of school. I became depressed and stopped doing my homework, going to the library, and reading all together.

My teacher was often angry with me. He would say things like, "Everybody in the class is doing their work, why aren't you?" and, "I can't understand why you come to school without your homework." And although he asked why my homework wasn't getting done, he never actually took the time to stop and find out the answer. Instead, he had an attitude that, to me, seemed as if he expected nothing more from me. His snide comments and uncaring attitude would eventually lead to my own feelings of apathy in regard to school. I recall, vividly, one event in particular. I came into class one morning after a rough night at home and my teacher asked me if I had done my homework, which for the first time in a long time, I had. I told him that I did it and had to get it from my back pack. The whole class waited in silence, I could feel their eyes watching me while I ran to the cupboards to get it, and at that moment, when I opened my back pack, I realized that I had left it at home. Feeling completely humiliated, standing there in front of the class, he said, "You don't have to lie, Laura. I know that you didn't do it." My heart sank into my stomach, heat radiated through my body, and my face turned red. I told him that I did do it and left it on the dresser in my bedroom. He continued to tell the other children in class, while I was standing there, that if they didn't do their homework, they would not be successful; he was telling them that I would not be successful. At that moment, I wanted to run and hide, but I didn't. I held back tears on the way to my seat and simply rested my head for the remainder of the period.

In his book, *Lives on the Boundary*, Mike Rose writes, "Students will float to the mark you set." Unfortunately for me, and for all of the students in my class, our teacher had set a very low mark. The school, located in a fairly affluent community, was a place of education for children of all socio-economic backgrounds. Maybe the teacher just figured all of his students were living an easy life and, at the age of 10 his students had no stresses or worries. He never made an attempt to learn these things, and instead of being inspirational and positive, he taught all of us a lesson about humiliation and failure. Because I had not met his definition of a successful student, I was mentally conditioned to think I would never be a success in life. He had no intentions of encouraging me or making me feel worthy. Instead of taking me aside and asking me why I wasn't doing my homework, or how things were at home, he used negative discipline in front of a classroom full of children to make me feel embarrassed, stupid, and scared. I needed to be encouraged. I needed support. I needed him to ask if I was ok.

In describing his own educational experience, Rose writes, "I got very good at watching a blackboard with minimum awareness." It's interesting that he described his experience as watching the blackboard. In itself, the word "watching" doesn't imply any sort of interaction or need for comprehension. Like Rose, I began to experience school passively, rather than actively. By the time middle school began, I was completely underprepared and overwhelmed. I would keep to myself and didn't speak much. Most of the time I was observing what was going on around me; watching as my classmates were being molded into the picture of educational success. In other words, they all sat at their desks, staring straight ahead, listening to directions and taking notes. They understood what was expected of them. I was far behind everyone else, feeling lost emotionally and academically. Because every day was a struggle, I wondered how I was supposed to catch up when I was lacking a basic support system. At home, no one took my education seriously, and at school no one bothered to question the support I should have been receiving at home. I was simply herded along with all of the other kids, from one grade to the next.

High school was very different from middle school. Classes were larger and teachers were even more demanding. I remember my first day of school well. I was more nervous than excited. When I arrived to first period, my English class, the teacher gave us an index card and told us to write down anything that we didn't understand or had struggled with. I wrote my name at the top of the index card and sat, with it blank, for about 20 minutes. Because I could not even imagine where to begin, I tried to peek over and see what the kid next to me was writing, but I couldn't make out his small handwriting. Not only did I not know what to write, but I didn't even have a solid understanding of what this teacher was asking. At the end of class, I handed in the index card blank.

I felt ashamed and useless. Each day I continued to go to class, expecting this teacher to say something to me, or even yell at me, about handing in the blank card. But she never said anything. It was like she never even looked at it—never wondering why one of her students, whose life she could have been enriching, had nothing to put on her card. Looking back, I find it ironic that this teacher, who made an initial effort to connect with her students and their needs, never took the time to follow up. I wish she could have seen that blank card as a call for help instead of a display of apathy, but I didn't know how to approach the issue back then.

Soon after that I started skipping classes. I would sit over at the "chain," a place where the "cool" seniors hung out and smoked cigarettes. They would often talk about how much school sucked, and sadly, I could relate. I found comfort with them—with other kids who felt unmotivated and overtired. We knew that there was more hardship to life than math homework or regents exams. As hard as I tried, I couldn't get a hold on school. I was absent over half of the school year and it wasn't because I felt like smoking cigarettes at the chain. I was absent because things started getting increasingly bad at home and I had no choice but to stay there and help with the realities of what life handed me.

After I completed my first year of high school, I received a letter in the mail stating that, because of my absences and lack of participation, I would have to repeat the 9th grade. I was so upset. I thought there was no way in hell I would do it over again. Soon after that, I received another letter from the school board stating that the school didn't feel that it was the right place for me. They instructed that I would attend Boces, a school for students who were no longer making the "right kind of progress" in their previous schools. Rose writes, "The vocational track, however, is most often a place for those who are just not making it, a dumping ground for the disaffected." This is what Boces was for me—a dumping ground in the most literal sense. The worst part is that, instead of getting positive attention and being helped back on the right track, everyone seemed to care even less than before. I learned nothing but how to defend myself from girls who wanted to fight. No one at the school was interested in the progression of my education, which left me wondering why I was there at all. I hated it. At that point I would have given anything to go back to my previous high school, but that wasn't an option. In the middle of that school year, my family was evicted from our apartment.

We moved to a town a few miles away and started a new, completely dysfunctional, life. I stopped going to school and started working full-time to help pay the bills. No one came to the new apartment to see why I wasn't in school. No one called or sent letters. Now, completely off the educational radar, I went about my business, raising my little brother and working full-time.

It wasn't until many years later, while working an unfulfilling job, that a few of my co-workers finally convinced me to take another shot at pursuing the education I had given up so long ago. They encouraged me to take the GED test and continue my education by going to college. Over and over I would say, "yeah, yeah, I'll get it," until one day I realized where my life was heading. I was tired of working all of the time and accomplishing nothing of what I wanted.

Getting my GED wasn't easy, even though the seed had been planted in my mind; I was still hesitant to take my next step. When I finally took the leap and took the test I was really surprised to find out that I had passed all but the math. Although I was feeling disappointed, I decided to enroll in a GED math program. In my class, there were people of all ages. The teacher was amazing, and cared deeply for all of her students. She would constantly tell us that we could pass the test and that she was sure that we'd all had to overcome harder things in life. This hit home for me. I had run into so many road blocks throughout my life but kept figuring out a way around them—all I had to do was figure out a way around this one. I knew at that moment, that if I worked hard enough, I could pass the test. It was her positive attitude that would take all of us on the road to success. A few months later I took the test and passed. I was in complete and utter shock. I had never realized how encouraging it was to have someone take the time to help me toward such an achievement.

The following spring, I enrolled at Nassau Community College. My heart dropped when I went to take the placement exam. I wanted to do well, but I didn't understand most of the questions that were on it. I placed into the Basic Education Program, which was a good first step, but because I had high expectations, it left me feeling discouraged. I just kept thinking that I was not smart enough. But, ultimately, I had a drive, and I decided to do whatever it would take to change my life and my education. I no longer needed to listen to teachers to validate me or my decisions. While teachers are an important part of my life, I have learned to not tie my feelings of success to their opinions. My self-esteem and confidence have grown because of this insight. My work was going to be for me, and my life was going to be my own.

Come September, I went to my classes and couldn't believe the experience I'd had. My professors were wonderful. They offered every ounce of help that they could give and became a strong support system for me, one that I never had before. My Writing professor was particularly encouraging to me. For all of the years I had spent doubting my ability to excel in school, she would read my work and make a point to tell me how well I was doing. She offered me positive feedback and would constantly find ways to improve my self-esteem. In her, I finally found what I was missing—a person who cared and who was committed to helping me. Because I had such encouraging professors, I was able to skip out of the Basic Education Program and earn credits as a full-fledged student.

When I started classes the following semester I was more overwhelmed than ever before. I could not believe that I was finally a college freshman. I continued to doubt my abilities, but the strong group of professors that I've had the pleasure of working with kept reassuring me that I could achieve my dreams. One professor in particular stood out to me. Unlike many of my teachers in the past, who had never demanded my respect or expected anything from me in return, this professor put me on an even playing field. She didn't care if I, or anyone else, was on a different level—she expected the same quality of work from all of us. For the first time in my life I felt like a real student, not just a body getting pushed along from one class to the next. It was her inspiration that has gotten me to do the work I'm doing now.

In college, I have realized that I have a passion to learn—maybe it's because I have had the most incredible professors, or maybe it's because I have grown up and have begun to understand my life in a way that I hadn't before. I now understand my experiences as having been impacted by larger, dysfunctional systems. Every year students are lost to emotional turmoil and teachers, with an ever-increasing need to raise test scores, are not emotionally connected to their students, resulting in unhealthy educational relationships.

Reflecting on that blank index card I encountered back in high school, I can only wonder how things might have been different if that teacher had noticed its blankness. If she had seen that I had nothing to write, and instead of, perhaps, assuming it was the act of a lazy or apathetic student, had asked why I'd left the card blank. Now, I can only make assumptions. Maybe my teacher was having a bad day. Or maybe like my 5th grade teacher who humiliated me in front of the entire class, she was untrained or uneducated about the emotional needs of her students. Maybe she just didn't care. Regardless of the reason, I now feel the need to speak about, not only the expectations that teachers have for their students, but in return, the expectations, we as students, have of our educators.

Choosing to Read Critically Questions

1. Who is Perez's audience, and what, do you think, is the point of this piece?
2. In your own words, describe the turning point in Perez's academic life.
3. Evaluate Perez's use of Mike Rose's book *Lives on the Boundary.* Why does she quote from Rose, and what, if anything, does it contribute to the article overall?
4. Evaluate Perez's tone. Do you find it effective?

Choosing to Respond Questions

1. Perez's article might be categorized as a "literacy memoir" or a first-person narrative of how an individual develops as a reader and writer. Using Perez's work as a model, write your own literacy memoir, describing your educational experiences generally and focusing in on crucial moments in your academic life.
2. In groups of three or four, discuss Perez's article. Do members of the group see any of their own experiences reflected here? If not, what do they think of the situations she describes? A scribe should take notes on each member's response to share with the entire class.

Wide Awake to Connections Questions

1. Conduct research into the philosophies and practices of vocational schools today. Are there effective and appropriate vocational high schools or, as Perez suggests, are vocational schools "dumping grounds" for "problem" students? Write an essay in which you define and evaluate vocational schools; if necessary, provide recommendations for improving the situation.

2. Imagine you are the principal of an elementary school and you are writing a report for new teachers, outlining for them some of the most effective and least effective teaching practices. Drawing on the above article, as well as Mike Rose's "Finding Our Way: The Experience of Education" and/ or John Taylor Gatto's "The Seven-Lesson Schoolteacher" (both included in this chapter), compose your thesis-driven report providing teachers with guidelines for dealing with their students.

Luis J. Rodriguez, An Essay in "An Activists Forum: Countertales"

>> Prereading Check-In

1. What was the racial or ethnic makeup of your high school? Did most of the people at your school have the same background as you do? Focusing on how racial/ethnic dynamics did or did not play a role, describe your educational experiences.

2. Do you believe that the schools an individual attends will determine his or her success in life? How and to what extent? (This is a big question, so you might choose to focus on just one aspect in your writing.)

Luis J. Rodriguez *(b. 1954) is a poet and essayist whose memoir* Always Running: La Vida Loca, Gang Days in L.A. (1994) *describes gang life in East Los Angeles. The following selection, which first appeared in William Ayers, Jean Ann Hunt, and Therese Quinn's anthology* Teaching for Social Justice *(1998) confronts some of the shortcomings of the public school system.*

An Essay in "An Activists Forum: Countertales"

There are messages in the classroom, overt and implied, that say more than all the lesson plans in the world. As a child, the messages I received amounted to this: I had little or no value in the larger scheme of things, except perhaps as a future factory worker, janitor, or prison inmate. If questioned, any teacher would probably deny this. But the net result would be the same.

My imagination and natural desire for learning were squashed into a single concept. As a working-class son of Mexican immigrants following the known historical path of such sons, it would be difficult for me to overcome what was expected of me.

History is a powerful force. It's a history, I'm quite aware, of having been conquered, of coming from a poor developing nation, of having dark Indian skin that—at the core of this land—signifies inferiority (none of which, of course, is accurate).

I was expected to fail; moreover, this was my lot.

Sure there are exceptions. I know many Chicano college graduates; I have a brother-in-law who is a California state assemblyman. But they are usually considered special, different, unlike the rest of us.

I don't blame all teachers. It's never that easy. I had great teachers/mentors who helped me realize the powers I possessed for knowledge, for strategy, for speaking, and later, for writing.

And I understand things have changed since I was a child—although not by much.

Recently, my wife and I removed my eight-year-old son Ruben from the neighborhood school in our largely Latino community. In kindergarten, Ruben had forty-one classmates. The school was so overcrowded, children were forced to sit in cloakrooms. His teacher was a caring person; she was simply overwhelmed. The next two years weren't much better. In second grade, Ruben's teacher had placed his desk in a corner of the room, facing the wall, for four months! He had apparently misbehaved. But the teacher's reasoning for keeping him there was that "Ruben liked it." In fact, he was being socialized to remove himself, not to participate, eventually to fail. Whatever mistake he made had begun to be woven into an almost inescapable web.

After consulting the school manual, we discovered that such discipline could not be done without the parent's knowledge. Also, these measures had to be instructive, not punitive. In our mind, there were clear violations. However, the principal spent most of the time at our joint meeting justifying the teacher's action. The teacher was not our main concern here. Yet our son's well-being seemed to be the least critical aspect as we adults worked out a convenient compromise.

I won't get into the other problems at the school (including preschool kids receiving bug bites from sitting in unclean bungalows, and teachers who called children out of their names, including one who had a habit of throwing keys at unruly students). To challenge the inequities, my wife along with other parents and concerned teachers contacted the media and later published a bilingual newsletter called "High Expectations." But with things worsening for our boy, we finally enrolled him at another school (with a focus on Native American culture). So far, he has done better.

The problem is this: The United States has long instituted multi-tiered schooling. Those families with money, in private schools or in public schools with high property tax rates, have for the most part the best teachers, resources, and "messages" that say you can and will succeed (which has its own problems). Working-class families, particularly in depressed urban and rural communities, have to endure lower levels of education that in the past ran the gamut of slave schools, segregated schools (including Indian boarding schools), and tracking.

This can be overcome, but we must do it for all children, not only the exceptional few. I ask of teachers and administrators: What messages are prevailing in your classrooms? For any child, the proper and consistent nurturing of their capacities for greatness makes all the difference in the world.

To me, this is the social justice in education for the new millennium.

Choosing to Read Critically Questions

1. Explain what you think Rodriguez means in stating that education is "the social justice issue for the new millennium."
2. What kinds of "messages" do schools send, according to Rodriguez? You may want to focus on what Rodriguez says about his son Ruben's experiences at school.
3. What is Rodriguez's tone? Did you find it compelling?
4. Why does Rodriguez begin with a discussion of his own educational experiences? Did you find this discussion interesting and effective? Why or why not?

Choosing to Respond Questions

1. What messages do you feel you received in school? Be as specific as possible in your response. You may also want to consider whether or not you feel your race or gender or any other personal characteristic influenced the ways your teachers responded to you.
2. Do you agree with Rodriguez that education is a "social justice issue"? Building on your answer to Reading Question #1, compose an essay in which you take a position on this question.

Wide Awake to Connections Questions

1. Rodriguez briefly mentions Indian boarding schools in this selection. Conduct some research about these schools. When did they exist, what was their purpose (stated or implicit), and what is their legacy today?

2. Choosing to Respond Question #2 asks you to evaluate Rodriguez's claim that education is a social justice issue. Drawing on your answer, as well as one or two articles from this or any other chapter in this reader, discuss the concept of social justice, what you perceive as pressing social justice issues in the 21st century, and how the various issues presented in this textbook (for example, education, the environment, accessibility) might be interrelated.

Joseph B. Tulman, "Time to Reverse the School-to-Prison Pipeline"

›› Prereading Check-In

1. Drawing on your own experiences and observations, describe how schools currently discipline students who display disruptive behavior. Do you think such measures are effective? Why or why not?

2. What have you heard about "zero tolerance" policies in schools? What are the benefits of "zero tolerance"? What are some of the potential problems?

Director of the University of the District of Columbia's David A. Clarke School of Law's Juvenile and Special Education Law Clinic, **Joseph B. Tulman** *(b. 1954) has worked as a lawyer for children in neglect and delinquency cases and has written extensively on special education advocacy and disability rights. The following article, which argues that understanding students' special education needs might help us to better understand and disrupt the "school-to-prison pipeline," appeared in March 2008's* Policy & Practice.

"Time to Reverse the School-to-Prison Pipeline"

Exactly 26 years ago, I began representing "Ronald," my first delinquency client. A child with at least a dozen prior cases, Ronald was prepared to stand alone as a judge ruled on pretrial detention. Ronald's mother was unavailable; his father, unknown. I asked Ronald who might come down to stand with him. He offered the name of a teacher. The teacher helped convince the judge that Ronald was on the right path, getting individualized special education services, including counseling and other related services, in a program for children with serious emotional disturbance and learning disabilities. I kept up with Ronald for a few years. Notwithstanding remarkably difficult life circumstances, he was staying out of trouble and working as a bicycle messenger.

I didn't absorb the lesson of Ronald's case until I had met and represented hundreds of similarly situated children. I learned that the vast majority of children in the delinquency system have unmet—and often undiagnosed—special education needs. On one occasion, I asked a room full of juvenile probation officers how many of them were supervising any children who were reading at grade level. No hands went up.

Studies suggest that approximately 70 percent of incarcerated children have education-related disabilities that qualify them for services under the Individuals with Disabilities Education Improvement Act. I have never seen, however, a study in which researchers randomly selected a statistically significant percentage of children in a juvenile prison and then evaluated them for special education eligibility. Based upon that kind of study, I would bet on a finding of over 90 percent eligibility.

I have asked the law students whom I supervise to excavate the school histories of our delinquency clients. Predictably, we find that these children gained little traction in elementary school and started to slip into tardiness, truancy, and disciplinary exclusions in middle school. Most were out of step with school and were fully engaged with the delinquency system by 15 or 16.

In the 1990s, two national trends accelerated the effects of the "school-to-prison pipeline." Forty-nine states and the District of Columbia changed their laws to try more children in criminal court and incarcerate more children in adult jails and prisons. During the same time period, school suspensions and expulsions rose dramatically as a consequence of national, state, and local zero-tolerance policies.

A few years ago, I observed a delinquency system in which two-thirds of new delinquency court referrals were from public schools. Old-timers in the court confided that these cases—school fights and the like—would never have penetrated the delinquency court "when we were kids." Furthermore, the delinquency judge pointed out that the children referred were virtually all African American, and the judge concluded ruefully that the net effect was a steady resegregation of the public schools. Across the country, the vast majority of children in the delinquency system are children of color who come from low-income and indigent families. Disproportionate minority contact and confinement is pervasive. Minority children and children with disabilities are disproportionately excluded from schools through disciplinary actions.

The time has come to reverse the "School-to-Prison Pipeline." State and local governments could save money, improve outcomes for at-risk youth and families, and make communities safer by providing appropriate special education, mental health, and related services. The surgeon general's Report on Youth Violence, published in January 2001, provides ample evidence of community-based alternatives to incarceration that are effective. Missouri has abolished large-scale juvenile incarceration facilities, relying instead on community-based services. When incarceration is necessary, they confine children in small, treatment-oriented facilities. Recidivism rates in Missouri have declined to single digits, and administrators around the country are noticing that the "Missouri Model" is working. Moreover, in late November 2007, the U.S. Centers for Disease Control and Prevention released a study concluding that sending children to the adult criminal system increases crime. Youth tried as adults are, on average, one-third more likely to recidivate than youth who remain in the delinquency system.

What is preventing policymakers from pushing the pendulum back? One factor is the lack of coordination between agencies (i.e., the failure to create systems of care). School personnel, child welfare caseworkers, probation officers, and others, shift children from more mainstreamed systems to deep-end systems in order, ostensibly, to obtain services for those children. A social worker or teacher juggling too many "difficult" kids and "needy" families triages by sending the most draining cases to expensive inpatient placements and detention centers. Members of public school multidisciplinary teams aren't budgeted to add intensive services to children's individualized educational programs. Administrators fail to maximize federal Medicaid reimbursement for services. The result is drop-outs, push-outs, and, in a few instances, children who end up in expensive residential treatment centers. More frequently, these children get locked up.

Based upon the U.S. Supreme Court's Burlington decision and provisions of the Individuals with Disabilities Education Improvement Act, the law students whom I supervise often persuade hearing officers to order private school placements for our clients. Remarkably, though, our clients would be happy to attend their neighborhood schools if they could receive there the specialized instruction and individualized services that lead to success. Meanwhile, I have learned from Ronald and my other clients that I can help them stay out of prison by getting them into appropriate special education programs.

Choosing to Read Critically Questions

1. What does Tulman mean when he describes students as "fully engaged with the delinquency system by 15 or 16"?
2. In your own words, describe the "Missouri Model."
3. Why does Tulman bring up Ronald's story at the beginning and the end of the article? Did you find this effective?
4. Circle or otherwise identify areas in which Tulman uses facts and statistics. Did you find these statistics convincing and compelling? Why or why not?

Choosing to Respond Questions

1. Were you surprised by the information provided here? In particular, what do you think of Tulman's claim that "Minority children and children with disabilities are disproportionately excluded from schools through disciplinary actions"?
2. Tulman discusses "two trends" that have led to higher rates of incarceration for young people. Explain what they are, what they were designed to accomplish, and why Tulman sees them as problematic.

Wide Awake to Connections Questions

1. Research the "school-to-prison pipeline." Write an essay in which you describe and evaluate the situation and then describe and evaluate programs and efforts to dismantle the school-to-prison pipeline. You might find the websites of The Advancement Project and the ACLU helpful; in

addition, you might peruse the articles available through UCLA's Civil Rights Projects as well as newspaper articles and editorials on this topic.

2. Drawing on this article and another article from Chapter 9, "Disability Studies," discuss the ramifications of Tulman's statement that "Studies suggest that approximately 70 percent of incarcerated children have education-related disabilities that qualify them for services under the Individuals with Disabilities Education Improvement Act." How might better special education programs and services lower the rates of incarcerated children?

Mike Rose, "Finding Our Way: The Experience of Education"

>> Prereading Check-In

1. Describe one positive educational experience or outcome during any of your time in school.

2. Do you agree that the schools exist, in part, to train individuals to become "good citizens"? Explain what you think a good citizen is and explain why you agree or disagree.

Educator and scholar **Mike Rose** *(b. 1944), whose books include* The Mind At Work: Valuing the Intelligence of the American Worker *(2004),* Possible Lives: The Promise of Public Education in America *(1995),* Lives on the Boundary *(1989), and* Why School? *(2009), from which the following excerpt is taken, has written extensively about the experiences of working-class students in academic settings. In the following article, Rose argues that education is valuable for promoting students' intellectual and personal growth.*

"Finding Our Way: The Experience of Education"

A good education helps us make sense of the world and find our way in it.

We are driven—as surely as we are driven to survive—to find meaning in our lives, to interpret what befalls us, the events that swirl around us, the people who cross our paths, the objects and rhythms of the natural world. We do this instinctively; it is essential to being human. So we do it with or without education.

But we are getting educated all the time, of course: by family, community, teachers, pals, bullies, and saints. Our education can be as formal as a lesson or as informal as a lesson learned. This [selection] focuses on education that happens in the schoolhouse, the college classroom, the apprenticeship. Education that the culture deems important enough to support and organize.

The question "Why go to school?" has been central to the way I make a living and define myself. And my own coming-of-age—my own journey from hardship to professional security—was made possible by a series of gifted and committed teachers. So I have lived this question about education as well as reflected on it.

We educate for a number of reasons, and people have written about them since the first decades of the republic: to pass on traditions and knowledge, to prepare the young for democratic life, to foster moral and intellectual growth, to enable individual and societal economic prosperity. All are legitimate, and a good education fosters each of them. But I'm interested here in the experience of education when it's done well with the student's well-being in mind. The unfortunate thing is that there is nothing in the standard talk about schooling—and this has been true for decades—that leads us to consider how school is perceived by those who attend it. Yet it is our experience of an institution that determines our attitude toward it, affects what we do with it, the degree to which we integrate it into our lives, into our sense of who we are. We need to pay attention to the experience of going to school.

Because education became such a source of meaning in my own life— saved it really—I've been attuned to the different ways children give expression to the sense that a particular teacher's classroom is a good place for them: "She's teaching us how to do things we couldn't do before." "Math'll take you a long way in life." "This room is something positive." I've heard this kind of thing in shop classes: New tools "will enable me to do new things, and I'm excited." In college classrooms: "She has helped me to see things that were always there that I never noticed." In graduate seminars: "I'm learning these habits of mind that are helping me write what I want to write." In literacy and job training programs: "Formal schooling will help me survive in the future." "I admire and respect knowledge, and those that have it are well blessed." "I thank God to be able to seek the dream I want."

Let me bring this home by reflecting on my own time in school, the kinds of things I learned, and the intimate relationship that developed between learning and my orientation in the world.

I've experienced classrooms as both places of flat disconnection and of growth and inspiration, and this mix has proved invaluable as I myself have gone on to teach. I grew up in a poor neighborhood in South Central Los Angeles; my father was quite ill and my mother kept us afloat by waiting tables. The schools I attended were not so great, and from my elementary grades well into high school I accumulated a spotty academic record and years of hazy disaffection. I was dreamy, unengaged, fearful of things that I didn't understand. But I was fortunate. Later in high school and during my first bumpy years at a small college, I met some teachers who had a lasting influence on the direction of my life. My best education came in the humanities and social sciences, but the gist of what I'm going to share could apply to a wide range of pursuits, from music to biology to crafts and trades.

The study of literature broadened my knowledge of the world. Much has been written about how fiction allows you to participate in imagined worlds. That was true for me, especially when I was younger and much in need of imaginative release, but over time the guided study of literature gave me something else as well. It fanned out to and fostered a knowledge of history—intellectual and social history particularly—philosophy, and art. Reading, let's say, European literature of the early twentieth century brought with it the era's social movements, the crisis in philosophy, the jolting color and form of expressionism and cubism. History then led to politics and economics—which, in turn, were given a human face through the novels I was reading. Abstractions about "political trends and economic forces" were embodied in the physical and emotional details of the French coal mine, the Chicago meatpacking house, the Nebraska prairie.

The study of psychology gave me a way to understand human behavior. If literature provided historical scope and sweep, psychology took me in close to motivation, perception, learning. I'm simplifying a bit here, for literature surely provides rich insight into human behavior. But my point is that psychology provided a system, a vocabulary to think about, for example, the precision as well as the fallibility of memory or the processes by which we organize information from sight or touch. And psychology gave me a set of perspectives with which to look back over my own life, the beliefs I absorbed growing up, the twists and turns of my development.

Both the humanities and social sciences provided a set of tools to think with. Reading and writing are the megatools. Though I was fortunate to learn to read and write in elementary school—read pretty well, write so-so—it wasn't until my reading and writing were put to use in substantial and meaningful ways that they became more powerful, weighty, and developed critical depth. I learned to search for and synthesize information, to systematically analyze it, to develop an argument with it. Learning to argue in a systematic way is quite a complex skill, and the various disciplines I was exposed to provided help here as well. There are the different ways philosophers or statisticians argue a point, how a literary critic draws on selections of text to support a claim, the questions an experimental psychologist raises about someone's research methodology, and so on. These tools of inquiry, debated and developed over time, carry with them principles of implementation, an ethics of practice, a right and wrong way to do things. They provided me with the means to probe the world and to push back on others' interpretation of it.

Reading and writing gave me skills to create with and to act on the world. The endless writing of papers—and the reading that accompanied them—over time, with feedback from teachers, enabled me to develop skill as a writer. This skill was tested in classrooms and seminar rooms: pretty esoteric stuff, like a high school paper on Conrad's use of imagery in *Heart of Darkness*, and a college paper on sociological theories of alienation. But through assignments like these I was learning how to marshal evidence and frame an argument. And I was also becoming more adept at handling a sentence, folding information into it, making a complex point without losing the reader. These skills played out again and again on different topics and in different settings, leading to the ability to write a research article, a memo advocating a course of action, a newspaper opinion piece, an essay like the present one.

Acquiring and using knowledge brings its own pleasures. It just feels good to know things and to use what you know. And knowledge of something, baseball to mathematics, heightens your appreciation of it. Also, once you develop an interest in a topic, you want to know more. It has been that way with me about a number of things I was introduced to in school—including the topic of learning itself. My first psychology course in learning was based on laboratory studies; subsequent courses in education explored learning in classrooms, closer to the tutoring and teaching I was beginning to do myself. Over time I was guided to related topics: cross-cultural studies of cognition, neuroscience, and "everyday cognition"—the thinking involved in child rearing, cooking, figuring out what's wrong with a faulty lamp. The acquisition of this knowledge began in school and led outward, a divining rod to the pleasures of the invitingly new.

All the foregoing helped me develop a sense of myself as knowledgeable and capable of using what I know. This is a lovely and powerful quality—cognitive, emotional, and existential all in one. It has to do with identity and agency, with how we define ourselves, not only in matters academic but also in the way we interact with others and with institutions. It has to do with how we move through our economic and civic lives. Education gave me the competence and confidence to independently seek out information and make decisions, to advocate for myself and my parents and those I taught, to probe political issues, to resist simple answers to messy social problems, to assume that I could figure things out and act on what I learned. In a sense, this was the best training I could have gotten for vocation and citizenship.

Choosing to Read Critically Questions

1. What does Rose mean when he describes reading and writing as "megatools"?
2. What do you think the title of this piece means, and how does it relate to Rose's larger point?
3. Evaluate Rose's use of personal history and experience in this selection.
4. What is Rose's purpose in writing this? What do you think he is advocating for and do you find yourself convinced?

Choosing to Respond Questions

1. Rose writes, "Reading and writing gave me skills to create with and to act on the world." Explain what Rose means and respond to his idea that these skills can be empowering. Have you used reading and writing in order to "act" on or in the world? How? Why or why not?

2. In paragraph 5, Rose describes some of the reasons given for education: "to pass on traditions and knowledge, to prepare the young for democratic life, to foster moral and intellectual growth, to enable individual and societal economic prosperity." Choose one or two of these reasons and examine them. Do you believe this is a purpose of education? Should it be? How does education facilitate the development of these traits or the achievement of these goals?

Wide Awake to Connections Questions

1. Interview some students about their experiences of school. These students may be your peers or, if you have access to students in elementary or high school, younger students. Why do they go to school? What are they learning? What would they like to learn? Synthesize your findings in an essay.
2. Compose an essay in which you put Rose's work in dialogue with that of Nel Noddings, whose "Place and Nature" is excerpted in Chapter 11 of this book, who argues that students should be taught, among other things, "love of place." In your essay, address any overlaps between these two authors' essays, as well as differences in their ideas.

Anya Kamenetz, "Adapt or Decline"

>> Prereading Check-In

1. Have you ever taken a class online? If yes, please describe your experience. If not, explain whether and why you would or wouldn't try online education.
2. What, beyond job training, does a college education provide? What should it provide?

Anya Kamenetz *(b. 1980), a columnist for* Fast Company *magazine and a former columnist for the* Village Voice, *has written two books:* Generation Debt: The New Economics of Being Young *(2006) and* DIY U: Edupunks, Edupreneurs, and the Coming Transformation of American Education *(2010), from which the following is adapted, and two ebooks,* The Edupunks Guide *(2011) and* Learning, Freedom, and the Web *(2011). In the following excerpt, Kamenetz traces the development of college as we know it, highlighting some of the most pressing problems in higher education today.*

"Adapt or Decline"

In a faraway colony, one in a thousand people—mostly young, rich, white men—are sent to live in isolated, rural Christian communes. Some are pious, learned, ambitious; others are unruly younger sons with no other prospects. The students spend hours every day in chapel; every few years, the entire community is seized by a several-days-long religious revival.

They also get into lots of trouble. In their meager barracks they drink, gamble, and duel. They brawl, sometimes exchanging bullets, with local residents, and bother local women. Occasionally they rebel and are expelled en masse or force administrators to resign. Overseen by low-paid clergymen too deaf or infirm to control a congregation, hazed by older students, whipped for infractions of the rules, they're treated like young boys when their contemporaries might be married with children. And, oh yes, they spend a few hours a day in rote memorization of fewer than a dozen subjects.

This was the typical 18th century American college, loosely modeled on England's Oxford and Cambridge, which date to the 13th century. Nine colleges were founded in the colonies before the Revolution, and they're all still in business: Harvard, William and Mary, Yale, Princeton, Columbia, Penn, Brown, Rutgers, and Dartmouth.

For universities, history is authority. It's no accident that America's most prestigious institution, Harvard, is also its oldest, or that some of the oldest organizations of any kind, worldwide, are universities.

Surveying the history of American colleges and universities with a jaundiced eye convinces me that many aspects of the current so-called crisis in higher education are actually just characteristics of the institution. It has always been socially exclusionary. It has always been of highly variable quality educationally. It has always had a tendency to expand. In fact, it is precisely because we are always asking more and more of education at all levels that its failures appear so tremendous.

Still, the United States does seem to have reached an impasse today, given escalating demand for higher education, spiraling costs, and limited resources. Unlike the 1860s and unlike the 1960s, there is little national will to grow our way out of this problem by founding more colleges or spending much more money on the ones we do have. Is this merely one more symptom of national decline? Have we hit some kind of natural limit for an educated population? Or is there a mismatch between the structures of the past and the needs of the present?

America can't remain a global economic powerhouse while it slides to the middle of the heap in education. Nor can we grapple with the challenges we face as a global community without meeting the world's burgeoning demand for education. Nor can college leaders get away with claiming that their hands are tied and only more taxpayer and tuition dollars can solve their problems.

There are two basic options the way I see it: fundamentally change the way higher education is delivered, or resign ourselves to never having enough of it.

The good news is that all over the world people are thinking big about how to change higher education. Brick, stone, and marble institutions with centuries of prestige behind them are increasingly being joined by upstarts, both nonprofit and for-profit, and even more loosely organized communities of educational practitioners and apprentices.

The open courseware movement started at the Massachusetts Institute of Technology in 2001, when the school decided to put its coursework online for free. Today, you can go online to MIT OpenCourseware and find the full syllabuses, lecture notes, class exercises, tests, and some video and audio for 1,900 courses, nearly every one MIT offers, from physics to art history. As of March 2010, 65 million people from virtually every country on Earth have raided this trove.

Open educational content is just the beginning. Want a personalized, adaptive computer tutor to teach you math or French? A class on your iPhone that's structured like an immersive role-playing game? An accredited bachelor's degree, in six months, for a few thousand dollars? A free, peer-to-peer Wikiuniversity? These all exist today, the beginnings of a complete educational remix. Do-It-Yourself University means the expansion of education beyond classroom walls: free, open-source, networked, experiential, and self-directed learning.

This opening world presents huge questions about the true nature of a college education: questions that are legitimate even when they are raised with self-interest by traditional educators.

. . . The "multiversity," as it was dubbed by the University of California president Clark Kerr in 1963, clumps teaching with research, vocational and technical education with liberal arts, sports, clubs, and parties with intellectual life, accreditation and evaluation with mentoring and friendship. For students "college" means very different things at different times: the place to grow up, be out on your own, make friends, take leadership roles, prepare for and find a good job, and even learn.

Technology upsets the traditional hierarchies and categories of education. It can put the learner at the center of the educational process. Increasingly this means students will decide what they want to learn, when, where, and with whom, and they will learn by doing. Functions that have long hung together, like research and teaching, learning and assessment, or content, skills, accreditation, and socialization, can be delivered separately.

There's no good way to measure the benefits of the old-fashioned face-to-face educational model; there's worry that something important will be discarded in the race ahead. More fundamentally, no one knows if it's possible to extend the benefits of higher education to the majority of a population without diluting its essence. But those are questions that educators ought to be testing and investigating rigorously. College leaders who want to be on the right side of history won't hold stubbornly to the four-year, classroom-hour-based "butts-in-seats, nose-to-nose, face to face" model as the only way to provide the benefits of a liberal arts education. They will innovate to meet students wherever they are, and they will reinvent assessment to provide much better transparency about what students are learning.

Here are four trends guiding this transformation, as they might look from the point of view of college leaders:

1. **The 80/20 Rule.** Is your institution part of the leading-edge 20 percent? How will you attract and serve the "nontraditional" student who is the new norm? Most of the growth in higher education over the next century will come from the 85 percent of students who are "nontraditional" in some way—older, working adults, or ethnic minorities. They will increasingly attend the 80 percent of institutions that are nonselective. This includes most mainstream public universities and particularly community colleges and for-profit colleges, which saw the sharpest growth in the 2000s.

   For-profit colleges are the only U.S. institutions that have both the resources and the mission to seriously expand their numbers in the foreseeable future. Community colleges already enroll half of all undergraduates. Both disproportionately enroll the demographic groups that dominate the next generation of Americans: Hispanics, all other minority groups, and first-generation college students. Some of the boldest thinking is happening in institutions that are far from the ideal of either the multiversity or the colonial "little college." Yet, they typically lack the opportunity for undergraduates to participate in original research, not to mention many of the intangibles of college life like dorms and extracurriculars. Concerns about quality and affordability in the new mainstream of higher education have to be addressed head-on. The answer is not for established institutions to exclude the upstarts from the conversation.

2. **The Great Unbundling.** Which services and departments are core to your mission? Where can you partner, outsource, or pool resources across the state, the nation, or the world for greater efficiency? Universities have historically combined many social, educational, and other benefits in one-stop shopping. Increasingly, some of these resources (e.g., faculty time) are strained, while others (like written course content) are approaching a marginal cost of zero.

As it has with industries from music to news, the logic of digital technology will compel institutions to specialize and collaborate, find economies of scale and avoid duplications.

Books can be freed from the printed page, courses freed from geographical classrooms and individual faculty, and students freed from bureaucratic obstacles to transferring course credit between institutions, or designing their own courses of study.

Could any of your departments flourish on its own? Stripped-down institutions that focus on instruction or assessment only, or on a particular discipline or area, will find more and more audience. The most cutting-edge sciences and the most traditional liberal arts can both flourish in a specialized, concentrated, and technologically enhanced setting. I have seen professors elevate the craft of teaching rhetoric, composition, and critical thinking to new heights using social media and applying cutting-edge research about learning.

3. **Techno-hybridization.** Are distance learning decisions confined to the IT office? Are you creating online courses through a cheap, hands-off

process, or are you experimenting across disciplines with the best ways to integrate online and offline experiences? How can you identify and support your internal innovators among faculty? Department of Education research shows that a blend of technology-assisted and traditional class instruction works better than either one alone. This blending can occur with institutions enrolling students on campus or off, in classrooms or online—studies have shown that students do a better job collaborating online if they meet in person even once.

4. **Personal Learning Networks and Paths.** How well does your college serve the transfer, dropout, and nontraditional student? How easy do you make it for students to design their own experiences? People who graduate from high school at 18 and go straight through four years of college are already a tiny minority of all young Americans, around one in ten. Pulling America out of its educational slump requires designing programs flexible and supportive enough to reach the 44 percent of students who currently drop out of college and the 30 to 35 percent who drop out of high school. These programs have to provide socialization, personal development, and critical thinking skills, not just job training.

***

. . . Education is an essentially conservative enterprise. If we didn't believe that one generation had something important to transmit to the next, we wouldn't need education. So changing education makes lots of people nervous, especially school leaders whose salary comes from the old model.

Still, in an ideal world, we can agree that opportunities to stretch your abilities, test your personal mettle, follow your natural curiosity, and jam intellectually with friends, colleagues, and mentors—all the good stuff that is supposed to happen in college—would be more open to more people at all ages and transition points in life. Traditional colleges will continue to find plenty of eager applicants who want the experiences only they can provide.

The 80 percent of American college students who currently attend nonselective institutions will have many more options, and so will the majority of young people, those who drop out or who never apply. Alternatives to the four-year bachelor's degree will get more visible and acceptable, which might help bridge one of the biggest social divides in American life. Tuition costs would reach sane levels due to increased use of technology, true competition, and better-allocated federal and state incentives. This would lower one of the most important barriers to educational access.

By modifying the economics of the nation's second largest industry, we'd save money, and tap the resources and energy of a whole new generation to tackle challenges like building a greener society, expanding the middle class, creating better jobs, and providing people with health care. Whether these incipient changes will lead to that kind of positive transformation, however, still hangs in the balance.

It depends largely on whether the guardians of existing institutions embrace transformation, or let history pass them by.

Choosing to Read Critically Questions

1. In your own words, explain what Kamenetz means when she writes in paragraph 5 that "it is precisely because we are always asking more and more of education at all levels that its failures appear so tremendous."

2. Kamenetz suggests that higher education is at a crossroads. In your own words, explain how Kamenetz thinks colleges and universities should change.

3. Evaluate the opening of this article. Were you surprised when it is revealed that Kamenetz is describing college life in the 18th century? Why or why not?

4. Using evidence from the article to back up your answer, explain who you think Kamenetz's audience is. To whom is she writing?

Choosing to Respond Questions

1. Does Kamenetz's description of the college experience, as one that offers a student "opportunities to stretch your abilities, test your personal mettle, follow your natural curiosity, and jam intellectually with friends, colleagues, and mentors" resonate with you? Has this been your experience in college? If yes, provide examples. If no, describe what you have experienced and examine why you haven't had the chance to participate in the kinds of activities Kamenetz describes.

2. What does "DIY" mean generally? How is it usually used, and how is Kamenetz using it here? What are some of the possibilities and/or contradictions of having a "DIY University"?

Wide Awake to Connections Questions

1. Find, read, and evaluate Kamenetz's *The Edupunks Guide* (it is available for free online). Did you find the ebook useful, interesting, or inspiring? Using specific quotes and details, explain your reaction to Kamenetz's work.

2. Kamenetz writes that "Technology upsets the traditional hierarchies and categories of education." Drawing on Kamenetz's work, as well as one or two articles from Chapter 13, write an essay exploring if, how, and why technology can radically transform political, educational, or social practices and institutions.

QUESTIONS AND SUGGESTIONS FOR FURTHER RESEARCH AND WRITING

1. Drawing on two or three of the selections in this chapter, compose a thesis-driven essay in which you identify and discuss some of the most pressing issues in American education today. In addition to using the articles, you may choose to watch a documentary such as 2010's *Waiting for Superman, The Elephant on Campus* (available online) or 2009's *The Providence Effect.*

2. A number of writers and viewers have observed similarities between Plato's "Allegory of the Cave" and the popular movie *The Matrix* (1999), which explores the idea that we are all walking around unaware of "reality." Other films have also explored this subject. Write an essay in which you develop a contemporary application for Plato's work. This may mean that you find another film or text from popular culture that you feel in some ways speaks to Plato's work or you identify an analogous situation in your own life or in American life in general that you feel can be better understood if discussed alongside an explication of Plato's work. Alternatively, you might choose a selection from this textbook that you feel can be better understood if it is discussed in light of Plato's work.

3. Conduct research into the laws surrounding access to education for individuals with disabilities. Your essay might have a historical focus (tracing the changes in the past several decades) or it might be argumentative (forwarding a point about the past or current state of affairs). In addition, you may draw on your own experiences and observations if you so choose.

4. A number of films deal with educational experiences, including *Dead Poet's Society* (1989), *Mona Lisa Smile* (2003), *Good Will Hunting* (1997), *Lean on Me* (1989), *Dangerous Minds* (1995), and *Freedom Writers* (2007).

   Choose one or two films to analyze. What do contemporary American movies suggest about the state of education in America? What kinds of solutions to educational obstacles do these films propose? Do you find these films realistic? Why or why not? As you compose your essay, remember to use specific details from the film. This means that you should not only bring in specific verbal quotes, but also details including soundtrack, lighting, and camera angles, as evidence for your claims.

5. Think about what a "democratic college campus" might look like. First, research the meaning and usage of the word "democracy" and make sure that you clearly define your terms early in the essay. (A helpful source might be Richard Sclove's *Democracy and Technology*. In addition, you might choose to refer to Chapter 11 of this textbook and to plan your campus so that it will be "green" as well). To broaden your perspective and gain insights, interview some fellow students as well as education professionals about what a democratic college campus would look like and how it would function. After collecting your data, use visual aids and written work to demonstrate how you would enact the principles of democracy in the design of your campus and, if you so choose, curriculum. You may choose to include your own argument concerning the state of your campus and any recommendations for changes you might have.

13 Chapter Thirteen

Social Networking:
The Promise and Pitfalls of a Web 3.0 World

>> **Prereading Check-In**

1. How important are the Internet, a cell phone, and/or text messaging to your social life?
2. Brainstorm: What impact has the development of the Internet had on individuals' lives?

As we enter the third decade of social networking, many writers have attempted to make sense of how and in what ways the Web has affected our lives, the way we think, and the way we interact with others. In a world in which celebrities tweet their whereabouts to their fans, in which texting among young people has replaced phoning, and in which upwards of 300 million people have Facebook accounts, human communication has undergone seismic shifts. These social media technologies contain both promise and danger: We are more connected to others around the globe than ever before, and we are also more likely to relinquish private information about ourselves, to anonymously attack others, or possibly to turn away from others and to wall ourselves in on the Web, pursuing only narrow personal interests.

These days, many of us think nothing of posting our thoughts online, texting messages to friends anytime, anywhere—even while driving, waiting in line at the post office, or sitting in a classroom—uploading pictures to public websites, and inviting people we have never spoken to or met face-to-face to "friend" us. How, then, do we maintain or exert control over these rapidly changing media? Should we even try?

The pieces chosen for this unit range from discussions of privacy to the use of personal information to the profound cultural changes that the Internet has engendered, encouraging you to think critically about how you use social media technologies as well as what impact the use of these technologies has on you, your sense of identity, your community, and the larger world.

Herbert Marshall McLuhan, from *Understanding Media*

❯❯ Prereading Check-In

1. Consider if and how you interact differently with individuals in face-to-face situations as opposed to in cyber-situations, such as Facebook, texting, or Twitter. (If you don't use these technologies, you may use talking on the telephone as your example.)

2. In general, do you see the explosion of social networking sites as a positive or a negative development? Explain your answer.

One of the most important figures in the development of media theory, **Herbert Marshall McLuhan** *(1911–1980) is credited with coining the term "global village" and with famously writing that "the medium is the message." The following brief excerpt from McLuhan's* Understanding Media *(1962) invites readers to consider how communications technologies alter familiar experiences.*

From *Understanding Media*

The telephone: speech without walls.
The phonograph: music hall without walls.
The photograph: museum without walls.
The electric light: space without walls.
The movie, radio, and TV: classroom without walls.

Choosing to Read Critically Questions

1. What do you think McLuhan means when he writes "telephone: speech without walls"?

2. Explain what McLuhan means when he writes "movie, radio, and TV: classroom without walls."

3. What does the colon (:) suggest about the relationship between the terms on each side (i.e., "telephone: speech without walls")?

4. What effect does this selection have on you? Why do you think it is written this way?

Choosing to Respond Questions

1. Building on your answer to Choosing to Read Critically Question #2, respond to McLuhan's statement, "movie, radio, and TV: classroom without walls." Would you add Internet to the list? Why or why not?

2. As mentioned above, McLuhan famously wrote that the "medium is the message." By medium, McLuhan indicates the means by which the message is communicated; i.e., the television is the "medium" or the book is the "medium." According to McLuhan, a cartoon, for example, asks the viewer to participate in making meaning, while a movie might allow a viewer to be passive. It is how the content or message is conveyed that influences how the viewer interacts with and understands the content. Building on this idea, brainstorm and discuss what you think the "message" of mediums such as the Internet or social networking sites are.

Wide Awake to Connections Questions

1. Read the first chapter of McLuhan's book *Understanding Media*. Summarize the ideas McLuhan presents and respond. Is McLuhan's work still relevant today? If so, how can we apply his ideas to our understanding of the Internet?

2. Using one or two articles from Chapter 12 of this book ("American Education"), further discuss McLuhan's contention that communications media such as television and radio are the new "classroom without walls." In addition, you might ask whether or not you feel that social networking can serve educational purposes. Explain your ideas.

Damien Pearse, "Facebook's 'Dark' Side: Study Finds Link to Socially Aggressive Narcissism"

>> **Prereading Check-In**

1. Do you belong to a social networking site such as Facebook? Why or why not?

2. How important do you think it is that a person or child develops high self-esteem?

Damien Pearse *is a reporter for the* Guardian *newspaper. In the following article, Pearse describes recent findings suggesting that social networking might foster narcissism.*

"Facebook's 'Dark' Side: Study Finds Link to Socially Aggressive Narcissism"

Researchers have established a direct link between the number of friends you have on Facebook and the degree to which you are a "socially disruptive" narcissist, confirming the conclusions of many social media skeptics.

People who score highly on the Narcissistic Personality Inventory questionnaire had more friends on Facebook, tagged themselves more often, and updated their newsfeeds more regularly.

The research comes amid increasing evidence that young people are becoming increasingly narcissistic and obsessed with self-image and shallow friendships.

The latest study, published in the journal *Personality and Individual Differences*, also found that narcissists responded more aggressively to derogatory comments made about them on the social networking site's public walls and changed their profile pictures more often.

A number of previous studies have linked narcissism with Facebook use, but this is some of the first evidence of a direct relationship between Facebook friends and the most "toxic" elements of narcissistic personality disorder.

Researchers at Western Illinois University studied the Facebook habits of 294 students, aged between 18 and 65, and measured two "socially disruptive" elements of narcissism—grandiose exhibitionism (GE) and entitlement/exploitativeness (EE).

GE includes "'self-absorption, vanity, superiority, and exhibitionistic tendencies" and people who score high on this aspect of narcissism need to be constantly at the center of attention. They often say shocking things and inappropriately self-disclose because they cannot stand to be ignored or waste a chance of self-promotion.

The EE aspect includes "a sense of deserving respect and a willingness to manipulate and take advantage of others."

The research revealed that the higher someone scored on aspects of GE, the greater the number of friends they had on Facebook, with some amassing more than 800.

Those scoring highly on EE and GE were also more likely to accept friend requests from strangers and seek social support, but less likely to provide it, according to the research.

Carol Craig, a social scientist and chief executive of the Center for Confidence and Well-being, said young people in Britain were becoming increasingly narcissistic, and Facebook provided a platform for the disorder.

"The way that children are being educated is focusing more and more on the importance of self esteem—on how you are seen in the eyes of others. This method of teaching has been imported from the United States and is 'all about me.'

"Facebook provides a platform for people to self-promote by changing profile pictures and showing how many hundreds of friends you have. I know of some who have more than 1,000."

Dr. Viv Vignoles, senior lecturer in social psychology at Sussex University, said there was "clear evidence" from studies in America that college students were becoming increasingly narcissistic.

But he added: "Whether the same is true of noncollege students or of young people in other countries, such as the United Kingdom, remains an open question, as far as I know.

"Without understanding the causes underlying the historical change in U.S. college students, we do not know whether these causes are factors that are relatively specific to American culture, such as the political focus on increasing self-esteem in the late 80s and early 90s or whether they are factors that are more general, for example, new technologies such as mobile phones and Facebook."

Vignoles said the correlational nature of the latest study meant it was difficult to be certain whether individual differences in narcissism led to certain patterns of Facebook behavior, whether patterns of Facebook behavior led to individual differences in narcissism, or a bit of both.

Christopher Carpenter, who ran the study, said: "In general, the 'dark side' of Facebook requires more research in order to better understand Facebook's socially beneficial and harmful aspects in order to enhance the former and curtail the latter.

"If Facebook is to be a place where people go to repair their damaged egos and seek social support, it is vitally important to discover the potentially negative communication one might find on Facebook and the kinds of people likely to engage in them. Ideally, people will engage in pro-social Facebooking rather than antisocial me-booking."

Choosing to Read Critically Questions

1. In your own words, describe the behaviors of individuals who display grandiose exhibitionism (GE) and entitlement/exploitativeness (EE).

2. Near the end of the article, Pearse includes Dr. Viv Vignoles' explanation of the "correlational nature of the study." Explain what correlation is and what Vignoles means.

3. Were you surprised by the information presented in this article? Why or why not?

4. Did you feel that the information was presented clearly in this article? Provide an example of a particularly strong or weak section of the essay and explain what you think worked well or didn't work well.

Choosing to Respond Questions

1. Do you feel that young people today are more narcissistic than in the past? Use specific examples to back up your contention.

2. Write a brief essay in which you weigh Facebook's beneficial and detrimental aspects. Announce your position in the first paragraph (i.e., "Although it has its problems, Facebook is a positive force in society."). In the second paragraph, present the counterargument and in the remaining paragraphs, lay out your evidence for how and why Facebook has a positive or a negative effect on society.

Wide Awake to Connections Questions

1. The article mentions Americans' emphasis on the importance of developing high self-esteem. Research "self-esteem" and American education and/or childhood. Have Americans overemphasized self-esteem? If yes, what should educators focus on instead?

2. Read the excerpt from Mark Bauerlein's *The Dumbest Generation* in this chapter and compose an essay in which you examine the possible negative effects of the Internet on education and learning.

Deanna Zandt, "Social Media: Peril + Promise"

>> Prereading Check-In

1. What are some of the potentially positive uses of social media? Can they and do they benefit society?

2. If you use social networking, do you find that you primarily associate with people like yourself online? That is, are most of your online relationships with people of the same age, racial or ethnic background, gender, or from the same geographical area as you are? Be as specific as possible in your answer.

Media consultant and technologist **Deanna Zandt** *is the author of*
Share This! How You Will Change the World with Social Networking
*(2010). In the following article, which was excerpted from her book
and which originally appeared on the website* In These Times, *Zandt
contends that social networking can have a positive effect on our world.*

"Social Media: Peril + Promise"

No doubt about it: Social networks have landed in our culture, and
they're planning to stay awhile. During late 2008 and early 2009,
Facebook doubled in size, growing from 100 million registered users to
200 million in eight months, and topped the 400 million mark by early
2010. Twitter's popularity also skyrocketed during 2009, jumping from
4.5 million visitors to more than 20 million.

And yet, for all those impressive numbers, and for all the horn-tootin'
over the disruptive and democratizing potential of the Internet, we're still
seeing the Big Important Conversations dominated by the same old, same
old. Despite the fact that women, for example, make up more than half
of the active users on most social networking sites, we still usually see
men served up as the expert voices on social networks, on blogs, and in
mainstream media. Or, even though African Americans are more likely to
use Twitter than white people, white people are given the role of experts,
speaking at conferences, on top 10 lists, and more.

The Internet is deceptively equal. We don't know, or we're not willing
to recognize, that we have transposed to the Internet the same social
structures we've been living with for hundreds, maybe thousands, of
years. We're painting our understanding of the offline world—with all our
prejudices, biases and hierarchies—onto the canvas of the Internet.

Just as in real life, people congregate at different services and networks online, and the reasons often have to do with our cultural and
social identity. When we pretend the Internet is a social utopia, we do a
disservice not just to each other, but also to younger generations and their
understanding of how social networks function. In a 2006–2007 study,
noted technology researcher danah boyd found that teen users on social
networks were not just seeking out those like themselves; they were also
displaying class and racial tensions toward users who didn't congregate
where they did—who weren't like them. "What happened," boyd writes,

"was modern day 'white flight.'" Whites and the educated were more likely to leave MySpace or choose Facebook. This is not a legacy we want to leave when there is so much potential for fundamental change.

Gender roles also play an important part in how we use social media. Women are more likely to use social networking to deepen their existing relationships rather than to make loose, acquaintance-like new connections. The focus on "deep" versus "many" connections can leave women out of the professional networking game in a big way, a dangerous proposition as our culture becomes increasingly reliant on relationships and connections formed online.

But this shift also enables us to build authority on the basis of the quality of our ideas, rather than on a stacked deck of influence based on social structures like gender, race, and class. To be dominant in older social hierarchies, we had to have a lot of things going for us, including how we looked or where we came from. In the social network sphere, we are the ones determining what and who is relevant and influential to the work we're doing and the lives we're living.

As social networks shift our perceptions of authority, we have to guard against the problems that can arise when large numbers of people have access to information without context. Institutional authorities provided this context in the past. Now that another, more organic kind of authority plays a larger role in how and how quickly we receive information, we have a new responsibility to ensure that the reporting we share is accurate.

If we can assume this responsibility, the potential for social justice movements may be limitless. Armed with the power to subvert traditional power structures by establishing our own authorities, we may be able to escape the hierarchies that have kept our stories from reaching one another. We can change whom and what we consider influential and—as long as we develop the skills we need to act responsibly in the face of a flood of new information—we can tackle the societal structures that constrain us.

This shift in authority offers opportunities for progress, but deep and lasting change won't emerge unless we also recognize the biases we bring to the table. The ease with which we share information enables us to engage with social justice issues at speeds previously unimaginable. But that speed can come with traps. If we want to connect with each other in ways that will support change in the world, we must learn to maneuver around old-style thinking that keeps us out of important discussions and around networks that unintentionally marginalize others.

The Internet's lack of institutional structure shouldn't be confused with equality. Funny thing: When you remove explicit structure from a group (leaders, hierarchies, process) it turns out that implicit structure arises—structure based on people's personal biases, prejudices, and class interests.

When implicit structure takes over, we run the risk of entering a series of vicious cycles that prevent fundamental, systemic change from emerging. By pretending that these implicit biases don't exist or don't matter, we ignore the voices of those most affected by the issues we care about, and we reinforce the very power structures that we seek to break down. In a seminal 1970 paper, feminist scholar and author Jo Freeman labeled this phenomenon of marginalizing minority-represented voices "the tyranny of structurelessness":

> This means that to strive for a "structureless" group is as useful, and as deceptive, as to aim at an "objective" news story, "value-free" social science or a "free" economy. A "laissez-faire" group is about as realistic as a "laissez-faire" society; the idea becomes a smokescreen for the strong or the lucky to establish unquestioned hegemony over others. . . . Thus "structurelessness" becomes a way of masking power.

Our tendency to congregate around like-minded folk is understandable and human, but it can be dangerous when organizing around issues for change. This doesn't mean reaching out to opposing viewpoints at every juncture. It does mean we need to look hard at who is most affected by the issues we're working on and ensure that they're being heard. Engaging with and listening to people who have different backgrounds from our own starts a fundamental process for change, and social networks hold a lot of promise for making the networks we belong to more diverse.

How do we engage with diverse groups of people in online public spaces? Generally, those with the largest audiences will continue to build their audiences exponentially. But we're not just talking about audience size—we're talking about multiple conversations, and effective ones at that. In order to have those conversations, though, we have to chart a course of action that acknowledges our biases, so we can then start reaching out and connecting with people who don't share our same points of reference. When we do this, we will change the world.

Choosing to Read Critically Questions

1. Explain what Zandt means when she argues that "Armed with the power to subvert traditional power structures by establishing our own authorities, we may be able to escape the hierarchies that have kept our stories from reaching one another."

2. What does the term "white flight" refer to in reference to social media? What other meanings or connotations does it have?

3. Explain the ideas that Zandt is responding to when she writes about "all the horn-tootin' over the disruptive and democratizing potential of the Internet." What do you think other authors are "horn tootin'" about?

4. Who is Zandt's audience? Use specific parts of the article to back up your claim.

Choosing to Respond Questions

1. This excerpt from Zandt's book relies heavily on generalizations. Develop some examples that either support or invalidate Zandt's claims. For example, have you found that the "quality" of one's ideas outweighs institutional authority in some parts of the Web?

2. Zandt claims that social networking has not yet fulfilled its potential as a political tool. In a group, brainstorm ways that Facebook and the Internet could have a "disruptive potential."

Wide Awake to Connections Questions

1. In paragraph 2, Zandt writes that "Despite the fact that women, for example, make up more than half of the active users on most social networking sites, we still usually see men served up as the expert voices on social networks, on blogs, and in mainstream media . . . even though African Americans are more likely to use Twitter than white people, white people are given the role of experts, speaking at conferences, on top 10 lists, and more." Have you found this observation to be true? Examine some recent reporting on technology and social media in order to test Zandt's claim.

2. Read Malcolm Gladwell's article "Why the Revolution Will Not Be Tweeted" (in this chapter) in addition to doing some research into the 2009 protests in Moldova or the "Arab Spring" of 2010. Compose a thesis-driven essay in which you consider the role of social media in political activism.

Malcolm Gladwell, "Why the Revolution Will Not Be Tweeted"

>> **Prewriting Check-In**

1. Brainstorm on uses of social media to advance political causes. Write down anything you have heard about individuals around the world using social networking as a political tool.

2. Have you or has anyone you know ever used the Internet to connect with or solicit the help of strangers? For example, have you ever sold something, posted about a lost item or pet, or advertised something on the Internet? If you haven't, would you? Why or why not?

A staff writer with the New Yorker *since 1996,* **Malcolm Gladwell** *(b. 1963) has written four books, each of which has been a best-seller:* The Tipping Point *(2000),* Blink *(2005),* Outliers *(2008), and* What the Dog Saw: And Other Adventures *(2009). The following excerpt is from an article that originally appeared in* The New Yorker *in which Gladwell describes what he perceives to be some of social media's shortcomings.*

"Why the Revolution Will Not Be Tweeted"

At four-thirty in the afternoon on Monday, February 1, 1960, four college students sat down at the lunch counter at the Woolworth's in downtown Greensboro, North Carolina. They were freshmen at North Carolina A&T, a black college a mile or so away.

"I'd like a cup of coffee, please," one of the four, Ezell Blair, said to the waitress.

"We don't serve Negroes here," she replied.

The Woolworth's lunch counter was a long L-shaped bar that could seat sixty-six people, with a stand-up snack bar at one end. The seats were for whites. The snack bar was for blacks. Another employee, a black woman who worked at the steam table, approached the students and tried to warn them away. "You're acting stupid, ignorant!" she said. They didn't move. Around five-thirty, the front doors to the store were locked. The four still didn't move. Finally, they left by a side door. Outside, a small crowd had gathered, including a photographer from the

Greensboro *Record*. "I'll be back tomorrow with A&T College," one of the students said.

By next morning, the protest had grown to twenty-seven men and four women, most from the same dormitory as the original four. The men were dressed in suits and ties. The students had brought their school-work and studied as they sat at the counter. On Wednesday, students from Greensboro's "Negro" secondary school, Dudley High, joined in, and the number of protesters swelled to eighty. By Thursday, the pro-testers numbered three hundred, including three white women from the Greensboro campus of the University of North Carolina. By Saturday, the sit-in had reached six hundred. People spilled out onto the street. White teenagers waved Confederate flags. Someone threw a firecracker. At noon, the A&T football team arrived. "Here comes the wrecking crew," one of the white students shouted.

By the following Monday, sit-ins had spread to Winston-Salem, twenty-five miles away, and Durham, fifty miles away. The day after that, students at Fayetteville State Teachers College and Johnson C. Smith College, in Charlotte, joined in, followed on Wednesday by students at St. Augustine's College and Shaw University, in Raleigh. On Thursday and Friday, the protest crossed state lines, surfacing in Hampton and Portsmouth, Virginia, in Rock Hill, South Carolina, and in Chattanooga, Tennessee. By the end of the month, there were sit-ins throughout the South, as far west as Texas. "I asked every student I met what the first day of the sit-downs had been like on his campus," the political theorist Michael Walzer wrote in *Dissent*. "The answer was always the same: 'It was like a fever. Everyone wanted to go.'" Some seventy thousand students eventually took part. Thousands were arrested and untold thou-sands more were radicalized. These events in the early sixties became a civil-rights war that engulfed the South for the rest of the decade—and it happened without e-mail, texting, Facebook, or Twitter.

***

The world, we are told, is in the midst of a revolution. The new tools of social media have reinvented social activism. With Facebook and Twitter and the like, the traditional relationship between political authority and popular will has been upended, making it easier for the powerless to col-laborate, coördinate, and give voice to their concerns. When ten thousand protesters took to the streets in Moldova in the spring of 2009 to protest against their country's communist government, the action was dubbed the Twitter Revolution, because of the means by which the demonstrators had been brought together. A few months after that, when student protests rocked Tehran, the State Department took the unusual step of asking Twitter to suspend scheduled maintenance of its Web site, because the administration didn't want such a critical organizing tool out of service at the height of the demonstrations. "Without Twitter the people of Iran would not have felt empowered and confident to stand up for freedom and democracy," Mark Pfeifle, a former national-security adviser, later wrote, calling for Twitter to be nominated for the Nobel Peace Prize. Where activists were once defined by their causes, they are now defined by their tools. Facebook warriors go online to push for change. "You are the best hope for us all," James K. Glassman, a former senior State Department official, told a crowd of cyber activists at a recent conference sponsored by Facebook, AT&T, Howcast, MTV, and Google. Sites like Facebook, Glassman said, "give the United States a significant competitive advantage over terrorists. Some time ago, I said that Al Qaeda was 'eating our lunch on the Internet.' That is no longer the case. Al Qaeda is stuck in Web 1.0. The Internet is now about interactivity and conversation."

These are strong, and puzzling, claims. Why does it matter who is eating whose lunch on the Internet? Are people who log on to their Facebook page really the best hope for us all? As for Moldova's so-called Twitter Revolution, Evgeny Morozov, a scholar at Stanford who has been the most persistent of digital evangelism's critics, points out that Twitter had scant internal significance in Moldova, a country where very few Twitter accounts exist. Nor does it seem to have been a revolution, not least because the protests—as Anne Applebaum suggested in the Washington *Post*—may well have been a bit of stagecraft cooked up by the government. (In a country paranoid about Romanian revanchism, the protesters flew a Romanian flag over the Parliament building.) In the Iranian case, meanwhile, the people tweeting about the demonstrations were almost all in the West. "It is time to get Twitter's role in the events in Iran right," Golnaz Esfandiari wrote this past summer in *Foreign Policy*. "Simply put: There was no Twitter Revolution inside Iran." The cadre of prominent bloggers, like Andrew Sullivan who championed the role of social media in Iran, Esfandiari continued, misunderstood the situation. "Western journalists who couldn't reach—or didn't bother reaching?— people on the ground in Iran simply scrolled through the English- language tweets post with tag #iranelection," she wrote. "Through it all, no one seemed to wonder why people trying to coordinate protests in Iran would be writing in any language other than Farsi."

Some of this grandiosity is to be expected. Innovators tend to be solipsists. They often want to cram every stray fact and experience into their new model. As the historian Robert Darnton has written, "The marvels of communication technology in the present have produced a false consciousness about the past—even a sense that communication has no history or had nothing of importance to consider before the days of television and the Internet." But there is something else at work here in the outsized enthusiasm for social media. Fifty years after one of the most extraordinary episodes of social upheaval in American history, we seem to have forgotten what activism is.

***

Greensboro in the early nineteen-sixties was the kind of place where racial insubordination was routinely met with violence. The four students who first sat down at the lunch counter were terrified. "I suppose if any- one had come up behind me and yelled 'Boo,' I think I would have fallen off my seat," one of them said later. On the first day, the store manager notified the police chief, who immediately sent two officers to the store. On the third day, a gang of white toughs showed up at the lunch counter and stood ostentatiously behind the protesters, ominously muttering epithets such as "burr-head nigger." A local Ku Klux Klan leader made an appearance. On Saturday, as tensions grew, someone called in a bomb threat, and the entire store had to be evacuated.

The dangers were even clearer in the Mississippi Freedom Summer Project of 1964, another of the sentinel campaigns of the civil-rights movement. The Student Nonviolent Coordinating Committee recruited hundreds of Northern, largely white, unpaid volunteers to run Freedom Schools, register black voters, and raise civil-rights awareness in the Deep South. "No one should go *anywhere* alone, but certainly not in an automobile and certainly not at night," they were instructed. Within days of arriving in Mississippi, three volunteers—Michael Schwerner, James

Chaney, and Andrew Goodman—were kidnapped and killed, and, during the rest of the summer, thirty-seven black churches were set on fire and dozens of safe houses were bombed; volunteers were beaten, shot at, arrested, and trailed by pickup trucks full of armed men. A quarter of those in the program dropped out. Activism that challenges the status quo—that attacks deeply rooted problems—is not for the faint of heart.

What makes people capable of this kind of activism? The Stanford sociologist Doug McAdam compared the Freedom Summer dropouts with the participants who stayed and discovered that the key difference wasn't, as might be expected, ideological fervor. "*All* of the applicants—participants and withdrawals alike—emerge as highly committed, articulate supporters of the goals and values of the summer program," he concluded. What mattered more was an applicant's degree of personal connection to the civil-rights movement. All the volunteers were required to provide a list of personal contacts—the people they wanted kept apprised of their activities—and participants were far more likely than dropouts to have close friends who were also going to Mississippi. High-risk activism, McAdam concluded, is a "strong-tie" phenomenon.

This pattern shows up again and again. One study of the Red Brigades, the Italian terrorist group of the nineteen-seventies, found that 70 percent of recruits had at least one good friend already in the organization. The same is true of the men who joined the mujahideen in Afghanistan. Even revolutionary actions that look spontaneous, like the demonstrations in East Germany that led to the fall of the Berlin Wall, are, at their core, strong-tie phenomena. The opposition movement in East Germany consisted of several hundred groups, each with roughly a dozen members. Each group was in limited contact with the others: at the time, only 13 percent of East Germans even had a phone. All they knew was that on Monday nights, outside St. Nicholas Church in downtown Leipzig, people gathered to voice their anger at the state. And the primary determinant of who showed up was "critical friends"—the more friends you had who were critical of the regime, the more likely you were to join the protest.

So one crucial fact about the four freshmen at the Greensboro lunch counter—David Richmond, Franklin McCain, Ezell Blair, and Joseph McNeil—was their relationship with one another. McNeil was a roommate of Blair's in A&T's Scott Hall dormitory. Richmond roomed with

McCain one floor up, and Blair, Richmond, and McCain had all gone to Dudley High School. The four would smuggle beer into the dorm and talk late into the night in Blair and McNeil's room. They would all have remembered the murder of Emmett Till in 1955, the Montgomery bus boycott that same year, and the showdown in Little Rock in 1957. It was McNeil who brought up the idea of a sit-in at Woolworth's. They'd discussed it for nearly a month. Then McNeil came into the dorm room and asked the others if they were ready. There was a pause, and McCain said, in a way that works only with people who talk late into the night with one another, "Are you guys chicken or not?" Ezell Blair worked up the courage the next day to ask for a cup of coffee because he was flanked by his roommate and two good friends from high school.

***

The kind of activism associated with social media isn't like this at all. The platforms of social media are built around weak ties. Twitter is a way of following (or being followed by) people you may never have met. Facebook is a tool for efficiently managing your acquaintances, for keeping up with the people you would not otherwise be able to stay in touch with. That's why you can have a thousand "friends" on Facebook, as you never could in real life.

This is in many ways a wonderful thing. There is strength in weak ties, as the sociologist Mark Granovetter has observed. Our acquaintances—not our friends—are our greatest source of new ideas and information. The Internet lets us exploit the power of these kinds of distant connections with marvelous efficiency. It's terrific at the diffusion of innovation, interdisciplinary collaboration, seamlessly matching up buyers and sellers, and the logistical functions of the dating world. But weak ties seldom lead to high-risk activism.

In a new book called *The Dragonfly Effect: Quick, Effective, and Powerful Ways to Use Social Media to Drive Social Change*, the business consultant Andy Smith and the Stanford Business School professor Jennifer Aaker tell the story of Sameer Bhatia, a young Silicon Valley entrepreneur who came down with acute myelogenous leukemia. It's a perfect illustration of social media's strengths. Bhatia needed a bone-marrow transplant, but he could not find a match among his relatives and friends. The odds were best with a donor of his ethnicity, and there were few South Asians in the national bone-marrow database. So Bhatia's business partner sent out an e-mail explaining Bhatia's plight to more than four hundred of their acquaintances, who forwarded the e-mail to their personal contacts; Facebook pages and YouTube videos were devoted to the Help Sameer campaign. Eventually, nearly twenty-five thousand new people were registered in the bone-marrow database, and Bhatia found a match.

But how did the campaign get so many people to sign up? By not asking too much of them. That's the only way you can get someone you don't really know to do something on your behalf. You can get thousands of people to sign up for a donor registry, because doing so is pretty easy. You have to send in a cheek swab and—in the highly unlikely event that your bone marrow is a good match for someone in need—spend a few hours at the hospital. Donating bone marrow isn't a trivial matter. But it doesn't involve financial or personal risk; it doesn't mean spending a summer being chased by armed men in pickup trucks. It doesn't require that you confront socially entrenched norms and practices. In fact, it's the kind of commitment that will bring only social acknowledgment and praise.

The evangelists of social media don't understand this distinction; they seem to believe that a Facebook friend is the same as a real friend and that signing up for a donor registry in Silicon Valley today is activism in the same sense as sitting at a segregated lunch counter in Greensboro in 1960. "Social networks are particularly effective at increasing motivation," Aaker and Smith write. But that's not true. Social networks are effective at increasing *participation*—by lessening the level of motivation that participation requires. The Facebook page of the Save Darfur Coalition has 1,282,339 members, who have donated an average of nine cents apiece. The next biggest Darfur charity on Facebook has 22,073 members, who have donated an average of thirty-five cents. Help Save Darfur has 2,797 members, who have given, on average, fifteen cents. A spokesperson for the Save Darfur Coalition told *Newsweek*, "We wouldn't necessarily gauge someone's value to the advocacy movement based on what they've given. This is a powerful mechanism to engage this critical population. They inform their community, attend events, volunteer. It's not something you can measure by looking at a ledger." In other words, Facebook activism succeeds not by motivating people to make a real sacrifice but by motivating them to do the things that people do when they are not motivated enough to make a real sacrifice. We are a long way from the lunch counters of Greensboro.

The students who joined the sit-ins across the South during the winter of 1960 described the movement as a "fever." But the civil-rights movement was more like a military campaign than like a contagion. In the late nineteen-fifties, there had been sixteen sit-ins in various cities throughout the South, fifteen of which were formally organized by civil-rights organizations like the NAACP and CORE Possible locations for activism were scouted. Plans were drawn up. Movement activists held training sessions and retreats for would-be protesters. The Greensboro Four were a product of this groundwork: all were members of the NAACP Youth Council. They had close ties with the head of the local NAACP chapter. They had been briefed on the earlier wave of sit-ins in Durham and had been part of a series of movement meetings in activist churches. When the sit-in movement spread from Greensboro throughout the South, it did not spread indiscriminately. It spread to those cities that had preëxisting "movement centers"—a core of dedicated and trained activists ready to turn the "fever" into action.

The civil-rights movement was high-risk activism. It was also, crucially, strategic activism: a challenge to the establishment mounted with precision and discipline. The NAACP was a centralized organization, run from New York City according to highly formalized operating procedures. At the Southern Christian Leadership Conference, Martin Luther King, Jr., was the unquestioned authority. At the center of the movement was the black church, which had, as Aldon D. Morris points out in his superb 1984 study, "The Origins of the Civil Rights Movement," a carefully demarcated division of labor, with various standing committees and disciplined groups. "Each group was task-oriented and coordinated its activities through authority structures," Morris writes. "Individuals were held accountable for their assigned duties, and important conflicts were resolved by the minister, who usually exercised ultimate authority over the congregation."

This is the second crucial distinction between traditional activism and its online variant: social media are not about this kind of hierarchical organization. Facebook and the like are tools for building *networks*, which are the opposite, in structure and character, of hierarchies. Unlike hierarchies, with their rules and procedures, networks aren't controlled by a single central authority. Decisions are made through consensus, and the ties that bind people to the group are loose.

This structure makes networks enormously resilient and adaptable in low-risk situations. Wikipedia is a perfect example. It doesn't have an editor, sitting in New York City, who directs and corrects each entry. The effort of putting together each entry is self-organized. If every entry in Wikipedia were to be erased tomorrow, the content would swiftly be restored, because that's what happens when a network of thousands spontaneously devote their time to a task.

There are many things, though, that networks don't do well. Car companies sensibly use a network to organize their hundreds of suppliers, but not to design their cars. No one believes that the articulation of a coherent design philosophy is best handled by a sprawling, leaderless organizational system. Because networks don't have a centralized leadership structure and clear lines of authority, they have real difficulty reaching consensus and setting goals. They can't think strategically; they are chronically prone to conflict and error. How do you make difficult choices about tactics or strategy or philosophical direction when everyone has an equal say?

The Palestine Liberation Organization originated as a network, and the international-relations scholars Mette Eilstrup-Sangiovanni and Calvert Jones argue in a recent essay in *International Security* that this is why it ran into such trouble as it grew: "Structural features typical of networks—the absence of central authority, the unchecked autonomy of rival groups, and the inability to arbitrate quarrels through formal mechanisms—made the PLO excessively vulnerable to outside manipulation and internal strife."

In Germany in the nineteen-seventies, they go on, "the far more unified and successful left-wing terrorists tended to organize hierarchically, with professional management and clear divisions of labor. They were concentrated geographically in universities, where they could establish central leadership, trust, and camaraderie through regular, face-to-face meetings." They seldom betrayed their comrades in arms during police interrogations. Their counterparts on the right were organized as decentralized networks and had no such discipline. These groups were regularly infiltrated, and members, once arrested, easily gave up their comrades. Similarly, Al Qaeda was most dangerous when it was a unified hierarchy. Now that it has dissipated into a network, it has proved far less effective.

The drawbacks of networks scarcely matter if the network isn't interested in systemic change—if it just wants to frighten or humiliate or make a splash—or if it doesn't need to think strategically. But if you're taking on a powerful and organized establishment you have to be a hierarchy. The Montgomery bus boycott required the participation of tens of thousands of people who depended on public transit to get to and from work each day. It lasted a *year*. In order to persuade those people to stay true to the cause, the boycott's organizers tasked each local black church with maintaining morale and put together a free alternative private carpool service, with forty-eight dispatchers and forty-two pickup stations. Even the White Citizens Council, King later said, conceded that the carpool system moved with "military precision." By the time King came to Birmingham for the climactic showdown with Police Commissioner Eugene (Bull) Connor, he had a budget of a million dollars and a hundred full-time staff members on the ground, divided into operational units. The operation itself was divided into steadily escalating phases, mapped out in advance. Support was maintained through consecutive mass meetings rotating from church to church around the city.

Boycotts and sit-ins and nonviolent confrontations—which were the weapons of choice for the civil-rights movement—are high-risk strategies. They leave little room for conflict and error. The moment even one protester deviates from the script and responds to provocation, the moral legitimacy of the entire protest is compromised. Enthusiasts for social media would no doubt have us believe that King's task in Birmingham would have been made infinitely easier had he been able to communicate with his followers through Facebook and contented himself with tweets from a Birmingham jail. But networks are messy: think of the ceaseless pattern of correction and revision, amendment and debate, that characterizes Wikipedia. If Martin Luther King, Jr., had tried to do a wiki-boycott in Montgomery, he would have been steamrollered by the white power structure. And of what use would a digital communication tool be in a town where 98 percent of the black community could be reached every Sunday morning at church? The things that King needed in Birmingham—discipline and strategy—were things that online social media cannot provide.

***

The bible of the social-media movement is Clay Shirky's *Here Comes Everybody*. Shirky, who teaches at New York University, sets out to demonstrate the organizing power of the Internet, and he begins with the story of Evan, who worked on Wall Street, and his friend Ivanna, after she left her smart phone, an expensive Sidekick, on the back seat of a New York City taxicab. The telephone company transferred the data on Ivanna's lost phone to a new phone, whereupon she and Evan discovered that the Sidekick was now in the hands of a teenager from Queens, who was using it to take photographs of herself and her friends.

When Evan e-mailed the teenager Sasha, asking for the phone back, she replied that his "white ass" didn't deserve to have it back. Miffed, he set up a Web page with her picture and a description of what had happened. He forwarded the link to his friends, and they forwarded it to their friends. Someone found the MySpace page of Sasha's boyfriend, and a link to it found its way onto the site. Someone found her address online and took a video of her home while driving by; Evan posted the video on the site. The story was picked up by the news filter Digg. Evan was now up to ten e-mails a minute. He created a bulletin board for his readers to share their stories, but it crashed under the weight of responses. Evan and Ivanna went to the police, but the police filed the report under "lost," rather than "stolen," which essentially closed the case. "By this point millions of readers were watching," Shirky writes, "and dozens of mainstream news outlets had covered the story." Bowing to the pressure, the NYPD reclassified the item as "stolen." Sasha was arrested, and Evan got his friend's Sidekick back.

Shirky's argument is that this is the kind of thing that could never have happened in the pre-Internet age—and he's right. Evan could never have tracked down Sasha. The story of the Sidekick would never have been publicized. An army of people could never have been assembled to wage this fight. The police wouldn't have bowed to the pressure of a lone person who had misplaced something as trivial as a cell phone. The story, to Shirky, illustrates "the ease and speed with which a group can be mobilized for the right kind of cause" in the Internet age.

Shirky considers this model of activism an upgrade. But it is simply a form of organizing that favors the weak-tie connections that give us access to information over the strong-tie connections that help us persevere in the face of danger. It shifts our energies from organizations that promote strategic and disciplined activity and toward those that promote resilience and adaptability. It makes it easier for activists to express themselves and harder for that expression to have any impact. The instruments of social media are well suited to making the existing social order more efficient. They are not a natural enemy of the status quo. If you are of the opinion that all the world needs is a little buffing around the edges, this should not trouble you. But if you think that there are still lunch counters out there that need integrating, it ought to give you pause.

Shirky ends the story of the lost Sidekick by asking, portentously, "What happens next?"—no doubt imagining future waves of digital protesters. But he has already answered the question. What happens next is more of the same. A networked, weak-tie world is good at things like helping Wall Streeters get phones back from teenage girls. *Viva la revolución.*

Choosing to Read Critically Questions

1. In your own words, summarize the position Gladwell is arguing against as well as Gladwell's position. Make sure to explain the two ways in which traditional activism differs from online activism according to Gladwell.
2. What does Gladwell mean when he writes, "Innovators tend to be solipsists. They often want to cram every stray fact and experience into their new model"?
3. Consider Gladwell's use of other authors' ideas, particularly in paragraph 7. How and why does Gladwell quote others? What is the point of this paragraph?
3. Evaluate Gladwell's opening. Do you find the description of the sit-ins at Woolworth's effective and compelling? Why or why not?

Choosing to Respond Questions

1. Explain and evaluate Gladwell's use of Shirky's work at the article's conclusion. What does "Viva la revolución" mean? What is Gladwell's tone here?
2. Has the value of the Internet for social activism been overstated? What do you think? In a short essay, respond to Gladwell's argument.

Wide Awake to Connections Questions

1. Using Gladwell's claim that "Activism that challenges the status quo—that attacks deeply rooted problems—is not for the faint of heart," research an activist or revolutionary movement not discussed here in order to investigate the role—or lack of role—that technologies played in that movement. (You might also want to look at Thomas L. Friedman's article "Facebook Meets Brick-and-Mortar Politics" in the June 12, 2012, *New York Times*.)

2. Drawing on the information in this article as well as at least one article from Chapter 14, "How to Be Happy: The Question of Choice," compose an essay in which you explore the importance of human connections and relationships.

Daily Mail Reporter, "'It Has to Go Away': Facebook Director Calls for an End to Internet Anonymity"

>> Prereading Check-In

1. Brainstorm the benefits and drawbacks of anonymity on the Internet.

2. What do you know about Internet civility or etiquette? Have any of your classes ever dealt with how to behave on the Internet? Do you think schools should teach "netiquette"?

The British publication the Daily Mail *is a "middle market newspaper," a newspaper that combines news and entertainment. The following article, which appeared in July 2011, reports on Facebook marketing director Randi Zuckerberg's critique of Internet anonymity.*

"'It Has to Go Away': Facebook Director Calls For an End to Internet Anonymity"

Facebook's marketing director has called for an end to online anonymity, saying Internet users would "behave a lot better" if everyone had to use real names when surfing or posting on the Internet.

Randi Zuckerberg, Facebook's marketing director and sister of multimillionaire founder Mark, made the comments during a round table discussion on cyberbullying.

The ubiquitous social networking site, which has been at the center of recent controversy over Internet privacy and bullying issues, currently requires all its members to use their real names and emails when signing on.

Mrs. Zuckerberg argued that the end of online anonymity could help curb the trend of trolling and harassment on the Web.

Speaking at a Marie Claire panel discussion on social media, she said: "I think anonymity on the Internet has to go away.

"People behave a lot better when they have their real names down. . . . I think people hide behind anonymity, and they feel like they can say whatever they want behind closed doors."

The comments echo those of former Google CEO Eric Schmidt who has previously labeled Internet anonymity a "dangerous" precedent, before predicting government intervention will one day lead to its demise.

Privacy advocates have however condemned previous attempts to dismantle online anonymity.

Critics complain that the forced introduction of some kind of "online passport" would damage the freedom of speech and blunt the Internet as a tool for dissidents to speak up against oppressive governments.

The panel also pressed Mrs. Zuckerberg to list what forthcoming safeguards the site has to protect security; she declined.

She added simply: "There's so much more we can do. We're actively trying to work with partners like Common Sense Media and our safety advisory committee."

The panel was joined by Erin Andrews, an ESPN anchor who had a naked video of her posted online by a stalker.

At times becoming emotional, Mrs. Andrews asked Mr. Schmidt why searches for her name still brought up images and videos of the offending tape, despite her repeated attempts to have them removed.

Adding that [even though] she was a woman in her 30's, . . . "It's still cyberbullying. Somebody needs to step in. As a family we're always asking, what is it going to take?"

Facebook has previously come under fire after founder Mark Zuckerberg said he would "fight" to allow under-13s to use the social networking website—despite warnings it would put the most vulnerable children at risk.

In America, the age limit, also 13, is dictated by laws designed to protect young children, but Facebook's 27-year-old billionaire creator believes the educational benefits of using the site mean the restrictions should be lifted.

Choosing to Read Critically Questions

1. Explain Randi Zuckerberg's contention that people would "behave a lot better" if there were less anonymity on the Internet.
2. What are some of the reasons to retain anonymity on the Internet?
3. Does the controversy reported on in this article surprise you? Why or why not?
4. Pretend you are the editor of the *Daily Mail* and provide feedback for the author of this article. What is he or she doing well? What would you like the author to further report on or to explain?

Choosing to Respond Questions

1. Drawing on your own experiences and observations, take a position on this issue. Would you like to see less anonymity on the Internet? Why or why not?
2. Part of the problem with Internet anonymity, the article suggests, is that it fosters cyberbullying. Define cyberbullying and provide an example— drawn either from your own experiences and observations or from research. Analyze your example, asking whether or not less anonymity on the Web would have made a difference. Why or why not?

Wide Awake to Connections Questions

1. Building on your answer to Choosing to Read Critically Question #2, continue writing about this issue. Research and report upon whatever issue or issues you would have encouraged the writer to explore further.
2. If you were a teacher (of any subject or grade of your choosing), how would you use computers and technology? Write an essay in which you explain your ideas.

Mark Bauerlein, from *The Dumbest Generation*

>> Prereading Check-In

1. Do you or did you ever have an older mentor? If yes, please describe the relationship. If no, explain why you think you have never met an older person who helped you in your intellectual or moral development.
2. What, do you think, are some of positive effects of increased Internet use among young people? What are some of the drawbacks?

In addition to The Dumbest Generation: How the Digital Age Stupefies Young Americans and Jeopardizes Our Future; Or, Don't Trust Anyone Under 30 *(2008),* **Mark Bauerlein** *(b. 1959) has written books including* Negrophobia: A Race Riot in Atlanta, 1906 *(2001),* Literary Criticism: An Autopsy *(1997), and* The Pragmatic Mind: Explorations in the Psychology of Belief *(1997) and has written articles for publications including the* Wall Street Journal, *the* Weekly Standard, *and the* Washington Post. *In the following excerpt from* The Dumbest Generation, *Bauerlein argues that young people spend their time online avoiding that which is new or difficult.*

"Online Learning and Non-Learning"

The enhanced connectivity, and the indulgence of teachers and journalists, feed [an] adolescent vice that technophiles never mention: peer absorption. Educators speak about the importance of role models and the career pressures facing kids, but in truth, adolescents care a lot more about what other adolescents think than what their elders think. Their egos are fragile, their beliefs in transition, their values uncertain. They inhabit a rigorous world of consumerism and conformity, of rebellious poses and withering group judgments. Boys struggle to acquire the courage and strength of manhood, girls the poise and strength of womanhood. They tease one another mercilessly, and a rejection can crush them. Life is a pinball game of polarized demands—a part-time job that requires punctuality and diligence, pals who urge them to cut up in class; a midterm forcing them to stay home and study, a friend who wants to catch a horror flick. For many of them, good standing with classmates is the only way to secure a safe identity, and so they spend hours on the channels of adolescent fare searching out the latest in clothes, slang, music, sports, celebrities, school gossip, and one another. Technology has made it fabulously easier.

And so, apart from all the other consequences of digital breakthroughs, for the younger users a profound social effect has settled in. Teens and younger adults now have more contact with one another than ever before. Cliques used to form in the schoolyard or on the bus, and when students came home they communicated with one another only through a land line restricted by their parents. Social life pretty much stopped at the front door. With the latest gadgets in their own room and libraries, however, peer-to-peer contact never ends. Email and Instant Messaging maintain high school friendships long after graduation. Social networking sites produce virtual buddies who've never met in person and live 3,000 miles apart, but who converse intimately from one bedroom to another. School secrets and bullying get amplified on a saucy sophomore's blog, and two dozen others chime in. As soon as one class ends, undergraduates scurry across the quad for their next class but still take time to check cell phones for messages. Twitter technology (debuting March 2006) enables users to send short updates on the spur of the moment through mobile phones. . . . The "tweets" can be as mundane as "Well, I'm stuck in traffic," the rationale, according to *twitter.com*, stemming from one simple query: "What are you doing?" That is the genuine significance of the Web to a 17-year-old mind, not the universe of knowledge brought to their fingertips, but an instrument of nonstop peer contact.

Votaries of screen media and the Web start from the truism that the Web delivers a phenomenal body of data, stories, facts, images, and exercises. A column by education writer Joel Turtel advises "Let's Google and Yahoo Our Kids' Education" for that very reason. While in-class exercises drown students in overscheduled drudgery, he argues, search engines permit his daughter to "explore any subject" and put "the whole world at her fingertips." Studying is joyful and economical. "She can learn about tulips, cooking, dinosaurs, fashion, arithmetic, model airplanes, how to play the piano, or story books by thousands of authors," Turtel enthuses. When she is older, she can search dozens of Internet libraries, including the Library of Congress, for information on any subject under the sun.

He's right, it's all there, the great books, masterpieces, old maps, encyclopedia entries, world newspapers, science facts, and historical events. But that's not where the kids go. Caesar conquered Gaul, Cleopatra seduced him, and Antony took his place after the assassination, but young Americans prefer to learn about one another. In

Nielsen/NetRatings for October 2006, nine of the top ten sites for 12-
to 17-year-olds offered content or support tools for social networking.
Chief Nielsen analyst Ken Cassar noted with surprise "the extent to
which a wide array of supporting Web sites has developed in conjunc-
tion with these bigger, more well-known Web destinations. MySpace
and YouTube have spawned a vibrant online ecosystem." The National
School Boards report "Creating and Connecting" opens, "Online social networking is now so deeply embedded in the lifestyles of tweens
and teens that it rivals television for their attention." It counted nine
hours a week of networking time. For college students, the numbers
are no better. . . . In early 2006, when Northwestern University communications professor Esther Hargittai polled 1,300 students at the
University of Illinois-Chicago on their online time and favorite destinations, their choices were all too predictable. At number one stood
Facebook (78.1 percent), followed by *MySpace* (50.7 percent). Only
5 percent regularly checked a blog or forum on politics, economics,
law, or policy. Only 1 percent had ever perused the leading left-wing
blog *dailykos.com.*

The acclaimed empowerment that Web 2.0 has fostered goes
almost entirely toward social stuff. Teens and young adults like
email and Instant Messaging and pornography, not www.si.edu
(Smithsonian Institution). The Web offers wondrous information and
images, but why would a high school senior download them when
he can read what his classmates say about what happened over the
weekend? People can watch shows from the PBS series *Nova* online
or find on *YouTube* a clip of Thelonious Monk playing "Blue Monk"
while Count Basie grins in front of the piano, but those clips pale
before the thrill of composing something about yourself, posting it
online, having someone, somewhere, read it and write something
back. That's the pull of immaturity, and technology has granted young
Americans ever more opportunities to go with it, not outgrow it. Back
in 2001, Pew Research issued a report titled "Teenage Life Online,"
and almost the entire document focused on social matters, friendships, and messaging. The word *knowledge* appeared only once in
the entire 46 pages, when it mentioned that one-quarter of teens use

the Internet to "get information about things that are hard to talk to other people about." Instead of opening adolescents and young adults to worldly realities, acquainting them with the global village, inducting them into the course of civilization, or at least the Knowledge Economy, digital communications have opened them to one another—which is to say, have enclosed them in a parochial cosmos of youth matters and concerns.

Maturity comes, in part, through vertical modeling, relations with older people such as teachers, employers, ministers, aunts and uncles, and older siblings, along with parents, who impart adult outlooks and interests. In their example, they reveal the minor meanings of adolescent worries, showing that the authentic stakes of life surpass the feats and letdowns of high school and college. The Web (along with cell phones, teen sitcoms, and pop music), though, encourages more horizontal modeling, more raillery and mimicry of people the same age, an intensification of peer consciousness. It provides new and enhanced ways for adolescents to do what they've always done in a prosperous time: talk to, act like, think like, compete against, and play with one another. Social life is a powerful temptation, and most teenagers feel the pain of missing out—not invited to the party, not having the right clothes, not making the sports team, not having a date for the dance. Digital technology is both a way into it and a way out. It keeps popular teens in the know and in the clique, providing connections that stabilize their popularity. . . . And it gives unpopular teens an outlet and an audience, for instance, the nerd who opens a blog and gripes about the day's displeasures . . .

In both cases, the absorption in local youth society grows, and adolescence appears ever more autonomous. For all of them, popular youths and marginal ones, the celebrated customization power of digital technology is disabling. Ordinary 18-year-olds love digital technology because it allows them to construct a reflexive surrounding. The part-time job tires them and the classroom irks them to death, but the blogs, games, shows, videos, music, messages, updates, phone calls . . . they mirror their woes and fantasies. It's a pre-packaged representation of the world, a "Daily Me," a rendition of things filtered by the dispositions of young users. . . . The things that bother and bore them are blocked

out. The people they don't know and don't want to know they don't
have to meet. A coup may have erupted in Central America, a transportation bill passed the House, a food scare just started, but if they don't
care about them they don't have to hear about them. Reality is personalized, and the world outside steadily tallies the ego inside. A 16-year-old
panelist at the 2006 Online News Association convention summed it up
perfectly. When a journalist in the audience asked if sticking solely to
RSS feeds made her miss the "broader picture," she snapped, "I'm not
trying to get a broader picture. I'm trying to get what I want." For most
adolescents, that means the horizon ends with their friends, music, TV
shows, games, and virtual contacts. The adult realities of history, politics, high art, and finance can wait.

The psychological delights are intellectually stultifying. For education
to happen, people must encounter worthwhile things outside their sphere
of interest and brainpower. Knowledge grows, skills improve, tastes
refine, and conscience ripens only if the experiences bear a degree of
unfamiliarity—a beautiful artwork you are forced to inspect even though
it leaves you cold; an ancient city you have to detail even though history puts you to sleep; a microeconomic problem you have to solve even
though you fumble with arithmetic. To take them in, to assimilate the
objects intelligently, the intellectual tool kit must expand and attitudes
must soften. If the first apprehension stalls, you can't mutter, "I don't get
it—this isn't for me." You have to say, "I don't get it, and maybe that's *my*
fault" . . .

Nobody savors this process, but mature adults realize the benefits.
Adolescents don't, and digital connections save them the labor of self-
improvement. . . . With the screen offerings, the intellectual barriers are
low and the rewards immediate.

This is precisely why young adults claim technology as their own,
and why we should reconsider the basic premise of digital learning: that
leisure time in front of screens forms an educational progress. Not reject
the premise, but examine it again, slow it down, set it in light not only
of the promise of technology, but in light of a demonstrable and all-too-
frequent outcome. For most rising users, screen time doesn't graduate
them into higher knowledge/skill states. It superpowers their social
impulse, but it blocks intellectual gains.

Choosing to Read Critically Questions

1. Describe some of Bauerlein's criticisms of the way that young people engage with communication technologies.

2. Explain the implications of Bauerlein's claim that "Digital technology . . . keeps popular teens in the know and in the clique, providing connections that stabilize their popularity. . . . And it gives unpopular teens an outlet and an audience, for instance, the nerd who opens a blog and gripes about the day's displeasures. . . . In both cases, the absorption in local youth society grows, and adolescence appears ever more autonomous. For all of them, popular youths and marginal ones, the celebrated customization power of digital technology is disabling."

3. Bauerlein is pretty unapologetic in his criticism of young people's priorities. Did you like his tone, or did you find it alienating?

4. Evaluate Bauerlein's use of evidence. Did you find the data and quotations he includes effective? Which ones and why?

Choosing to Respond Questions

1. Drawing on your experiences and observations, discuss whether or not Internet use results in young people's immersion in "a parochial cosmos of youth matters and concerns."

2. In a group, discuss Bauerlein's contention that "Maturity comes, in part, through vertical modeling, [such as] relations with older people." Have you found this to be true? Record the various experiences and opinions of the group members and present them to the larger class.

Wide Awake to Connections Questions

1. Read the rest of Bauerlein's book *The Dumbest Generation.* Alternately, you might go to the book's website at thedumbestgeneration.com and read some reviews and articles. Compose an essay in which you discuss and respond to Bauerlein's ideas about technology and the youth culture.

2. Bauerlein writes that "For education to happen, people must encounter worthwhile things outside their sphere of interest and brainpower. Knowledge grows, skills improve, tastes refine, and conscience ripens only if the experiences bear a degree of unfamiliarity—a beautiful artwork you are forced to inspect even though it leaves you cold; an ancient city you have to detail even though history puts you to sleep; a microeconomic problem you have to solve even though you fumble

with arithmetic. To take them in, to assimilate the objects intelligently, the intellectual tool kit must expand and attitudes must soften. If the first apprehension stalls, you can't mutter, 'I don't get it—this isn't for me.' You have to say, 'I don't get it, and maybe that's *my* fault.'" Drawing on one or two articles from Chapter 12 of this textbook, evaluate and respond to Bauerlein's characterization of the process of learning.

QUESTIONS AND SUGGESTIONS FOR FURTHER RESEARCH AND WRITING

1. Drawing on articles from this chapter as well as one or two articles from Chapter 12, "American Education," compose an essay in which you discuss the positive or negative effects of technological developments on school and learning in the twenty-first century. Bauerlein's "Online Learning" and *Science Daily's* "Children With Home Computers" (available online) might be good places to start your reading.

2. As of this writing, Facebook and Instagram have made controversial changes to their privacy policies (Instagram ultimately decided against a plan that would allow them to sell users' photographs). Research these changes, the controversies leading up to and surrounding them, and compose an essay taking a position on the company's policies.

3. There are a number of books and films that describe the loss of personal privacy. *1984* by George Orwell, *Brave New World* by Aldous Huxley, and Suzanne Collins' recent *Hunger Games* series are gripping and accessible novels dealing with the imposition of a totalitarian power that governs every aspect of life. The feature film, *Paparazzi* (2004), deals with a Hollywood actor's reaction to the paparazzi who threaten his wife and children. *The Net* (1995) details how a computer programmer's identity is stolen, endangering her life. *FeardotCom* (2002) and *Pulse* (2006) exploit teenagers' fascination with and fear of cyberspace. 2010's *The Social Network* describes the creation—and controversy around—the website Facebook. Avail yourself of some of these sources and research other book and filmic representations of the absence of privacy to compose a response to literary and/or cinematic representations of the invasion of privacy.

4. Several of the selections in this chapter discuss the possibilities for political and activist engagement on the Web; others discuss the dangers of incivility, cruelty, and sloppy thinking on the Web. After identifying and familiarizing yourself with a handful of blogs and news sources that cover urgent issues, read and analyze the

comments that follow important stories. What kinds of trends do you observe? For example, how is the comment section different on a feminist blog such as feministing.com from a news site such as drudgereport.com? Drawing on articles from this section, analyze the data you collect in order to compose a thesis-driven essay.

14 Chapter Fourteen

How to Be Happy:
The Question of Choice

>> **Prereading Check-In**
1. Are you happy? Why or why not?
2. The Declaration of Independence states that all Americans have the right to "life, liberty, and the pursuit of happiness." What does the "pursuit of happiness" mean to you?

Happiness is perhaps the ultimate human goal, the reason that many of us give as the hoped-for result of our conscious choices. What, however, is happiness? Wherever did 21st-century Americans get the idea that we have some sort of right to be happy?

The Declaration of Independence states that all Americans have the right to "life, liberty, and the pursuit of happiness." The American Supreme Court has taken up the question of what the "pursuit of happiness" is in several cases; one way of looking at the ability to pursue happiness is the ability to have choices. If we cannot control our own lives with regard to where we will live, whom we will live with, where we will work, and why, then our ability to pursue happiness is curtailed. Yet, as Vicki Haddock points out in "The Happiness Quotient: Do High Expectations and a Plethora of Choices Make Women Miserable?," included in this chapter, too many choices can also have a negative effect on our happiness levels.

In some respects, the pursuit of happiness may be understood as the goal underpinning all of the readings in this textbook (and perhaps most of the readings in most composition anthologies) in that many of the articles advocate or try to convince readers of a certain course of action or a certain way of seeing the world. For example, what is the ultimate goal of education, environmental conservation, or using social media to maintain friendships? Thus, it is possible to approach the readings in *Wide Awake* as each attempting to identify, understand, and manage important aspects of our lives and experiences.

This chapter contains discussions of what it means to be happy as well as cutting-edge research into how to understand and increase our happiness. Can we think our way to happiness? What kinds of situations increase happiness—and what kinds decrease it? This chapter will give you an opportunity to explore a topic that has inspired many philosophers, writers, and artists, and which has more recently become a popular subject for scientific study.

Marcus Aurelius, from *Meditations*

⟩⟩ Prereading Check-In

1. How do you feel about changes in your life? Does change tend to make you happier or less happy? Explain.
2. To what extent do you think you can determine your own happiness? Explain.

Marcus Aurelius *(121 A.D.–180 A.D.) was the Roman emperor from 161–160. His* Meditations *articulate what is known as "stoic philosophy," which encouraged self-discipline and virtue. In this excerpt from* Meditations, *Aurelius recommends a reliance on the self as a key to tranquility and happiness.*

From *Meditations*, **Book Four:**

Men seek retreats for themselves, houses in the country, at the seashore, and in the mountains; and you tend to desire such things very much. But this is a characteristic of the most common sort of men, for it is in your power whenever you will to choose to retreat into yourself. For nowhere either with more quiet or more freedom from trouble does a man retreat than into his own soul, particularly when he has within him such thoughts that by looking into them he is immediately perfectly tranquil; and I affirm that tranquility is nothing other than the proper ordering of the mind.

Do not act as if you were going to live ten thousand years. Death hangs over you. While you live, while it is in your power, be good.

How much trouble he avoids who does not look to see what his neighbor says or does or thinks, but only to what he does himself, that it may be just and pure; or as Agathon says, do not consider the depraved morals of others, but cling to the straight and narrow path without deviating from it.

He who has a powerful desire for posthumous fame does not consider that every one of those who remember him will himself also die very soon; then again also they who have succeeded them, until the whole remembrance shall have been extinguished as it is transmitted through men who foolishly admire and then perish. But suppose that those who will remember are even immortal, and that the remembrance will be immortal, what good will this do you?

What is evil in you does not subsist in the ruling principle of another; nor in any part or transformation of your physical body. Where is it then? It is in that part of you which has the power of forming opinions about evils. Let this power then not form such opinions, and all is well. And if that which is nearest to it the poor body is burnt, filled with excrescences and decay, nevertheless let the part which forms opinions about these things be quiet; that is, let it judge that nothing is either bad or good which can happen equally to the bad man and the good. For that which happens equally to him who lives contrary to nature and to him who lives according to nature, is neither according to nature nor contrary to nature.

Constantly regard the universe as one living being, having one substance and one soul; and observe how all things have reference to one perception, the perception of this one living being; and how all things act with one movement; and how all things are the cooperating causes of all things which exist; observe too the continuous spinning of the thread and the structure of the web.

You are a little soul carrying about a corpse, as Epictetus used to say.

It is no evil for things to undergo change, and no good for things to come into being as a consequence of change.

Time is like a river made up of the events which happen, and a violent stream; for as soon as a thing has been seen, it is carried away, and another comes in its place, and this will be carried away too.

If any god told you that you shall die tomorrow, or certainly on the day after tomorrow, you would not care much whether it was on the third day or on the next, unless you had a very degraded spirit, for how small is the difference? So think it no great thing to die after as many years as you can count rather than tomorrow.

. . . Be like the cliff against which the waves continually break, but which stands firm and tames the fury of the water around it.

Choosing to Read Critically Questions

1. In your own words, explain what Aurelius is suggesting in the first paragraph of this excerpt.

2. Aurelius invokes another philosopher, Epictetus, when he writes, "You are a little soul carrying about a corpse." What do you think Aurelius means by this? Discuss whether or not you agree with this understanding.

3. Why, do you think, does Aurelius spend so much time discussing death?

4. The *Meditations* were written in the second century; do you feel they still have something to offer us today?

Choosing to Respond Questions

1. Aurelius writes that "tranquility is nothing other than the proper ordering of the mind." Explain what you think he means by this and whether or not you agree.

2. Working in a group, discuss why this piece is included in a chapter on happiness.

Wide Awake to Connections Questions

1. Further research the life and accomplishments of Marcus Aurelius and write an essay in which you try to understand how his thinking was manifested (or was not manifested) in his personal and political life. In other words, do you think that Aurelius practiced what he preached? Give concrete examples to back up your claims.

2. Using Aurelius's claim that "He who has a powerful desire for posthumous fame does not consider that every one of those who remember him will himself also die very soon" and drawing on articles from the previous chapter, "Social Networking," compose an essay in which you discuss contemporary interest in fame, even if that fame is extremely short-lived. Why do people want to be famous? How are they going about getting famous these days?

Charles Schulz, "Peanuts"

>> Prereading Check-In

1. How much is your personal happiness dependent on other people?

2. Here's a tough one: What, do you think, is the meaning of life?

Cartoonist **Charles Schulz** *(1922–2000) is best known for* Peanuts, *a long-running cartoon focused on the daily life and foibles of Schulz's character Charlie Brown. During his long career, Schulz was awarded a Reuben, two Peabodys, and five Emmys for his work. Below, Charlie and his friend/antagonist Lucy discuss the "purpose of life."*

PEANUTS by Charles M. Schulz

Choosing to Read Critically Questions

1. Explain Charlie Brown's attitude toward other people.
2. Explain Lucy's perspective.
3. Is this cartoon funny to you? Why or why not?
4. Schulz uses images and words to convey meaning. What is the meaning of the third frame? (What are Lucy and Charlie doing?) What visual elements tell you what they are doing?

Choosing to Respond Questions

1. Which character are you more like? Which attitude do you sympathize with?
2. Evaluate the perspectives in this cartoon as a springboard into a discussion of the "purpose of life." How much do we owe other people? What should we expect from them?

Wide Awake to Connections Questions

1. In his later life, Schulz referred to himself as a "secular humanist." Research secular humanism and see if this philosophy is reflected in the above cartoon.
2. Using this cartoon and another article from this chapter, write an essay in which you discuss the importance of connections to others for personal happiness.

Eric Weiner, from *The Geography of Bliss*

>> **Prereading Check-In**

1. Do you sometimes think that you would be happier if you lived somewhere else? Where and why?
2. If you had to guess, what country do you think has the happiest citizens? Explain your answer.

A correspondent for National Public Radio and a journalist who has reported for the New York Times, **Eric Weiner** *(b. 1963) traveled the world researching his book* The Geography of Bliss: One Grump's Search for the Happiest Places in the World *(2009), from which the following selection is excerpted. In the piece, Weiner examines Americans' relationship to home and happiness.*

From *The Geography of Bliss: One Grump's Search for the Happiest Places in the World*

America's place on the happiness spectrum is not as high as you might think, given our superpower status. We are not, by any measure, the happiest nation on earth. One study, by Adrian White at the University of Leicester in Britain, ranked the United States as the world's twenty-third happiest nation, behind countries such as Costa Rica, Malta, and Malaysia. True, most Americans—84 percent, according to one study—describe themselves as either "very" or "pretty" happy, but it's safe to say that the United States is not as happy as it is wealthy.

Indeed, there is plenty of evidence that we are less happy today than ever before, as psychologist David Myers has shown in his book *The American Paradox: Spiritual Hunger in an Age of Plenty.* Since 1960, the divorce rate has doubled, the teen suicide rate tripled, the violent crime rate quadrupled, and the prison population quintupled. Then there are the increased rates of depression, anxiety, and other mental health problems. (There is robust evidence that what we're witnessing is a genuine increase in these disorders and not merely a greater willingness to diagnose them.)

What about all that money? We are the wealthiest country in the world, the wealthiest nation ever. On the one hand, all this cash is good. Basic survival is not an issue for most Americans. Wealthier Americans are, on average, (slightly) happier than poorer ones. Yet one fact bedevils the money-equals-happiness argument: As a nation, we are three times richer than we were in 1950 yet no happier. What's going on?

Clearly, one dynamic at work is rising expectations. We compare ourselves not to the America of 1950 but the America of today and, more specifically, to our neighbors of today. We give lip service to the notion that money can't buy happiness but act as if it does. When asked what would improve the quality of their lives, Americans' number-one answer was money, according to a University of Michigan study.

The self-help industrial complex hasn't helped. By telling us that happiness lives inside us, it's turned us inward just when we should be looking outward. Not to money but to other people, to community and to the kind of human bonds that so clearly are the sources of our happiness.

Americans work longer hours and commute greater distances than virtually any other people in the world. Commuting, in particular, has been found to be detrimental to our happiness, as well as our physical health. Every minute spent on the road is one less minute that we can spend with family and friends—the kind of activities, in other words, that make us happy.

Political scientist Robert Putnam makes a convincing case in his book *Bowling Alone* that our sense of connection is fraying. We spend less time visiting family and friends; we belong to fewer community groups.

Increasingly, we lead fragmented lives. The Internet and other technologies may salve our loneliness, but they have not, I believe, eliminated it.

Over the past fifty years, America's happiness levels have remained remarkably stable, unperturbed by cataclysmic events. After the attacks of September 11, 2001, researchers found no marked decrease in U.S. happiness levels. The 1962 Cuban missile crisis precipitated a brief *increase* in national happiness. Most people of the world derive happiness from the quotidian. Historian Will Durant has said, "History has been too often a picture of the bloody stream. The [real] history of civilization is a record of what happened on the banks."

We remain a profoundly optimistic nation. Two-thirds of Americans say they are hopeful about the future. Hopeful, I guess, that we will be happier.

When it comes to thinking about happiness, pondering it, worrying about it, cogitating over it, bemoaning our lack of it, and, of course, pursuing it, the United States is indeed a superpower. Eight out of ten Americans say they think about their happiness at least once a week. The sheer size and scope of the self-help industrial complex is testimony to both our discontent and our belief in the possibility of self-renewal.

No other nation's founding document so prominently celebrates happiness. Of course, the Declaration of Independence only enshrines the right to *pursue* happiness. It's up to us, as Benjamin Franklin once quipped, to catch it.

Choosing to Read Critically Questions

1. What, according to this excerpt, really does make people happy?
2. In your own words, explain the following passage. If necessary, look up any unfamiliar words:

   > Most people of the world derive happiness from the quotidian. Historian Will Durant has said, "History has been too often a picture of the bloody stream. The [real] history of civilization is a record of what happened on the banks."

3. Explain the relationship between wealth and happiness.
4. In a parenthetical remark about the rise in mental health problems, Weiner states, "There is robust evidence that what we're witnessing is a genuine increase in these disorders and not merely a greater willingness to diagnose them." Why, do you think, does Weiner include this comment? What kinds of responses is he perhaps hoping to head off?

Choosing to Respond Questions

1. What, if anything, did you find surprising or interesting in Weiner's article? Explain your reaction.

2. Do you, personally, imagine that if you were wealthier you would be happier? Describe your perspective on the relationship (or lack thereof) between having money and being happy.

Wide Awake to Connections Questions

1. Using the Web, conduct your own research on global happiness. Compose an essay synthesizing and commenting on your findings. You might start your research by Googling "gross national happiness" or looking at maps that purport to illustrate how happy people are in different parts of the world.

2. Drawing on this article and one or two selections from Chapter 13, construct an argument about the relationships between technology and happiness.

Vicki Haddock, "The Happiness Quotient"

>> **Prereading Check-In**

1. Describe one of the happiest times in your life.

2. What role, do you think, does choice play in happiness? Is it important for you to have lots of choices in different areas of your life?

Vicki Haddock *is a freelance journalist who has written for the* San Francisco Chronicle. *The below article, which originally appeared in the* Chronicle, *describes recent studies that suggest women's happiness levels have decreased in recent years.*

"The Happiness Quotient: Do High Expectations and a Plethora of Choices Make Women Miserable?"

Exactly what does it take to make a woman happy?

One of the first to record her answer to that conundrum was the Marquise du Chatelet, whom history has recollected as the jilted mistress of Voltaire. That is short shrift: The brilliant marquise was a mother, a shopaholic, a passionate lover—and most significantly, a revolutionary scientist and mathematician who suspended wooden spheres from the rafters of her country estate to test Newton's theories, and who scribbled her insights until the candles burned to nothingness, plunging her hands into ice water to jolt herself awake. Her intellectual feverishness prompted the philosopher Immanuel Kant to sneer that such a woman "might as well have a beard," and Voltaire himself, having received solo title-page credit for a book he privately admitted she practically dictated to him, declared that the marquise was a great man whose only shortcoming was having been born female.

Thus duly boxed in by the gender conventions of 18th-century France—and by an unplanned pregnancy at age 43 that she presciently regarded as a death sentence—the Marquise du Chatelet brought a unique perspective to a treatise she titled "Discourse on Happiness."

To be truly happy, she ruefully concluded, "one must be susceptible to illusions, for it is to illusions that we owe the majority of our pleasures. Unhappy is the one who has lost them."

So where are we nearly three centuries later? Recalibrate for feminism, which aimed to liberate women from the constricting corsets of sexist roles. Factor in an unprecedented level of education, greater earning power, more economic independence, more reproductive control and access to virtually any career, from CEO to soldier to leader of the free world. In theory, at least, a woman's prospects for happiness have never looked brighter.

Yet the paradox: Two recent studies reveal that a majority of American women are finding the holy grail of happiness more elusive. Researchers were startled to find that women now report less happiness than in the early 1970s; and where they once indicated greater levels of happiness and life satisfaction than men, that's now reversed.

"Aha!" opposing sides in the culture wars declared, glomming onto the findings to bolster their own takes on gender conflict. But this newly identified "happiness gap" is hardly a prima facie indictment of feminism for having worsened the lot of women, given that most women adamantly oppose a return to rigid gender roles. Nor could it be attributable mainly to the notion that men are slacking while women work a second shift—full time in the workforce and a second full-time job at home. The results show that women are spending the same number of hours working now, on average, as in the 1970s, although a greater percentage is outside work. As for housework, men have picked up a greater, though still minority, share. Much of the cooking and cleaning is "hired out" or simply goes undone (Americans now spend $26 billion more each year on restaurants than grocery stores).

Even so, men today report spending less time on activities they regard as stressful and unpleasant than a few decades ago. Women still spend about 23 hours a week in the unpleasant-activity zone—which was about 40 minutes more than men four decades ago, and now amounts to 90 minutes more than men.

And feeling guiltier in the process.

. . . Measuring human happiness is tricky science: There is no "happy thermometer" to tuck under one's tongue. So while happiness research is booming, researchers wrestle with how to measure it and how to account for data dependent on self-reporting of debatable reliability (although scientists find that people who describe themselves as happier also show outward signs validating that description—for example, they smile more). In recent years, they have puzzled over why 45 percent of Republicans say they'e "very happy" when only 30 percent of Democrats do, or why married people report more happiness than singles, or why an index claimed the "happiest Zip code" belongs to Branson, Mo.

But a gender-based "happiness gap" is particularly complicated, given that men tend to see "Are you happy?" as a yes-or-no proposition. For women, it's an essay question.

In one recent study, two economists at the University of Pennsylvania analyzed 35 years of data from the widely regarded General Social Survey and other assessments, including the Virginia Slims American Women's Poll and the Monitoring the Future survey of teenagers.

Since 1972, women's self-described levels of happiness have fallen a few percentage points and now rest below that of men, on average, in every age category. It is particularly pronounced in those ages 30 to 44— not coincidentally, women dealing with child rearing and aging parents, while reaching a critical point in their careers.

This drop in female happiness is pervasive—it also holds true regardless of marital status, education, and employment. The only exception researchers were able to tease out was among African Americans. No one's certain why African American women report higher levels of happiness than they did in the 1970s, but it's an intriguing aberration that merits follow-up.

While the gap is not huge, research co-author Betsey Stevenson said it was stunning given that by objective measures, the status of women's lives has improved in recent decades. "We would have expected their happiness to shoot up, not fall," she said.

Perhaps the most persuasive explanation for the happiness gap is . . . [h]aving choices means that women actually must choose. Or, as Bob Seger would put it, what to leave in, what to leave out. Acknowledge the axiom of the time-space continuum: A woman can only be in one place at a time, and any given day cannot contain more than 24 hours.

"My grandmother used to say too many choices make you sick," said Mary Nolan, taking in the view from her Financial District office. "I get this from my business bent, but I do believe we're too afraid to be wrong. We're afraid that if we make a wrong choice, we can't turn around and change it. Which is really unfortunate, because courage often comes from recognizing the wrong choice and reversing direction."

Of course, choice is relative: The spectrum narrows for poor women living paycheck to paycheck. But for the first time in history, women confront a wider array of life alternatives than men, who rarely contemplate, for example, putting their careers on hold to care for children or aging parents. We're still adjusting to this shift in the cultural paradigm.

When researchers ask teenage girls what is important to them—finding a successful job, staying close to their friends, having a family, looking good and so on—they discovered that their answer was "everything." They ranked nothing as less important than it had been in the past.

The unquestioned modern mantra is that freedom comes through maximizing choice. Swarthmore psychology Professor Barry Schwartz says that's why supermarkets stock 75 salad dressings, why a single electronics store's product line allows buyers to construct more than 6 million stereo systems. And it's why someone, somewhere is busy creating a combo MP3 player/nose hair trimmer/crème brûlée torch.

"More choices are better, but more and more choices are not. Too much choice produces not liberation but paralysis," says Schwartz, the author of "The Paradox of Choice: Why More Is Less."

The same principle applies to women's life choices.

"Even if you overcome paralysis and make a choice, you end up less satisfied than if you had fewer options," Schwartz contends. "Whatever salad dressing you choose, it won't be perfect, and you end up thinking about the ones you didn't buy. And the imagined alternative induces you to regret the decision you made. Not only that, but when you have no choice and things aren't perfect, you can blame the world.

"But when you have all these choices and you still feel regretful and unsatisfied, you end up blaming yourself. Hence, guilt."

"The reason things seemed better back when they were worse," Schwartz says, "is because people with few choices and lowered expectations could expect to be pleasantly surprised." That also might explain why the World Values Survey of 65 countries found the happiest people in Nigeria, a country lacerated with instability and poverty, while the United States lagged in 16th place.

Many women also set stratospheric expectations for themselves, and for each other—reinforced by the cult of Martha Stewart, a slew of self-improvement books, the prevalence of plastic surgery. We've come to regard our work lives, our home lives and our private lives as projects to be endlessly tweaked in pursuit of perfection.

. . . If nothing else, the declaration of a happiness gender gap is generating provocative conversation. The researchers themselves note that because men traditionally were less happy, perhaps women's happiness has diminished as they've entered into their world and are now bedeviled by the same woes that have long depressed men.

Or maybe the happiness gap isn't actually new at all. "Freakonomics" author and economist Steven Levitt suggests "there was enormous social pressure on women in the old days to pretend they were happy even if they weren't."

Like the Marquise du Chatelet, perhaps now we're abandoning our illusions and simply being more honest.

Choosing to Read Critically Questions

1. According to the article, what are some of the possible causes of women's decreased happiness?

2. Explain Professor Barry Schwartz's claim that "Too much choice produces not liberation but paralysis."

3. Haddock writes, "If nothing else, the declaration of a happiness gender gap is generating provocative conversation. The researchers themselves note that because men traditionally were less happy, perhaps women's happiness has diminished as they've entered into their world and are now bedeviled by the same woes that have long depressed men." In your own words, explain what Haddock is suggesting and decide whether or not you agree with this point.

4. Haddock writes that "Measuring human happiness is tricky science: There is no 'happy thermometer' to tuck under one's tongue. So while happiness research is booming, researchers wrestle with how to measure it, and account for data dependent on self-reporting of debatable reliability." In light of Haddock's admission that researchers are dealing with subjective experiences, do you find the evidence and reasoning presented here convincing? Why or why not?

Choosing to Respond Questions

1. Drawing on your personal experiences as well as the above article, discuss the stress and difficulty that often accompanies having choices. Is it better to not have choices? Explain your answer.

2. Haddock reports that only "African American women report higher levels of happiness than they did in the '70s" and that this is "an intriguing aberration that merits follow-up." Speculate on why this is so, developing reasons for why this population might have different experiences of happiness or report on their happiness differently than other populations.

Wide Awake to Connections Questions

1. Write an essay in which you discuss the Marquise de Chatelet's contention that one must have illusions to be happy alongside the depiction of learning and enlightenment in Plato's "The Allegory of the Cave." Is ignorance bliss? What are the rewards of not having illusions?

2. Drawing on this article and the next one, Leonhardt's "For Blacks, Progress in Happiness," compose an essay in which you discuss how race, ethnicity, gender, or class might affect happiness. (You also might choose to discuss a group not mentioned in these articles; you might look, for example, at recent findings that Latina girls and women in the United States have some of the highest rates of attempted suicide.)

David Leonhardt, "For Blacks, Progress in Happiness"

>> **Prereading Check-In**
1. Reread the title and write a paragraph anticipating what Leonhardt will discuss in this article.
2. Do you think your racial or ethnic background has any effect on your personal happiness?

Pulitzer prize-winner **David Leonhardt** *(b. 1973) has been writing columns on economics and business for the* New York Times *since 2000. In the following article, which originally appeared in the Business section of the* Times, *Leonhardt describes recent findings with regard to evaluations of happiness levels among African Americans.*

"For Blacks, Progress in Happiness"

Set aside some prominent success stories, like the current occupant of the White House, and the last few decades have not been great ones for African-American progress.

In 1975, per capita black income was 41 percent lower than per capita white income. Since then, the gap has shrunk only modestly, to 35 percent. The black unemployment rate today is nearly twice as high as the white rate, just as it was in 1975. And by some measures—family structure, college graduation, incarceration—racial gaps have actually grown.

But now a new study has found that there is one big realm in which black Americans have made major progress: happiness.

White Americans don't report being any more satisfied with their lives than they did in the 1970s, various surveys show. Black Americans do, and significantly so.

Betsey Stevenson and Justin Wolfers, the University of Pennsylvania economists who did the study, point out that self-reported measures of happiness usually shift at a glacial pace. The share of whites, for example, telling pollsters in recent years that they are "not too happy"—as opposed to "pretty happy" or "very happy"—has been about 10 percent. It was also 10 percent in the 1970s.

Yet the share of blacks saying they are not too happy has dropped noticeably, to about 20 percent in surveys over the last decade, from 24 percent in the 1970s. All in all, Mr. Wolfers calls the changes to blacks' answers, "one of the most dramatic gains in the happiness data that you'll see."

The new study is part of a deluge of happiness research by economists, who are discovering what the rest of us have long known: money isn't everything. To get a true sense for people's quality of life—the most basic mission of economics—you have to try to peek inside the human mind.

Money clearly has a big effect on the mind, just as it has a big effect on health, education and almost everything else. The rich report being happier than the middle class on average, and the middle class report being happier than the poor. The income and wealth gaps between whites and blacks, in turn, explain a big part of the happiness gap.

But they don't explain all of it. Among whites and blacks making the same amount of money, whites tend to be happier. This unexplained gap, however, has shrunk.

Ms. Stevenson and Mr. Wolfers have a good way of making this point. In the 1970s, a relatively affluent black person—one in a household making more than nine out of 10 other black households, or at the 90th percentile of the black income spectrum—was earning the same amount as someone at the 75th percentile of the white spectrum. That's another way of saying blacks were making less than whites.

But blacks were far less satisfied with their lives than could be explained by the income difference. People at the 90th percentile of the black income spectrum were as happy on average as people just below the 10th percentile of the white income spectrum, amazingly enough.

Today, people at the 90th percentile of the black income spectrum are still making about as much as those at the 75th percentile of the white spectrum—but are now as happy on average as people in the dead middle, or the 50th percentile, of the white income spectrum. The income gap hasn't shrunk much, but the happiness gap has.

In the paper, which is awaiting peer review, the two economists acknowledge that they cannot be sure what is causing the change. But it is consistent with patterns that other happiness researchers have noticed, and there are some plausible explanations.

The most obvious is the decrease—though certainly not the elimination—in day-to-day racism. "The decline in prejudice has been astounding," says Kerwin Charles, a University of Chicago economist who has studied discrimination. Well into the 1970s, blacks faced "a vast array of personal indignities that led to unhappiness," he noted. Today, those indignities are unacceptable in many areas of American life.

Old polls bear this out. In the early 1970s, 39 percent of Americans said they favored laws against marriage between the two races, according to one long-running poll. When the question was last asked, earlier this decade, the share had fallen below 10 percent. The number saying they are unwilling to vote for a black presidential candidate has also plummeted. That shift is a reminder that jobs once closed to blacks—Fortune 500 chief executive, A-list movie star, secretary of state, attorney general or president—no longer are.

It isn't hard to see how the decline in discrimination improves people's lives, above and beyond their pay.

And the decline in discrimination may even be lifting black wages, despite the meager gains in the overall statistics. Jonathan Guryan, a Northwestern University economist, points out that the last three decades have brought a wave of forces that could have led to a widening of the black-white pay gap.

Union membership has dropped, and black workers are more likely to be unionized. Income inequality has risen, and black households are more likely to be middle class or poor. The economic returns of a college degree have soared, and the college graduation gap between whites and blacks has grown. Nonetheless, the black-white pay gap has shrunk slightly.

One intriguing footnote to the new paper is how different it seems from an earlier Stevenson-Wolfers paper about women and men. It found that women have become less happy over the last few decades, in spite of big economic, educational and social progress. Ms. Stevenson argues—persuasively, I think—that the combined job and family expectations for women today may have left many less than fully satisfied.

By contrast, the happiness gains for black women have been a bit bigger than for black men, who are still more satisfied than they were in the 1970s, but less so than a decade ago.

With both the race and the gender findings, you get a sense of how much fairer the American economy has become, and yet how unfair it can still be.

A rich vein of research has shown that racial discrimination remains a part of daily life, albeit a reduced one. To take just one example, an experiment found that résumés with typically black names lead to fewer job interviews than similar résumés with different names. Combine the discrimination with the toll of bad schools and broken families, and you end up with those huge lingering black-white gaps.

Closing the gaps would clearly help the economy—moving families out of poverty, freeing up talent and, in the long run, probably lifting growth. But these wouldn't be the only benefits. There would also be some on which it's hard to put a price.

Choosing to Read Critically Questions

1. Without using statistics, restate the findings Leonhardt describes in paragraphs 9, 10, and 11.
2. Describe and explain how Leonhardt opens the article. Do you find the opening effective?
3. In your own words, explain how discrimination might be different now than it was 30 or 40 years ago.
4. Why did this article originally appear in the "Business" section of the newspaper?

Choosing to Respond Questions

1. Leonhardt writes that "day-to-day" racism has decreased in America. Does this ring true to you? Explain.
2. Making reference to Leonhardt's article and, in particular, his final paragraph, discuss the relationship between money and happiness.

Wide Awake to Connections Questions

1. Leonhardt mentions a study which "found that résumés with typically black names lead to fewer job interviews than similar résumés with different names." This experiment is also discussed in Steven Levitt and Stephen Dubner's book *Freakonomics: A Rogue Economist Explores the Hidden Side of Everything.* Read *Freakonomics,* or find another source that discusses the study, in order to get a more complete understanding

of what the experiment was designed to demonstrate or discover. Then, write an essay in which you summarize and respond to the data. Is this experiment compelling to you? Do you find the outcomes surprising? Why or why not?

2. Drawing on this article, as well as one or two other articles in this text-book (you may look at Gladwell's "The Revolution Will Not Be Tweeted"), write an essay exploring the ways in which individuals' personal experiences are affected by larger social forces, such as environmental policy or institutionalized racism.

Eve Savory, "Meditation: The Pursuit of Happiness"

>> Prereading Check-In

1. How much control, do you think, do you have over your own emotions?

2. If you could change one thing about your life in order to be happier, what would it be?

Canadian reporter **Eve Savory** *has written extensively on science and medicine for CBC news; the following article appeared on CBC News online. In this excerpt, Savory describes how the research of psychologist Richard Davidson is changing what we know about attaining happiness.*

"Meditation: The Pursuit of Happiness"

Dharamsala is the home in exile to thousands of Tibetans who followed the Dalai Lama, after China occupied Tibet.

For 25 centuries Tibetan Buddhists have practiced and refined their exploration. For generations they probed their inner space with the same commitment with which western science explored the external world and outer space. The two inhabited separate worlds.

But now, they are finding common ground in a remarkable collaboration.

In March 2000, a select group of scientists and scholars journeyed to Dharamsala. They came to share insights and solutions—to human distress and suffering.

Among them was Richard Davidson, a neuroscientist from the University of Wisconsin. He finds nothing contradictory about doing science with Buddhists.

"There is almost a scientific-like attitude that is exemplified by Buddhist practitioners in investigating their own mind," he says. "Their mind is the landscape of their own experimentation, if you will."

The westerners had been invited by the Dalai Lama himself to his private quarters.

For five days, monks and scientists dissected what they call "negative emotions"—sadness, anxiety, jealousy, craving, rage—and their potential to destroy.

One of the participants, Daniel Goleman, author of the book *Destructive Emotions*, says, "As we were leaving the U.S. to come here, the headline was a six-year-old who had a fight with a classmate and the next day he came back with a gun and shot and killed her. It's very sad."

Why would the scientists seek answers in Tibetan Buddhism?

Because its rigorous meditative practices seem to have given the monks an extraordinary resilience, an ability to bounce back from the bad things that happen in life, and cultivate contentment.

Richard Davidson's lab is one of the world's most advanced for looking inside a living brain. He's recently been awarded an unprecedented $15-million grant to study, among other things, what happens inside a meditating mind.

"Meditation is a set of practices that have been around for more than 2,500 years, whose principal goal is to cultivate these positive human qualities, to promote flourishing and resilience. And so we think that it deserves to be studied with the modern tools of science," Davidson says.

A little over a year later, in May 2001, the Dalai Lama returned the visit to Davidson's lab in Madison, Wis.

His prize subjects—and collaborators—are the Dalai Lama's lamas, the monks.

"The monks, we believe, are the Olympic athletes of certain kinds of mental training," Davidson says. "These are individuals who have spent years in practice. To recruit individuals who have undergone more than 10,000 hours of training of their mind is not an easy task and there aren't that many of these individuals on the planet."

The Dalai Lama has said were he not a monk, he would be an engineer.

He brings that sensibility—the curiosity and intellectual discipline—to the discussion on EEGs and functional MRIs.

But this isn't really about machines.

And it isn't about nirvana.

It's about down-to-earth life: about the distress of ordinary people—and a saner world.

"The human and economic cost of psychiatric disorder in western industrialized countries is dramatic," says Davidson. "And to the extent that cultivating happiness reduces that suffering, it is fundamentally important."

The monk and the scientist are investigating—together—the Art of Happiness.

"Rather than thinking about qualities like happiness as a trait," Davidson says, "we should think about them as a skill, not unlike a motor skill, like bicycle riding or skiing. These are skills that can be trained. I think it is just unambiguously the case that happiness is not a luxury for our culture but it is a necessity."

But we believe we can buy happiness . . . if we just had the money. That's what the ad industry tells us. And we think it's true.

People's theories about what will make them happy often are wrong. And so there's a lot of work these days that shows, for example, that winning the lottery will transiently elevate your happiness but it will not persist.

There's some evidence that our temperament is more or less set from birth. So and so is a gloomy Gus . . . someone else is a ray of sunshine—that sort of thing.

Even when wonderful or terrible things happen, most of us, eventually, will return to that emotional set-point.

But, Davidson believes, that set point can be moved.

"Our work has been fundamentally focused on what the brain mechanisms are that underlie these emotional qualities and how these brain mechanisms might change as a consequence of certain kinds of training," Davidson says.

His work could not have been done 20 years ago. "In fact, 20 years ago, we had dreams of methods that allow you to interrogate the brain in this way, but we had no tools to do it."

Now that we have the tools we can see that as our emotions ebb and flow, so do brain chemistry and blood flow. Fear, depression, love . . . they all get different parts of our brain working.

Happiness and enthusiasm, and joy—they show up as increased activity on the left side near the front of the cortex. Anxiety, sadness—on the right.

Davidson has found this pattern in infants as young as 10 months, in toddlers, teens and adults.

Davidson tested more than 150 ordinary people to see what parts of their brains were most active.

Some were a little more active on the left. Some were a little more active on the right.

A few were quite far to the right. They would probably be called depressed. Others were quite far to the left, the sort of people who feel "life is great."

So there was a range. Then Davidson tested a monk.

He was so far to the left he was right off the curve. That was one happy monk.

"And this is rather dramatic evidence that there's something really different about his brain compared with the brains of these other 150 people. This is tantalizing evidence that these practices may indeed be promoting beneficial changes in the brain."

Here, the Olympic athletes of meditation meet the Cadillac of brain scanners.

Khachab Rinpoche, a monk from Asia, came to Madison to meditate in perhaps the strangest place in his life: the functional MRI.

It lets scientists watch what happens inside his brain when he switches between different types of meditation.

They want to know how his brain may differ from ordinary people, and whether that change is related to the inner contentment the monks report.

So they test how subjects react to unpleasant sounds and images flashed into the goggles they wear in the MRI.

Normally when we're threatened one part of the brain is tremendously active, but in the monks, "the responsivity of this area is specifically decreased during this meditation in response to these very intense auditory stimuli that convey strong emotions," Davidson says.

It's very preliminary work, but the implication may be that the lamas are able to move right through distressing events that overwhelm the rest of us—in other words, one of the keys to their happiness.

It may tell us something about our potential. "Our brains are adaptable, our brains are not fixed. The wiring in our brains is not fixed. Who we are today is not necessarily who we have to end up being," Davidson says.

Tibetan Buddhism is said to be one of the most demanding mental endeavors on the planet. It takes 10,000 hours of meditation and years in retreat to become adept. Few of us can imagine such a commitment.

But that doesn't mean the benefits of meditation are out of our reach.

Zindal Segal is a psychologist at the Centre for Addiction and Mental Health in Toronto. He uses meditation to treat mood disorders.

It's based on Buddhist teachings and its called mindfulness.

"Very few of us can sit for 10,000 hours to be able to do this but the interesting thing is that we don't need to. These capacities are available to all of us," Segal says. "We're talking about paying attention, we're talking about returning wherever our minds are to this present moment. These are things that we all have. We don't have to earn them, we just have to find a way of clearing away the clutter to see that they are already there."

Meditation is now out of the closet. The word is, it eases stress, drops blood pressure, helps put that bad day at the office in perspective.

Meditation is being mainlined by the mainstream, from corporate offices to factory floors.

"Meditation has been around for 2500 years so it's not like a new practice," Davidson says. "But science is catching up to an old tradition and the evidence seems to be emerging that meditation can change the pattern of brain chemistry or blood flow in the brain."

And now there's proof meditation can change the brains of ordinary people and make them healthier.

Promega is a biotech company in Madison, Wis., where the researchers from the Brain Imaging Lab recruited typical stressed out workers—office staff, managers, even a skeptical research scientist, Mike Slater.

"Things were chaotic and crazy. We had a newborn. We had three deaths in the family. So it was a pretty topsy-turvy time," Slater says.

All the subjects had activity in their brain measured . . . and half—including Mike Slater—were given an eight-week course in meditation.

Then everyone — meditators and controls — got a flu shot, and their brains were measured a second time.

The meditators' brain activity had shifted to that happy left side. Mike Slater was almost too successful.

"I was pretty happy all the time and I was worried that maybe I was masking some stuff that might really be irritating me so I stopped it and my wife noticed an increase in my irritability, so, you know, I have both sides of the experiment now. It calmed me down and I stopped doing it and my irritability increased," he says.

That wasn't all. Their immune systems had strengthened.

"Those individuals in the meditation group that showed the biggest change in brain activity also showed the biggest change in immune function, suggesting that these were closely linked," Davidson says.

Davidson and his team had shown meditation could shift not just mood—but also brain activity and immunity in ordinary people.

And they'd answered a potential flaw in the monk study.

"Someone may say, well, maybe these individuals are that way to start out with. Maybe that's why they're attracted to be monks," Davidson says. "And we actually can't answer that on the basis of those data, but with the Promega study, we can say definitely that it had to do with the intervention we provided."

There are reasons to believe the insane pace and many aggravations of daily life can be dangerous to the health of our minds and our bodies.

We can't push the delay button on a busy world and we can't bail out.

But perhaps meditation is a way to encourage a sense of well-being—a deep breath in the center of the whirlwind.

"As the Dalai Lama himself said in his book *The Art of Happiness*, we have the capacity to change ourselves because of the very nature, of the very structure and function of our brain," Davidson says. "And that is a very hopeful message because I think it instills in people the belief that there are things that they can do to make themselves better."

Choosing to Read Critically Questions

1. In your own words, describe what Davidson's research is suggesting about the connection between meditation and happiness.
2. What, according to Davidson, does the Promega study prove and how?

3. Davidson states that "happiness is not a luxury for our culture but it is a necessity." What do you think he means by this, and do you agree with this statement?

4. Elsewhere, Davidson has said that practicing meditation can have "an effect on the brain in the same way golf or tennis practice will enhance performance." Explain how practicing a sport may improve performance and what the limitations of practice are, then discuss and evaluate the analogy that Davidson is using.

Choosing to Respond Questions

1. There's a cliché that people don't ever really change. However, the research above suggests that people are, in fact, capable of change. Drawing on your own experiences and observations, discuss a change you have witnessed in yourself or someone else and explain how that change took place.

2. Elsewhere in Davidson's work, he suggests that our capacity for compassion is related to our capacity for happiness. Drawing on this article, as well as your own experiences and observations, compose an essay in which you explore this connection.

Wide Awake to Connections Questions

1. After conducting some more research on Davidson's work, perform your own experiment. That is, using Davidson's experiment as a model, practice meditation every day for two or three weeks. Record how you feel before, during, and after you meditate, as well as any other information or events that you think are relevant. Synthesize your findings in an essay about your experience.

2. Drawing on this article and another article from this chapter (perhaps Haddock's "The Happiness Quotient"), write an essay in which you discuss happiness in contemporary society. Why are people unhappy? How can people increase their happiness?

QUESTIONS AND SUGGESTIONS FOR FURTHER RESEARCH AND WRITING

1. Scholars have noted similarities between Marcus Aurelius's ideas and that of Buddhist philosophy. Research the central tenets of Buddhism and write an essay in which you compare and contrast what you find with this selection from Aurelius's *Meditations*. Alternately, you might choose to look up Epictetus, a philosopher Aurelius invoked in *Meditations*. What does Epictetus have to say about attaining happiness, and how do his ideas correspond with or contrast with Aurelius's?

2. Investigate the overlap between happiness and one of the other topics dealt with in this anthology. (These topics include education, disability studies, the environment, privacy, and food politics.) For example, you might ask: In general, are people with higher educational degrees happier or are they less happy? Why do people with disabilities often report being just as happy as those without disabilities? How can the environment impact happiness?

3. If you Google the words "happiness" and "test," you'll find a number of websites offering you the chance to take an exam that will ostensibly tell you how happy you are. Look at a few of these tests and write an essay analyzing the questions. What kinds of questions are asked? Are the results surprising? Why or why not? Did you discover anything about yourself? How useful do you find these types of exercises?

4. Typically, films tend to present happiness as the outcome of a huge—yet predictable—change in one's sense of self. Films such as *A Christmas Carol* (any version), *Sister Act, Regarding Henry, Confessions of a Shopaholic, Funny People,* and *About a Boy,* feature self-absorbed characters who have to experience an extreme turn of events in their lives in order to become less selfish and more compassionate and ultimately happier. Select a film or films from the above list (or come up with your own film that depicts happiness and unhappiness) and discuss the realism of these depictions in an age when buying bigger and better things occupies so much of our energies.

5. Conduct interviews of two of the happiest people you know and two of the unhappiest people you know. (Of course, your judgments of their levels of happiness might be inaccurate; perhaps you will discover that you've misinterpreted their demeanors.) Using the answers to your interview questions as your data, compose an essay in which you address fundamental questions about emotional well-being. What is happiness? Is it an inborn trait, or is it possible for an individual to choose to be happy? What kinds of things contribute to individual happiness? You may draw on some of the articles in this chapter in order to supplement your findings.

Credits

Chapter 2

Page 13 (Top): Turan, Kenneth. "Review of Harry Potter and the Deathly Hollows — Part 2," The Los Angeles Times, 2011; **13 (Bottom):** Excerpted from "The Social Network" by Peter Travers, Rolling Stone, October 14, 2010. Copyright © 2010 Rolling Stone LLC. All Rights Reserved. Reprinted by Permission.; **16:** Vanderbilt, Tom. "Traffic: Why We Drive the Way We Do and What it Says About Us," 2008.

Chapter 4

Page 33: Balko, Radley. "Health Care Should Be a Personal Responsibility." Wide Awake: Thinking, Reading, and Writing Critically. 1st Ed. Sara Hosey. New York: Pearson Longman, 2013.; **34:** Wray, Laura and Flanagan, Constance. "An Inconvenient Truth About Youth," The Washington Post, 2006.

Chapter 5

Pages 44–45: Starr, Douglas. The Killer of Little Shepherds: A True Crime Story and the Birth of Forensic Science. Knopf, 2010.

Chapter 6

Pages 57–58: Blanton, DeAnne and Lauren M. Cook. They Fought Like Demons: Women Soldiers in the Civil War. Vintage, 2003.; **66:** Douglass, Frederick. Narrative of the Life of Frederick Douglass, An American Slave. 1845.

Chapter 7

Page 79 (Top): Krugman, Paul. "Free to Choose Obesity?," New York Times, 8 July 2005. Nytimes.com. Web. 28 September 2009.; **79 (Bottom):** Plaza, Carla I. "State's Public Health Initiatives Address Nutrition, Obesity, and Physical Education." 1 September 2004. Allbusiness.com Web. 29 September 2009.

Chapter 8

Pages 89–90: Wills, Garry. Lincoln at Gettysburg: The Words that Remade America. New York: Simon and Schuster, 1992.

Chapter 9

Pages 98–100: Keller, Helen. The Story of My Life, 1905.; **102–103:** By Graham Pullin. "An Introduction to Universal Design" Dwell 2010, ©2010. This article was first published in the March 2010 issue of Dwell ® Magazine. Dwell is a registered trademark of Dwell Media LLC; **104–106:** Zulu, Winston. "I Had Polio. I Also Have Sex." New York Times, 2011.; **107–110:** Author: G.E. Zuriff, © 1996, in Zuriff, G.E. "Medicalizing Character." The Public Interest. 1996, © 1996 http://www.nationalaffairs.com/public_ interest/detail/medicalizing-character **115–120:** Clare, Eli. "Exile and Pride: Disability, Queerness and Liberation." South End Press, 1999.

Chapter 10

Pages 132–135: Copyright © 1990 Wendell Berry from What Are People for. Reprinted by permission of Counterpoint.; **137–140:** Brownell, Kelly and Katherine Battle Horgen. Food Fight: The Inside Story of the Food Industry, America's Obesity Crisis and What We Can Do About It. 2003; **142–144:** Balko, Radley. "Health Care Should Be a Personal Responsibility." Health Care. Ed. Jan Grover. Detroit: Greenhaven Press, 2007; **146–153:** "Remarks by the First Lady to the NAACP National Convention in Kansas City, Missouri" (2010); **155–157:** Gunlock, Julie. "Federalizing Fat."

National Review Online, 2010.; **158–161:**
Winter, Amy. "The Biggest Losers & the
Lies They Feed Us." Off Our Back, ©2004

Chapter 11
Pages 165–170: Ch 11 Walden. http://www
.gutenberg.org/files/205/205-h/205-h.htm;
171–173: Jacoby, Jeff. "The Waste of
Recycling." The Boston Globe. 9/22/2010.;
175–176: Noddings, Nell. Happiness and
Education. Cambridge University Press
(December 6, 2004). 320pp.; **178–181:**
Clark, Ward M. "Why Hunt?" Wildfowling
Magazine International.; **182–186:**
Gore, Al. "Nobel Peace Prize Acceptance
Speech." Nobel Foundation. © 2007.;
187–189: Wray, Laura, and Constance
Flanagan. An Inconvenient Truth About
Youth. The Washington Post. 2006.; **190–192:**
By The Christian Science Monitor Editorial
Board. Reprinted with permission from
the April 20, 2012 issue of The Christian
Science Monitor. © 2012 The Christian
Science Monitor (www.CSMonitor.com)

Chapter 12
Pages 200–204:http://www.gutenberg
.org/files/1497/1497-h/1497-h.htm#link2H_
4_0004; **205–213:** Gatto, John Taylor.
"Dumbing Us Down." New Society
Publishers. 1992.; **215–221:** Bush, George
W. "President Bush Discusses No Child
Left Behind." General Philip Kearny
School, Philadelphia, Pennsylvania. 2009.;
222–228: Courtesy of Laura Perez. Perez,
Laura. "A Forgotten Child Remembers:
Reflections on Education."; **229–231:**
Rodriguez, Luis J. "There are messages in
the classroom..." from Always Running: La
Vida Loca: Gang Days in L. A.: Curbstone
Press, 1990. 610 word excerpt; **232–235:**
Joseph B. Tulman, "Time to Reverse
the School-to-Prison Pipeline" in Policy
and Practice Magazine, March 2008.
POLICY AND PRACTICE -WASHINGTON-
AMERICAN PUBLIC HUMAN SERVICES
ASSOCIATION-2008, VOL 66; NUMB 1,
pages 22. © 2008 American Public Human
Services Association.; **236–240:** Excerpt

from "Why School" Copyright ©2009 by
Mike Rose. Reprinted by permission of
The New Press. www.thenewprss.com;
242–247: Anya Kamenetz

Chapter 13
Page 251: McLuhan, M. (1964).
Understanding Media: The Extensions of
Man. New York: McGraw-Hill.; **253–254:**
Damien Pearse, "Facebook's 'Dark Side':
Study Finds Link to Socially Aggressive
Narcissism." Copyright Guardian News
& Media Ltd 2012.; **256–259:** Reprinted
with permission of the publisher. From
No Doubt About It, copyright© 2010
by Zandt, Deanna., Berrett-Koehler
Publishers, Inc., San Francisco, CA. All
rights reserved. www.bkconnection
.com; **260–271:** "Small Change: Why
the Revolution Will Not Be Tweeted," by
Malcolm Gladwell. Copyright © 2010 by
Malcolm Gladwell. Originally published in
The New Yorker. Reprinted by permission
of the author.; **272–273:** The Daily Mail
Online. Dailymail.co.uk July 28, 2011.
Copyright: Associated Newspapers Ltd.;
274–279: "Online Learning and Non-
Learning," from The Dumbest Generation
by Mark Bauerlein, copyright © 2008 by
Mark Bauerlein. Used by permission of
Jeremy P. Tarcher, an imprint of Penguin
Group (USA) Inc.

Chapter 14
Pages 284–285: Trans. George Long,
revised by Paul Birans, from Reading
About the World, ed. Paul Brians,
vol 1, ©1999; **288–290:** From the
Geography of Bliss by Eric Weiner.
Copyright © 2008 by Eric Weiner. By
permission of Grand Central Publishing.
All rights reserved.; **291–295:** Haddock,
Vicki. "The Happiness Quotient." The San
Francisco Chronicle. 2007.; **297–300:**
Leonhardt, David. "For Blacks, Progress
in Happiness." The New York Times.
2010.; **301–306:** Savory, Eve. "Meditation:
The Pursuit of Happiness." CBC News.
2004.

Index